Buying In or Selling Out?

Buying In
or Selling Out?

The Commercialization of the American Research University

EDITED BY DONALD G. STEIN

RUTGERS UNIVERSITY PRESS

New Brunswick, New Jersey, and London

Library of Congress Cataloging-in-Publication Data

Buying in or selling out? : the commercialization of the American research university
/ edited by Donald G. Stein.
     p.   cm.
  Includes bibliographical references and index.
  ISBN 0–8135–3374–0 (hardcover : alk. paper)
  1. Education, Higher—Economic aspects—United States. 2. Research—Economic
aspects—United States. 3. Universities and colleges—United States—Finance. I.
Stein, Donald G.
   LB2326 .3.B89 2004
   338.4'3378—dc21

                                   2003009387

British Cataloging-in-Publication data record for this book is available from the
British Library.

Manufactured in the United States of America

Contents

Acknowledgments   *vii*

Chapter 1   A Personal Perspective on the Selling of Academia   *1*
DONALD G. STEIN

Chapter 2   College Sports, Inc.: How Big-Time Athletic
Departments Run Interference for College, Inc.   *17*
MURRAY SPERBER

Chapter 3   The Benefits and Cost of Commercialization of
the Academy   *32*
DEREK BOK

Chapter 4   Increased Commercialization of the Academy
Following the Bayh-Dole Act of 1980   *48*
MARY L. GOOD

Chapter 5   Delicate Balance: Market Forces versus the Public Interest   *56*
JAMES J. DUDERSTADT

Chapter 6   Pushing the Envelope in University Involvement
with Commercialization   *75*
RONALD A. BOHLANDER

Chapter 7   Conflicting Goals and Values: When Commercialization
Enters into Tenure and Promotion Decisions   *89*
KAREN A. HOLBROOK AND ERIC C. DAHL

Chapter 8   Buyer and Seller Views of University-
Industry Licensing   *103*
JERRY G. THURSBY AND MARIE C. THURSBY

Chapter 9   The Increasingly Proprietary Nature of Publicly Funded
Biomedical Research: Benefits and Threats   *117*
ARTI K. RAI

Chapter 10   The Clinical Trials Business: Who Gains?   *127*
                MARCIA ANGELL

Chapter 11   Reforming Research Ethics in an Age of Multivested
                Science   *133*
                SHELDON KRIMSKY

Chapter 12   The Academy and Industry: A View across the Divide   *153*
                ZACH W. HALL

Chapter 13   Responsible Innovation in the Commercialized
                University   *161*
                DAVID H. GUSTON

                Contributors   *175*
                Index   *179*

Acknowledgments

I thank William F. Chace, president of Emory University; Howard Hunter, provost of Emory University; and Senator Sam Nunn and his colleagues at Bank of America for their financial support of the Conference on Commercialization of the Academy, held in April 2002, which led to this edited volume. Frank Karel, former vice president of the Robert Wood Johnson Foundation, and the foundation itself both graciously contributed to the planning and financial support necessary for both the book and the conference. This project would not have been possible without the initial and continued support of the Robert Wood Johnson Foundation, and I am deeply grateful for its help and its recognition of the need to examine the influence of private corporations and economic interests on higher education and research. Finally, I am deeply appreciative of the careful, excellent work done by my editorial assistant, Lauren Hoffmann, and, in the later stages of the manuscript, my office assistant, Leslie McCann.

Buying In or Selling Out?

Chapter 1

A Personal Perspective on the Selling of Academia

DONALD G. STEIN

Why Compile a Book about the Commercialization of Academia?

It has now been almost four decades since I started my career, first as a university professor and laboratory researcher in the field of psychobiology and neuroscience; then, much later, as a dean of graduate studies and a vice provost/vice president for research. Before returning to research and teaching, I had the good fortune to serve for thirteen years in senior administration at both Rutgers University and Emory University, two distinguished research institutions. At both, I was charged with the administration of graduate programs and many of the faculty's research activities. These administrative responsibilities gave me the opportunity to see first hand how the control, use, and sale of intellectual property at the universities were affecting the values and principles associated with research, teaching, and scholarship across all traditional disciplines and schools involved in graduate and undergraduate education.

While working as a dean and a research administrator, I also continued to teach and conduct research; so like everyone else in the sciences, I sought external funding for my projects. Trying to balance research and teaching with administration meant that I struggled with the same day-to-day issues that faculty members also addressed as they tried to balance their teaching and service duties to the university with their research interests and obligations. Frankly, I did not like what I was seeing, either as an administrator or as a member of the faculty. What began to concern me was not the pursuit of "extra," or external, funding but the overwhelming emphasis on the pursuit of

money through the sale of intellectual property as well as the changes in academic attitudes and values that this chase was producing. In a sense, every
professor involved in basic research or scholarship eventually has to recognize that he or she is part scholar, part salesperson. When professors try to
persuade department chairs, deans, foundation executives, or federal bureau-
crats to give them money for research, for time off from teaching, for more
time to consult, and so on, they are selling their ideas with the promise that
something "good" will result from their efforts. This reality has been part of
academic life for as long as I've known it. Every candidate seeking a job in a
research-oriented institution understands it, so why does there now seem to
be a greater problem with marketing our work, perhaps more efficiently and
effectively than we've done in the past? At scientific professional meetings
and informal gatherings, I've noticed that discussions now focus primarily on
the increasing pressures on faculty to support themselves at work. Senior investigators in the entrepreneurial loop have complained to me that they per-
sonally have almost no time to conduct research because so much of their
effort is devoted to finding new revenue streams. They do this by negotiating
contracts with the business sector to pursue research that essentially helps to
develop new techniques or devices that have commercial potential. Thus, in
return for their support, the companies get exclusive first rights to anything
developed in that laboratory.

There are those who argue that academic scholars should profit just as
much from their work as anyone else does in the business, sports, or medical
communities. Indeed, many university administrators do not acknowledge that
a problem even exists, and their positions are well represented in this book.
Others believe that the situation has been overdramatized by less successful
and less productive members of the academic community, who are trying, in
times of change, to protect their tenure. The "Nota Bene" section of *Academe* (September/October 2001), the bulletin of the American Association
of University Professors, featured a brief article on the Business–Higher Education Forum's report suggesting that there ought to be stronger ties between
academia and industry for a variety of reasons. The note points out, however,
that "although research universities have long collaborated with industry to
their mutual benefit, collaborations have never been free of concerns that the
financial ties of researchers or their institutions to industry may exert improper
pressure on the design and outcome of research. This is especially true of research that has as its goal commercially valuable innovations, which is the
most common type of industry-sponsored research" (*http//:www.aaup.org/
publications/Academe/01SO/SO01NB.HTM#9*). In this book, I attempt to provide a balanced perspective on these questions. But why would a distinguished

group of former and present research university presidents, deans, government officials, and business leaders find it worthwhile to come together to produce this volume?

What Environmental Pressures Lead to Commercialization of the Academy?

During the past ten or fifteen years, faculties at the major research institutions have come under increasingly explicit as well as implicit demands to generate income and external research support for the institutions that employ them. When I began my work as a scientist in the 1960s, federal funding was a wonderful way to purchase needed equipment, test new ideas, and generate extra income during the summer while allowing me to devote all my time to research. During the academic year, laboratory work had to be balanced with the demands of teaching, committee work, student supervision, community involvement, and personal commitments. Now, especially in the health sciences but also in the basic sciences, faculty are often recruited at research universities with the understanding that they will have to generate part or all of their salaries through external funding for the duration of their careers at the university. At some institutions, arts and sciences faculty who are successful at obtaining external grants and contracts can "buy off" their teaching to the point that they never have to see an undergraduate or participate in the day-to-day activities of college life. Such academic stars are highly desirable to recruiters because they bring luster and income to institutions trying to enhance their own prestige, but these successful faculty members are like free agents in sports: they sell themselves to the highest bidder and have no particular sense of commitment to the places that hire them. Through corporate contracts and federal grants, some of these faculty have forty or more postdoctoral research associates working exclusively on a single faculty member's research. To replace these stars in the classroom, department chairs often have to employ adjunct faculty, who roam from place to place on a part-time basis. In some prestigious and costly institutions, faculty associates cover 25 percent of all the course offerings and teach all the freshman and sophomore courses. Both young and more seasoned faculty members know that the reward structure of the university often favors those who bring in the cash; so the cycle repeats itself at every level, leading to competition rather than collegiality, paperwork rather than productivity, and increasing pressure to do what will sell rather than what is intellectually stimulating, innovative, and important to teach and learn.

Pressures to generate more external income run counter to the primary mission of the university, which is to teach and to generate new knowledge and discovery in an unbiased manner, free from commercial pressure and special interests. The pressures are particularly blatant in the sciences and information technologies; but they are growing in the arts and humanities, where faculty are encouraged to consult, develop, copyright, and sell their lecture notes and syllabi or to develop and sell distance learning courses over the Internet—with the university, of course, taking a piece of the action. According to Gary Rhoades (2001), "from one institution to the next, the intellectual products of professors are being translated into commodities sold in the marketplace. The type of intellectual property varies from community colleges to research universities and from education to engineering departments. The University of California, for example, sought to require professors to post course materials on the Web so that it could sign a contract with a company to deliver the courses through distance education" (38). In such cases who will evaluate the quality of work aside from its commercial value? Where does one draw the line between commercially viable product development and straightforward scholarly research? Who decides whether such work is worthy of widespread dissemination? Who controls the advertising and sale of such information? And finally, where does the money go? And who decides how it will be used? Given these economic incentives and pressures, it hardly comes as a surprise that a number of highly visible and distinguished author-historians were recently found to have plagiarized the work of other scholars and falsified historical data to promote their own books and products to the public. In these cases, the pursuit of scholarship appears to have taken second place to the pursuit of commercialization and media exposure.

Commercialization and commodification have other insidious effects on academic life. Less popular courses, such as those in classics or literature, may be dropped in favor of courses that are more marketable to students. Faculty are sought who work in areas for which federal and corporate funding is available rather than in areas that might enhance the intellectual quality of the institution. Very often, attractive start-up packages are offered to faculty members who may have the capacity to generate large grants or contracts. Those whose work is considered esoteric, even though they may be excellent teachers, are often stripped of space and facilities for their work because their research will not generate corporate interest or federal funding. It is not uncommon these days for universities to commit hundreds of millions of dollars to creating new research buildings in the hope of attracting faculty who hold important patents or have the potential for developing them. If the gamble fails, the entire institution then pays the price of covering the overhead and the costs of maintaining the facility. This often comes at the expense of other programs throughout the institution, which then cannot grow or develop.

Faculty members whose research and expertise can generate substantial income are often treated very differently from their counterparts who focus on teaching and the pursuit of esoteric knowledge of no interest to the marketplace. Entrepreneurial professors who have a history of successful patent generation are often treated like sports figures, commanding much higher salaries, more staff support, commitments to large amounts of start-up money, and often complete freedom from any teaching responsibilities, while their less business-oriented colleagues have to pick up the extra teaching loads and day-to-day committee work required for university functions. Faculty whose work has commercial value are often encouraged by their institutions to seek venture capital to form start-up companies, often with the institution itself investing in the start-up in return for equity positions or exclusive licensing rights. Institutions have been known to invest so heavily in biotechnology and information technology start-ups that their endowments and other important university functions have been threatened. Some faculty members spend so much time "consulting" for their own companies or sitting on the boards of companies in which they have commercial interest that they are rarely on campus.

Although such activity may not be viewed as a conflict of interest, it certainly implies a conflict of commitment, especially if 100 percent of a professor's salary is paid by the university. On the one hand, such situations may be more easily justified in a private university, where the administration and the trustees can use their discretion in how their monies are spent, even if alumni and parents of students think this is not the best use of tuition dollars. On the other hand, when state and public institutions play this game, the issues become more complex because both taxpayer and tuition dollars subsidize the business ventures of individual faculty in the hope of some future gain. It is interesting to note, however, that only a few such ventures have returned substantial profits to the institutions that funded them.

Overall, if the public begins to feel that it cannot trust its tax-supported universities to be objective and free from commercial pressures to produce products, confidence in the institutions that take this route of development may be substantially eroded. Given the recent crises produced by companies like WorldCom and Enron, there is reason to be concerned that the commercialization of scholarship also may be associated with serious pitfalls. If commercialization of the academy affected only a few tenured professors who had no business in the classroom under any circumstances, encouraging their research and business activities might at least help to recover some of the costs of retaining them under the terms of their lifetime contracts. But I don't think this is the case. Junior faculty as well as graduate students and sometimes even undergraduates have come under the influence of commercialization pressures.

During my tenure as dean, I had the opportunity to interview many young Ph.D.s seeking their first or second jobs in the arts and sciences as well as in professional schools such as medicine, public health, nursing, and business. From the first, these candidates are told that if they are to succeed in getting tenure, they must generate grants and contracts, both federal and private. At Emory University's School of Medicine, for example, untenured basic sciences faculty are told they must generate at least two federal contracts or grants if they expect to be considered for tenure. Federal contracts are preferred to those from private industry or foundations, not because the work is necessarily better or more innovative but because government contracts can generate considerable indirect income to the university. For example, for every federal dollar provided for the direct costs of research, about fifty-five cents is added as an indirect cost return to the university; private foundations and companies will not usually provide this indirect funding. In some institutions faculty are expected to generate a certain number of indirect cost dollars per square foot of laboratory space they receive. If their grant income falls below this "rent," they may be moved to lesser quarters or lose their space altogether, a sure prescription for the downward spiral of failure and the eventual denial of tenure. In some medical schools physician faculty members earn large sums for themselves and their laboratories by supervising numbers of clinical trials that test new drugs under contract to pharmaceutical companies. Marcia Angell discusses some of the problems and pitfalls of this type of collaboration, in which the risks of loss of objectivity and potential conflicts of interest often compete with the possibility of substantial financial gain for the parties involved in the trials.

The pressure to generate their own income and fringe benefits leaves younger faculty with little time to spend with their students or in other forms of collegial activities. Every free moment is spent seeking outside funding or trying to protect their intellectual property through patents and copyrights. Is it worth the effort? First, lackluster teaching is the likely result of this pressure to raise money for research and to commodify what faculty members do. Professors who have to spend the great majority of their time seeking multiple sources of outside funding simply don't have enough time left to spend in the classroom. For this reason, many of our better biomedical and life scientists seek positions in medical schools where teaching requirements are minimal. With so little emphasis on undergraduate teaching, who is left to do it? Most is done by graduate students with no teaching experience, who rarely have a clue about what is expected of them. Is it any wonder that American undergraduates no longer pursue science-based careers?

Second, many universities hold hundreds of patents and spend a good deal of money in filing patent applications that could go to other worthy projects, such as scholarships, fellowships, or community service initiatives. Rarely do universities have the financial or staff resources to market the patents aggressively, so most of them languish in offices of technology transfer. Only a very few universities have ever made substantial dollars from patents held by faculty. Some wags have said that institutions would be better off investing in state lotteries because the probability of success in the Big Game is greater than hitting the jackpot with a faculty patent.

The problem for both junior and senior faculty is that they often are forced to do "bread and butter" research—that is, safe, noncontroversial research that generates high indirect cost returns and the possibility of a patent—rather than follow their own interests. And this is just one part of the problem. To survive in today's academic setting, scientists must go where the money is, which means that they cannot take chances on doing novel research or spending too much time with their students or participating in other outside activities. In addition, biomedical scientists are constantly seeking support from biotechnology or pharmaceutical companies, both of which have specific commercial agendas for developing new patentable products that they can then sell in the marketplace. When faculty accept contracts from these companies, they are often prohibited from sharing their findings with colleagues, publishing, disclosing the results of their research at scientific meetings, or discussing their work with students in the classroom. Such work can conflict with the values of academic freedom and the open discussion of ideas, which are at the heart of the university's mission.

It is no longer uncommon to hear a panelist at a professional meeting tell the audience that she cannot state explicitly what she is doing because her work is under patent review. One can only wonder why such researchers come to the meeting in the first place! According to Julia Liebeskind (2001), in the biomedical sciences "patenting has changed collegial relations in the field. Scientists interested in patenting, for example, may restrict the size of their research teams to minimize disputes over claims to inventions. Some scientists are even reluctant to engage in casual conversation with their colleagues, present new ideas at meetings, or even have students, or other faculty, work in their laboratories on a visiting basis" (52).

Not only are faculty hesitant to share their ideas if there is any chance that they might have commercial value; they are also unwilling to share techniques, reagents, chemicals, or cells that in the past would have been given freely to colleagues working on similar projects. Often the institutions of the individual investigators insist that a material transfer agreement between the donor and the recipient colleague be signed before any potentially useful material is exchanged. Colleagues from different universities who want to collaborate are sometimes required by their respective institutions to sign nondisclosure and confidentiality agreements limiting when papers can be presented or published. At this point, university lawyers become involved; and often months pass before any work can be done, if it is ever done at all. In this context, collegiality and intellectual exchange are sacrificed for potential commercial gain, even though the odds are small that any financial gain will be realized.

In my own laboratory, for example, we wanted to purchase some new gene-chip technology from a faculty colleague who had a small biotechnology company situated at another university. We were offered a reduced price for the materials if we would agree to give authorship to and share oversight of publication with the provider of the technology on any of the research that we published using his chip. Although it sounds simple, this agreement would have required us to share control of any intellectual property generated by our research with someone whose only relation to the work was the sale of a piece of technical equipment.

In another recent case, we hoped to obtain tissue samples from a colleague at another school to use in our research on stem cells and recovery from brain injury. The material transfer agreement we were asked to sign to have access to the tissue required us to refrain from comparing the donated cells to any other types of cells for safety and efficacy in case we found that the donated tissue was less effective or potentially harmful to the subjects into which they were placed. If strong financial interests had not been at stake, one would guess that the provider of the unique cells would have been delighted to know whether or not the tissue was useful. This is just another example of how commercialization of academia has affected the quality of research and scholarship. We refused to accept the agreement.

So where is all this evidence leading? First, the objectivity, quality, and type of research in the United States suffer if the primary motive for research and scholarship is profit. If we go too far down this road, where will there be a place for innovation and the quest for knowledge without any immediate payoffs? Businesses have every right to expect that research will lead to product development and increased market share, but should our universities switch to this model as well? Second, in the sciences at least, the pressure to "publish or perish" is being supplanted in too many cases by the pressure to "publish, patent, or perish." This is one reason why fewer of our top students are choosing to enter graduate programs and pursue careers in basic research. The pressures are just too much for the salaries offered. At least in the sciences, the academic community is changing dramatically. One has only to look at the fact that more than 50 percent of our postdoctoral research fellows in university laboratories are from abroad, mostly India and the People's Republic of China.

In a number of institutions, postdoctoral fellows are beginning to organize for collective bargaining because their working conditions are so unsatisfactory. They accrue no seniority, rarely get decent benefits, have temporary visa status, and often work for salaries that are substantially less than that of other university workers with fewer skills and less training. They are sometimes required to teach in less popular laboratory classes. The result is that college undergraduates feel neglected by their professors, see the pressures that they are under, hear their complaints, and choose to earn degrees in business or go on to medical school.

For all these reasons, the time seemed ripe to bring together a group of distinguished individuals from academia, government, and industry to discuss the issues and problems associated with the commercialization of academia. The participants represent a range of opinions on the matter at hand. Some argue that commercializing academic intellectual property is exactly the role that universities should be playing to promote the public good. Others argue that the price of commercialization is simply too high because traditional academic values and principles are being sacrificed to the profit motive. The purpose of the book, however, is not simply to provide a platform for the pros and cons of commercialization. The participants recognize that commercialization is the current reality for our institutions and that it has progressed too far for us to return to the good old days. Despite markedly different perspectives, most of the authors believe that guidelines governing commercial activities should be established so that our institutions of higher learning can continue to sustain the free and open inquiry, scholarship, and collegiality that remain core academic values.

The Conference on Commercialization of the Academy was held 5–7 April 2002 at Emory University. A planning grant for the meeting, travel stipends, and honoraria for the participants were graciously provided by the Robert Wood Johnson Foundation of Princeton, New Jersey. John Stone of Emory University's School of Medicine, a consultant to the Robert Wood Johnson Foundation; and Frank Karel, then vice president of the foundation, were enthusiastic in their support for the meeting because of their concerns about the issues. As the structure of the conference developed, the president's office at

Emory suggested incorporating the symposium under the auspices of the Sam Nunn/Bank of America Policy Forum. Former U.S. senator Sam Nunn has had a longstanding interest in policy issues shaping American life and security. Each year the forum is held at one of three institutions in Georgia: the Georgia Institute of Technology, the University of Georgia, or Emory University. It fell to Emory to host the 2002 forum, and Emory's president, William Chace, felt strongly that the topic of commercialization of the academy was both appropriate and timely. The range of sponsorship demonstrates that a broad spectrum of policymakers, in both government and academia, recognizes that the issues of commercialization of academic life can have a serious impact on American educational policy and practice.

Given the importance of higher education in driving the economy of the United States, it is imperative to make those who shape and implement such policies and practices aware of and sensitive to the forces determining what present and future generations of our students will think and do. Institutions of higher learning also need to give some thought to what they want to be. For example, how does one combine the desire to promote an entrepreneurial spirit among faculty and students while focusing on the essential differences between a university and a software or biotechnology company? What are the essential values that our universities and colleges need to teach our future generations, and what do institutions of higher learning want to be remembered historically for having accomplished? What is the moral responsibility of the institution to its faculty and students? Is the university to become a guild of skilled craftspeople marketing their wares to the highest bidder? Or is there something more collegial and special about the college experience for all who participate in it? Commercialization of education, research, and scholarship is clearly a challenge to the very essence of the historical role of nonvocational higher education. This challenge will require considerable discussion and debate, and all participants in the university community have a stake.

Emory University is in a unique position to serve as a kind of laboratory for developing and testing new guidelines to shape how commercialization at this institution will proceed. Emory is distinctive in several ways. First, it is a private institution with a relatively substantial endowment that allows it to take innovative risks if its faculty and administration choose to do so. Second, Emory has no political agendas to meet, as is the case at state institutions, and thus has much more flexibility of operation and management. Third, at the moment, Emory University is in a state of flux. The president and the executive vice president for finance have both announced their retirements. The positions of provost, dean of the college, and dean of the graduate school also are open. While certainly there is some concern about all these changes, they do provide a wonderful opportunity for the faculty and the board of trustees to ask candidates where they stand on the issues and what they plan to do about them. Admittedly, this inquiry can be only one part of a much larger set of parameters that will affect the future of the institution, but it will be an important part of faculty hiring decisions and of Emory's choice of direction in the years ahead. If this book can help in the discussion, it will have accomplished its goal.

Chapter 2, written by Murray Sperber of Indiana University in Bloomington, is a delightful and somewhat cynical historical review of commercialization of the academy, starting with its impact on college sports at the beginning of the twentieth century. Sperber describes how commercialization of college athletics set the stage for commercialization of all other aspects of university life, including scholarship and research. The issue of how college athletics can affect the priorities and directions of the university has been publicized in an article titled "How Football Can Crush a College," published in the *New York Times*, 22 December 2002, which describes the hidden costs to academic programs and priorities when universities get carried away with paying huge salaries to coaches and spend prolifically to build and recruit teams.

In chapter 3, the former president of Harvard University, Derek Bok, addresses both the benefits and the costs to universities of growing commercialization. He points out that, in the final analysis, very few universities benefit from large-scale profit-making ventures. Bok suggests that commercialization from athletics to research often demands costs that are higher than returns and that such attempts may be a form of pandering to market demands. He further suggests that, while commercialization does not always bring out the best in people, universities that try not to play the game are often left behind in their ability to recruit top faculty and students. Bok concludes his chapter by recommending that faculty members and administrators pay more attention to evaluating the risks of commercialization before they commit their university to this path.

In chapter 4, Mary Good, formerly chief executive officer of Allied Signal Corporation and now dean of engineering at the University of Arkansas in Little Rock, reviews the background and context of the twenty-year-old Bayh-Dole Act, which allows university faculty on taxpayer-supported research grants to patent and license their discoveries to private industries rather than put the information into the public domain. She argues that it is exactly the mission of the state universities, especially those that were originally land-grant schools, to interact with business and develop new products for the public welfare. According to Good, Bayh-Dole became law because it was essential to strengthening the U.S. economy just as the country was embracing globalization of industry and commerce. While she acknowledges that problems have emerged, Good believes that Bayh-Dole has been immensely helpful and can be improved by appropriate dialogue between academic and industrial leaders.

Former president of the University of Michigan James Duderstadt asks in chapter 5 whether it makes sense that the Bayh-Dole Act still grants patent rights to universities for government-sponsored research. Does transferring intellectual property to commercial interests benefit the public and the institutions in which the work was developed? What is the fundamental mission of the public university, and how does it serve the public interest by selling its intellectual property to the highest bidders? If higher education is a public good, how does this notion fit with the sale of its intellectual property?

In chapter 6, Ronald Bohlander of the Georgia Institute of Technology in Atlanta describes the steps that institution has taken to manage issues of technology transfer and commercialization of the faculty's intellectual property. The Georgia Tech Research Institute (GTRI) was mandated by the Georgia legislature to promote research and encourage industrial and economic development for the state. As Bohlander shows, the GTRI model is one of many university attempts to address how faculty translate their research into corporate products. Questions concerning who benefits, how much they benefit, and whether any public good will come of the efforts are issues facing many research institutions, which must convince policymakers, alumni, parents, and prospective donors that a university's overall mission and direction will not be compromised by its commercial ventures.

Karen Holbrook, president of Ohio State University, and Eric Dahl of the University of Georgia point out in chapter 7 that we have gone too far to turn back in developing relationships between higher education and business. In 2000, more than $1.25 billion in university revenues was generated in licensing fees and options; and this wealth creation, along with the increased number of jobs created by technology transfer, is considered an important sign of the success of the commercialization endeavor. Holbrook and Dahl discuss how the entrepreneurial spirit is evaluated in the context of promotion and tenure decisions at the university. Is there a different set of expectations for faculty whose work generates wealth for the university as opposed to those who hew to the more traditional academic values of scholarship and the creation of knowledge for its own sake? For junior faculty, should the commercialization of their technology and discoveries be considered as a part of the tenure and promotion criteria? Are scholar entrepreneurs the wave of the future for higher education? The answers to the questions raised in this chapter will have an important impact on the focus and direction of American universities in the years ahead.

Jerry Thursby and Marie Thursby, of Emory University and Georgia Institute of Technology respectively, look at some hard data, surveying in chapter 8 how university industry licensing has affected income streams and how successful such interactions have been in promoting and developing technology transfer. Has licensing of intellectual property been effective in generating substantial income for the universities? Has there been a substantial increase in product development because of such licensing? Have faculty benefited from these agreements? These authors also report that, about half the time, corporate sponsors of university research reserve the right to withhold or block publication to protect industry secrets. Should a university engage in this kind of research? For instance, should it accept limits on its control of information that do not endanger national security?

Arti Rai is an attorney specializing in intellectual property rights. In chapter 9 she reviews how our legal system encourages academics working in the field of biotechnology to attempt to patent just about everything they can. She also discusses the financial impact of product licensing on university activities and the role that such licensing plays in restricting the flow of communication essential to the conduct of good science. She also considers whether or not exclusive patenting is financially beneficial or whether models other than exclusive patenting may be more effective in promoting product development.

In chapter 10, Marcia Angell, a physician and former editor of the *New England Journal of Medicine*, discusses her concerns about how accepting pharmaceutical-company funding to test new drugs at academic medical centers has dramatically changed the mission and focus of these medical schools. She highlights the real and potential conflicts of interest that emerge for both physicians and the institutions that employ them with the commercialization of academic medicine and recommends steps to correct the abuses.

Sheldon Krimsky of Tufts University discusses in chapter 11 the growing symbiosis between academia and commerce and, in this context, the need for developing new policies on research ethics. Krimsky presents an excellent review of the literature in the field and provides data showing that intense commercialization is slowing the progress of both basic and applied research in universities and the corporate sector. He also discusses why greater attention must be paid to both potential and actual conflicts of interest. Krimsky's chapter shows cause for concern about how unbiased biomedical and basic research is being challenged by commercial influences on the process and product of the work.

Like Mary Good, Zach Hall has worked as both a university administrator and an executive in a biotechnology company. In chapter 12, he suggests that academic institutions and private companies need each other and can provide highly symbiotic and beneficial working environments that benefit society at large. Hall claims that the key to success in these relationships is for both parties to recognize that they may have different needs, agendas, and missions. As long as the distinctions are preserved and recognized, Hall sees no conflicts, arguing that both sides succeed in advancing the research necessary to remain competitive at both the intellectual and economic levels.

In chapter 13, David Guston, a professor of public policy at Rutgers University, addresses the future, asking how the ethics of commercialization affect both the public and the academic community and proposing that research universities develop special centers to evaluate responsible innovation so that commercialization does not corrupt the academic mission. He offers a number of interesting and specific suggestions for the development of norms and guidelines that would shape the commitment of funds and other university resources to product development and innovation.

Conclusion

So where do we go from here? This book presents a number of thought-provoking chapters, each with its own perspective on how best to approach commercialization of the academy. There is no question that industry-academic relationships will continue to grow, especially if federal funding decreases in the years ahead and if there is a growing trend toward training students for specific vocations rather than educating them primarily to be informed and well-rounded citizens.

Maybe I'm old-fashioned, but I don't like to think of the university as just another service or commodity business. If we accept that some commercialization of the academic enterprise is probably a good thing, what steps should be taken to protect both students and their teachers from pressures that might diminish the quality of teaching and the objective search for truth that should be the bedrock of academic research and scholarship? There are no easy answers to this debate, but I would like to offer some suggestions based on the readings. These opinions are mine and should not be taken to represent those of the contributing authors or other members of the Emory faculty and administration.

- Universities collectively and individually need to examine and evaluate their specific mission and clearly state to their public what that mission is and how they intend to implement it.

- At least every ten years, that mission ought to be reevaluated by the university community to determine whether the objectives have been met. The impact of commercialization on faculty and student values and morale ought to be carefully evaluated as a part of the self-study.
- Every university should create a broadly based committee of faculty and trustees to review the impact and relevance of commercialization on the university's mission and purpose. The committee should establish guidelines about acceptable and unacceptable forms of commercialization activity. These norms may vary from institution to institution.
- The criteria for faculty hiring, promotion, and tenure ought to be clearly stated. If entrepreneurial activity is valued, as Karen Holbrook and others represented in this book say it should be, then this preference ought to be made clear to candidates at the time of hiring. To provide effective balance, teaching and basic scholarship ought to be given as much, if not more, weight in the promotion and tenure process.
- To promote research and scholarship, universities need to wean themselves from dependence on external commercial support and federal funding. If research and scholarship are primary missions of the institution, they should not be left to the mercy of corporate needs and agendas or the whims and fancies of federal and private funding agencies. If universities are truly in the business of scholarship, then scholarship and research ought to be considered as much a part of university costs as presidential salaries, football coaches, heating, gyms, and athletics. Perhaps in this context, prospective donors need to be more effectively persuaded that support of scholarship has as much intrinsic value to the university as a new gym, a football team, or a student union.
- In this same context, schools of medicine ought to decide whether they want only to train physicians or whether they also want to engage in research. If the latter, they should consider providing adequate support for this endeavor on a continuing basis and as a cost of doing business. At the risk of sounding self-serving, support for basic biomedical research is just as important as year-end bonuses for clinical medical staff. Forcing researchers to cover the costs of their own salaries and research creates a situation full of potential for conflicts of interest and commitment in a teaching institution. Even worse, it often results in pedestrian research

because it forces researchers to go where the money is rather than pursue interesting leads and more innovative problems.

• Universities' tendency to put up new buildings in the hope of becoming more attractive to big-money scholars and donors may be less effective than spending resources on faculty and staff who have devoted a good part of their lives to their respective institutions. In other words, universities need to pay more than lip service to helping long-term faculty lead more productive and active academic lives.

No doubt, the reader will have other suggestions. These points are just the beginning of the dialogue, by no means the end.

References

Liebeskind, Julia. 2001. "Risky Business: Universities and Intellectual Property." *Academe* 87 (September/October): 49–53.

"Nota Bene: University-Industry Partnerships Touted." *Academe* (*http://www.aaup.org/publications/Academe/01SO/SO01NB.HTM#9*).

Rhoades, Gary. 2001. "Whose Property Is It? Negotiating with Universities." *Academe* 87 (September/October): 38–43.

Chapter 2

College Sports, Inc.

How Big-Time Athletic Departments
Run Interference for College, Inc.

MURRAY SPERBER

History

Almost every sports historian agrees that the first intercollegiate athletic event
in American history was a boat race between Harvard and Yale in 1852 on
Lake Winnepesaukee in New Hampshire. Crew was becoming popular as a
club sport in the United States, in both gentlemen's clubs and student clubs.
Because of the fame of the Oxford-Cambridge boat race in England and the
anglophilia of schools like Harvard and Yale, it was inevitable that a boat race
between the two would occur. But why at this time and place?

The superintendent of the Boston, Concord, and Montreal Railroad,
James M. Elkins, who had invested capital in land, tracks, and equipment at
the New Hampshire lake, wanted to develop the area as a summer resort. He
had the bright idea that a boat race on the lake between the two most famous schools in the nation would attract newspaper coverage and publicity
for his resort area. He wrote to the crew people at the schools: "If you will get
up a regatta on the lake between Yale and Harvard, I will pay all the bills"
(Smith and Lucas 1978, 197). Apparently, for the owner of the railroad, "the
first intercollegiate contest was entirely a commercial venture" (197).

Historians have examined the student records at Yale and Harvard for
this period and have determined that a number of members of both crews were
not registered students at the schools; probably they were professional rowers
who hired themselves out to gentlemen's clubs in Boston and New York. On

this day they were ringers hired to help their employers (Yale or Harvard) win the race (Smith 1988, Rader 1983). Thus, in the very first college sports contest in American history, even before the starting gun went off or an oar hit the water, two elements were at play: the event was totally commercial, and the participants were cheating. The history of intercollegiate athletics has gone downhill from there.

Crew remained the most popular college sport for a number of decades and was always highly commercial. Then football replaced it as the number-one sport in American collegiate athletics. Again commercialism reigned, as did ringers and tramp athletes—men who went from school to school selling their services for a football season or a game or two. Professional football did not exist, and the colleges provided tramp athletes with a nice income. One famous athlete was James Hogan, considered the best player at the turn of the twentieth century, employed by no less a luminary than Yale's legendary Walter Camp, the man who wrote the basic rules of football and invented such elements as the All-America team.

Hogan was already twenty-seven years old when he started playing at Yale. He lived in luxurious accommodations provided by Yale alumni; never attended classes; and (most profitably for him) was given the American Tobacco Company concession for New Haven, receiving a commission from every cigarette pack sold in the city. Of course, the company also used his name and picture to promote its products. In addition, Hogan was in charge of the game programs for all Yale home football contests and took a cut of the advertising sold for them, much of it from the tobacco companies. In this way, the American Tobacco Company identified itself with one of the most prestigious universities in the country.

American Tobacco and Yale was not a singular tie-in. Looking through football game programs and student publications from the first decades of the twentieth century, the reader can see the omnipresence of tobacco companies, which promoted an abundance of cigarette brands and tied most of the ads to images of the healthiest young men on campus: the athletes who endorsed the products. The Carnegie Foundation issued a famous report in 1929 on intercollegiate athletics, noting: "The advertiser [particularly the cigarette manufacturers but also other companies] has been among the most persistent exploiter of college athletics" and college athletes (Savage et al. 1929, 276).

Thus, the first corporations to consistently use colleges and universities for their own ends were tobacco companies. Throughout the first half of the twentieth century, cigarette company advertising emphasized youth and healthiness; and their advertising agencies purchased key locations in college football programs and other student publications, everything from the student newspaper and yearbook to playbills for the drama club's productions. Even though scientific studies on the lethality of smoking came much later, Americans have long known about its dangers; "coffin nails" and "death sticks" were popular early twentieth-century nicknames for cigarettes. But the tobacco industry countered this awareness with ads featuring handsome, fit young men and women smoking its products. College athletes were featured often because in the 1920s college football had exploded in popularity, becoming the second most popular sport in the United States, just behind professional baseball.

Cigarette advertising gained momentum in the 1930s at a time when economic depression made smoking a cheap pleasure. During World War II, the tobacco industry tied much of its advertising to both sports and patriotism. In a typical wartime advertising campaign, which appeared in a full season of football programs, Liggett and Myers showed a male collegian in an Army Reserve uniform bicycling across the middle pages of the program, his left hand gripping both the handlebar and a cigarette. The logo "Chesterfield," in large type, occupies the upper half of the page; the team rosters appear in tiny print within the bike wheels. Not just the uniform indicated patriotism; because of the gas shortage, so did the bicycle (Sperber 1998).

The volume and slickness of cigarette advertising, as well as its ubiquity, help explain college students' increasing consumption of and, for many, addiction to nicotine from the 1920s on. Moreover, cigarette companies urged female students to smoke, with the goal of making smoking acceptable for all women; previously, females who smoked were considered déclassé. Significantly, neither the college sports establishment nor any individual school objected to the cigarette ads or even the prominence of brand logos compared with school logos. The amount of money generated by the tobacco industry was already so large and its support of college sports so important, especially during the Depression and World War II, that higher education authorities not only failed to question the ethics of tobacco industry advertising but actively solicited it for game programs and other campus publications. Student newspapers and magazines, traditionally underwritten by the school, were willingly shifted to commercial advertisers.

Meanwhile, university researchers had started to study the effects of smoking; and scientific journals as well as some national magazines relayed the early, generally negative, findings. Thus, in the 1940s and 1950s, university personnel, even more than most Americans, knew about the dangers of smoking. Nevertheless, partly because of the tobacco industry's financial support of college sports and student publications, they did not act on their knowledge.

More than a half-century later, why should we care about these historic tobacco ads in campus publications? Wasn't it a good thing that cigarette advertising sustained various student periodicals? Wouldn't many of them have gone under without the support of advertisers? Without these publications, wouldn't many budding journalists or authors have had their careers aborted? These same arguments continue today: schools need money, so why not accept corporate sponsorship? For answers, let's begin with the Carnegie Report of 1929 and its condemnation of commercialism in college sports and college life. The report summed up the sins of college sports in the 1920s, noting an increasing number of large stadiums, the media hype that surrounded football games, and the increase in importance of coaches like Knute Rockne: "Commercialism has made possible the erection of fine academic buildings and the increase of equipment from the profits of college athletics, but those profits have been gained because colleges have permitted the youths entrusted to their care to be openly exploited. At such colleges and universities, the primary emphasis has been transferred from the things of the spirit or the mind to the material" (Savage et al. 1929, 306–7).

The authors of the report came from private liberal arts colleges and lacked sympathy for large land-grant institutions with their mandate for public service. Nevertheless, they did believe that colleges and universities were special places separated from the ordinary commerce of society. The authors did not deny that profits from college sports had made many campus buildings possible. They did, however, question the entire commercial sports enterprise, wondering whether colleges and universities had departed too far from their educational missions by providing entertainment for the public. The report authors argued:

> It is the undergraduates who have suffered most, and will continue to suffer most, from commercialism, and its results. More than any other force, it has tended to distort the values of college life and to increase its emphasis upon the material and the monetary. Indeed, at no point in the educational process has commercialism in college athletics wrought more mischief than in its effect upon the American undergraduate. And the distressing fact is that the college, the Fostering Mother, has permitted and even encouraged it to do these things in the name of education. (306–7)

In other words, the university proponents of college sports, particularly university presidents and boards of trustees, claimed that the function of sports is educational. Disputing that claim, the report also attempted to refute an argument still put forth today:

> The argument that commercialism in college athletics is merely a reflection of the commercialism of modern life is specious. It is not

the affair of the college or the university to reflect [absolutely contemporary] modern life. If the university is to be a socializing agency worthy of the name, it must endeavor to ameliorate the conditions of existence, spiritual as well as physical, and to train men and women who shall lead the nations out of bondage to those conditions. To neither of these missions does commercialism in college athletics soundly contribute [nor do other elements of commercialism on campus]. (306–7)

We could not write these words today; in the postmodern era we have become more cynical. Yet for all of the antique phrases and sentiments in the Carnegie Report, its vision of colleges and universities as special and unique places unsullied by commercialism, its view of undergraduates as different from other cohorts of the population, and its assertion of the special meaning of a college education are still meaningful. For that reason, the report remains a central document in the history of American higher education.

Coaches

In the 1920s, the Carnegie investigators recognized that football coaches were important engines for the commercialism of college sports; and the report discusses coaches' high salaries (already higher than the most important professors at their institutions) and their endorsement deals for various products, including cigarettes. The most famous coach of the era and the leading entrepreneur in his profession was Knute Rockne of the University of Notre Dame. I was the first researcher to discover Rockne's papers, in a sub-basement of the Notre Dame Library. They had been in storage since his death in a plane crash in 1931. The papers contained more than 25,000 items, of which nearly one-fourth concerned his commercial ventures, including correspondence about those ventures, contracts, and ads featuring the coach.

Rockne endorsed just about everything his agent recommended. That man was Christy Walsh, history's first sports agent, who also represented Babe Ruth. In a typical letter, Walsh wrote to Rockne: "Babe Ruth has frequently let me use his signature to endorse various things. Now I am anxious to get an endorsement [from you] for him in connection with his Mail Order Health Service which we are just starting off." Rockne replied, "The endorsement you mention for Babe Ruth's Health Service is perfectly O.K." Considering the Bambino's physical excesses and ailments, including gonorrhea, buying the Babe Ruth Health Service, even on Knute Rockne's blind recommendation, might have proven an interesting adventure (Creamer 1974). Safer and cheaper were such Rockne-endorsed products as Studebaker automobiles and

Barbasol Shaving Cream: "It's the right play at the right moment—that's why I use Barbosal." In fact, because the Studebaker factory was in South Bend, Indiana, near Notre Dame, Rockne became a spokesman for the company, touring the country and earning large sums of money for promoting Studebakers. The company even named a car after him. Before his untimely death, Rockne had raised his annual income to $75,000, well over $1 million a year in today's dollars and far greater than the income of any other coach, professor, or college president of the period. Like many visionary entrepreneurs, Rockne saw the commercial potential of college sports and exploited it (Sperber 1993).

In the late 1920s, the Fighting Irish football team became immensely popular all over the country, filling huge new stadiums from Los Angeles to New York, and making the University of Notre Dame a household word. Obviously, corporations like Studebaker wanted to associate themselves and their products with a successful football coach like Rockne (he was the winningest coach of his era) and the popular image of his employer, the University of Notre Dame. Rockne pioneered so many entrepreneurial practices that university administrators had no policies on how to handle him. They tended to treat him and his deals benignly, rarely objecting to any of his endorsements. Similarly, when other coaches did commercial tie-ins, their schools rarely objected. This established a pattern for many generations, and hundreds of Rockne's successors followed in his wake.

Because of the Depression and World War II, no college coach equaled Rockne's $75,000 annual salary until Bear Bryant began winning national championships at the University of Alabama in the 1960s. Like Rockne, "the Bear" would endorse almost any product. All over the state of Alabama, billboards showed Bryant's face and signature houndstooth hat with the proclamation, "The Bear says buy . . . ," the sentence being filled in with a wide range of brand names (Bryant and Underwood 1975). Through the 1960s and 1970s, coaches continued to associate themselves with various corporations and endorse a multitude of items. Coaches' endorsements of Coca-Cola products were everywhere for a time; but coaches also endorsed local, regional, and national products. Don Nehlen, long-time football coach at West Virginia University, for example, always endorsed Mister Bee, a local potato chip. In the late 1970s, Indiana University football coach Lee Corso, now an analyst on ESPN, endorsed South African kruggerands.

Corso pushed the coins on Indiana television, raising a troubling point: in television endorsements, whom do university coaches represent—themselves or their school? Usually an ad features the coach, often one of the most prominent personalities at the school, pitching the product. In this way, the coach appears to represent the university. Indeed, in many ads, the coach seems to be a public spokesperson for the institution. Therefore, when the coach endorses a product, the implication is that the school also stands behind this commercial item.

Some coaches deny that the public makes this connection; but with the visual trappings of the university in the ads, the tie-in between the school and the product appears very real. Certainly, corporate advertisers believe that the connection exists and pay large sums of money based on this belief. Until the 1990s, there was a simple test for coaches' claims that they represented only themselves. If, in a television ad, a professor of medicine stood in a lab coat in her department's laboratory with her name, title, and the university's name on the bottom of the screen and endorsed a nonprescription cold medicine, the university would reprimand her. She also would receive a letter from the university's legal counsel about her actions. In addition, the school would demand that the commercials stop immediately. Few colleges or universities, however, were willing to rein in coaches' endorsement deals.

The situation changed in the 1990s, when schools began to allow faculty and staff members to endorse products so long as the institution received a cut of the corporate remuneration. Thus, College Sports, Inc., pioneered the world of commercial endorsements and sponsorships for College, Inc. But in an ironic twist, schools also changed the rules for some of the coaches' endorsements, not severing the tie with corporate America but demanding a cut for themselves.

Nike Schools

The first such change occurred with coaches' contracts with sporting-goods companies. In the late 1970s, a Las Vegas promoter named Sonny Vaccaro, who had a passion for college basketball, wanted to promote basketball tournaments and approached Nike to sponsor them. At the time, Nike was a small company in Beaverton, Oregon, that manufactured mainly track shoes but was interested in the basketball shoe market. Vaccaro asked Nike to provide free shoes for the players as a way of promoting the company's shoes and to give money to the coaches to ensure that the players on their teams wore the free Nikes. The company was skeptical but agreed to try Vaccaro's scheme. In March 1979, when *Sports Illustrated* featured a cover photograph of Larry Bird, then a college player, with his Nike shoes clearly visible, the company realized the value of Vaccaro's concept. Sales exploded after the Bird photos, and Nike became a major sponsor of college athletics. Its competitors, particularly Reebok and Adidas, quickly followed, vying with Nike to sign coaches, especially those in charge of teams that frequently appeared on television (Strasser and Becklund 1993).

In the early 1990s, the shoe endorsement money for a top coach reached a half-million dollars a year; and even lesser known coaches received six figures, causing a number of schools to step in and work out direct deals with corporate sponsors. Although the coach would still receive his or her money, the school would sign an exclusive contract with the corporation, the latter supplying all of the school's teams with equipment and paying the university for the privilege. The schools even claimed that this was a major college sports reform: they now had control of their coaches because the latter could not independently sign contracts with shoe companies but had to exist under the school's umbrella contract with corporate sponsors. The coaches liked the new arrangement—almost always a sign of non-reform—because they continued to receive the big bucks from the companies and now avoided the hassle of dealing with them directly.

The University of North Carolina at Chapel Hill was one of the first institutions to become a "Nike school." In 1993, it signed a five-year deal with Nike worth an estimated $11 million to the university, and Nike placed its swoosh logo on all UNC Chapel Hill team uniforms and shoes as well as on all coaches' jackets, hats, and other apparel—in short, on any UNC item that might appear on a telecast of a Tarheel game in any sport (*http://gazette. unc.edu/archives/01Oct24/file.5.html*). Television executives estimated that if UNC played another Nike-outfitted school such as the University of Michigan in a late-round National College Athletic Association (NCAA) men's basketball tournament game or a major bowl game, viewers would see the swoosh for about twenty minutes during the broadcast. At 1990s ad rates, that exposure was worth about $20 million. Considering that the sale of collegiate goods and apparel averaged $2.5 billion a year in the United States in the 1990s, Nike and its competitors were benefiting nicely from the university tie-ins.

Nike's director of college sports marketing, Kit Morris, commented, "The college market is one of our key target audiences. Outfitting college sports teams gives Nike authenticity and sends a strong message to consumers" (*Raleigh [N.C.] News and Observer*, 9 November 1997). The key word is *authenticity*. How could Nike translate the image of sneakers, sweatshirts, and warm-up suits, all of them inexpensive to make, into products for which young people will pay sizable sums of money? Nike's solution was to associate the company with an institution that represents authenticity, to mingle Nike's name with that of a prestigious university such as UNC Chapel Hill. In the *News and Observer*, Morris proudly explained that the company liked "the association with one of the premier universities in this country, a university that distinguishes itself in the classroom, on the playing field and court, and in the production of leaders. That's a very enviable association that's attractive for us."

After the company had signed up a number of distinguished universities as Nike schools, the law of unintended consequences caught up with Nike. Students at these institutions, better informed and more politically inclined than collegians at other big-time college sports schools, became concerned about how the shoes were made—specifically, about Nike's labor practices in Asia. The students learned that women in Nike's Asian factories usually worked very long hours for very little pay to produce the shoes. UNC Chapel Hill students organized campus rallies protesting Nike's labor practices; and the media picked up the story, giving Nike reams of unwanted negative publicity. Students at other Nike schools joined the protest movement. The *News and Observer* summed up the situation: "Having lent their athletic teams to Nike, dignified universities are finding themselves identified with an unpleasant image, that of poor Asians earning a few dollars a day working overtime to sew $100 sneakers."

Officials at UNC Chapel Hill and other schools answered students and the media with a very old argument, essentially saying that the schools needed Nike money and could not support their athletic departments without the company's sponsorship. A coach at North Carolina State University explained that college sports is a business that must generate money in any way it can. The coach was correct. He failed, however, to state that college athletics is one of the most dysfunctional businesses in the United States. No matter how much revenue it generates, it spends more, often because of waste and mismanagement as well as its "athletics arms race": the habit of building new and often unnecessary multimillion-dollar facilities because rivals are constructing them. In the *Albany [N.Y.] Times Union,* 24 December 2000, the marketing director of Syracuse University's athletic department summed up the financial situation honestly: "Only 7 percent of NCAA Division I programs operate in the black . . . this is a multi-million dollar business. The reality is that the expenses are such that only a rare number of schools actually turn a profit. So it's either eliminate sports or try to enhance revenue with marketing and sales."

The truth is that schools do not need all the intercollegiate sports they play. For instance, twenty-six intercollegiate sports are played at the University of Michigan at a time of very tight educational budgets. It's difficult to understand why college administrators are willing to cut academic programs, even whole departments, yet rarely rein in athletic department growth and expenditures, even though they know that athletic department budgets are frequently in the red. In the *News and Observer* article, the chancellor of UNC Chapel Hill, Michael Hooker, offered a typical response to questions about Nike's tie-in with his university and athletic department: "I have misgivings about the propriety of a university being in the entertainment business, but that's what college athletics have become, and it's too late to turn back. The Nike contract falls within the context of the operation of the modern athletic department." This argument—accept the inevitability of affliction—has never carried much weight, but for a university president to make it is sad.

The most interesting aspect of the Nike case is its ethical dimension and what that says about the commercialization of the university. UNC Chapel Hill and other prestigious schools, including the University of Michigan, allied themselves with a corporation engaged in questionable labor practices. In the *News and Observer* piece, a student critic put the case succinctly: "college sports teams have been walking billboards for a company which is synonymous with the exploitation of young female workers." Obviously, this view casts an unfavorable light on the Nike schools; and as a UNC Chapel Hill faculty member said in the same article, "To the extent that we [this university] remain silent, we open ourselves to moral censure, if not ridicule." Universities should stand for positive values and ideals, not the exploitation of young Asian women and a corporation's manufacturing, marketing strategies, and bottom line. In a final irony, North Carolina was willing to tarnish its good name for a paltry sum of money. Considering the size of the school and its annual budget, Nike's $11 million over five years amounted to "chump change," and UNC played the role of the chump.

The Nike contract with these schools raises other important issues, including the nature of corporate sponsorship and the impact of the alliance with corporate America on the traditional independence of the university. The standard sporting-goods company contract contains clauses whereby universities agree to take reasonable steps necessary to address any remark by any university employee that disparages the company or its products. Obviously, this requirement runs counter to the university tradition of free speech.

One of academia's most cherished traditions is freedom of speech and research; indeed, tenure guarantees those freedoms. But corporate America has never valued those freedoms and sees little point in upholding them when it signs a contract with a university. Not surprisingly, during the Nike labor practice protests, Nike invoked the gag rule clause whenever possible, even asking St. John's University in New York, a Nike school, to fire an assistant soccer coach because he spoke out against Nike's Asian labor practices and refused to wear Nike apparel on the job. The university complied, and the coach filed a lawsuit that is now in litigation (Sperber 1990, 2000).

Aware of the prestige of a tie-in with an Ivy League institution, Nike signed a deal with Brown University. Brown's students, however, were particularly active in protesting the company's Asian labor practices; so the company pulled out of the deal. Observers in higher education saw Nike's move as a clear warning to other Nike schools: end campus protests, or lose their Nike contract.

Other clauses in the standard Nike contract with schools bear close examination. Not only must athletes and coaches wear Nike equipment and apparel at all times, even if they prefer products sold by other sporting-goods companies, but they must also appear at various functions to promote Nike merchandise. Sporting-goods companies are not the only ones who make such stipulations. For example, the football players at Ohio State University are not allowed to celebrate an important victory by dousing their head coach with Gatorade, as professional football teams do. The players must use PowerAde because Coca-Cola, the company that makes PowerAde, has exclusive contracts with Ohio State (Sperber 1990, 2000). In essence, the athletes become part of the company's marketing strategy, losing independence of action in the bargain.

Even the incentive clauses in the standard contracts have a negative aspect. In addition to making an annual payout to the school, sporting-goods companies promise universities six-figure bonuses if their teams make the final rounds of the NCAA Division I basketball tournaments or play in major bowl games. At one level, the companies are simply rewarding schools for providing them with additional television and print exposure for their products. These clauses, however, like similar ones in coaches' contracts, also increase the importance of winning. Not surprisingly, some coaches and athletic departments respond to these inducements by placing student athletes in less rigorous courses to allow more time for sports training.

Nike's contracts with various universities, as well as the labor practice issue, illustrate the perils of corporate sponsorship in higher education. However, the Nike controversy did not discourage schools from pursuing corporate sponsors. After Nike made improvements in its Asian factories, the labor practice issue died down; and athletic departments pursued corporate sponsorships with increasing zeal, seemingly without concern for the nature of the corporation or the tie-in's impact on the school's educational mission. In the *Columbus [Ohio] Dispatch*, 6 December 1998, a long-time observer of higher education noted, "If you go back to the mid-1980s, the mind-set in the collegiate world was to go out and negotiate a deal with corporate America only when there was a serious financial need. Now the college decision-makers hustle every deal that they can."

The University of Connecticut at Storrs is a typical participant in big-time college sports. In the 1989–90 season, the university generated about $250,000 from corporate sponsors. By the mid-1990s, the amount surpassed $1 million a year; and by the beginning of the twenty-first century, UConn had contracts with corporate sponsors worth more than $4 million (Sperber 1990). Corporate sponsorship at the University of Nebraska at Lincoln includes contracts with Pepsi, Ford, Embassy Suites, and others; and the unending list of corporate sponsors often turns off many alumni. In a letter to the editor of the *Omaha [Nebr.] World Herald*, 29 October 1999, an out-of-state visitor who had recently attended a game in Lincoln complained:

> It made me ill to see how commercialized Nebraska football was. . . . they must have 40 different sponsors, ranging from widescreen monitors to Jennie O's. Every instant replay on the two widescreen monitors in the stadium was brought to us by a different sponsor. . . . Throughout the game, they played shameless video footage promoting not just their football team but mainly the sponsors that gave them the money.
>
> [These] are staples of professional games. But I was not at a professional game; I was at a college game. . . . College sports are, and have always been, secondary to academics. Most people go to college to learn and earn a degree. If he or she can go to a few games or even play in a few games while there, then that is added enjoyment. The money that is generated by an athletic program should first be used to further the academic goals of the institution.

Conclusion

Many Americans share the letter writer's view of universities and intercollegiate athletics. They believe in the primacy of academics over college sports, and they also mistakenly think that intercollegiate athletics generates revenue for universities and that these revenues are an excellent way of funding academic programs. In reality, college sports lose millions of dollars and siphon off money from academic programs when, at the end of each fiscal year, schools zero out their athletic department books with dollars from general operating funds. The public is unaware of the financial reality of college sports; and the media, which depend on the spectacle of intercollegiate athletics for large portions of newspaper sports sections and telecasts, do not inform the public of the harsher realities.

Financially, corporate sponsorship of college sports probably hurts universities more than it aids them. Many studies chart the public's increasing unwillingness to fund higher education; other studies show that the average taxpayer believes that college sports generates millions for many universities and that these schools do not need tax dollars. Economist Andrew Zimbalist (1999) argues that, for every dollar a corporate sponsor puts into an athletic department coffer, at least two taxpayer dollars are lost. Because the corporate dollars never go past the athletic department, the bottom line is a large loss of public funding for academic programs.

Colleges and universities in big-time college sports never seem to pause to examine the financial and ethical realities of corporate sponsorship. Many schools engage in a race for sponsorships, with no corporate sponsor considered out of bounds. Some universities even allow beer companies to sponsor their arenas and events, even though binge drinking is currently a major concern on American campuses; and many college teams play in city arenas where beer ads are omnipresent. Moreover, the main advertisers during the NCAA men's basketball tournament and all major bowl games are beer companies. Yet the NCAA and all the schools have anti-alcohol policies and claim that they are trying to curb student binge drinking.

Not surprisingly, the marketing of college sports has also spawned special consultants and agencies, some of which are subsidiaries of large corporations. For example, Creative Sports, Inc., is owned by ESPN, which is owned by ABC-TV and the Disney Corporation. A few years ago the agency signed a deal with the University of South Florida in Tampa to promote the school's college sports program. In the *Tampa [Fla.] Tribune*, 11 May 1997, a Creative Sports, Inc., executive enthused, "We are now part of the USF athletic department. . . . Yes, we will go head-to-head with the pro sports dollar. But we will maximize our [college] product. I think that every university athletic department understands the value of marketing and promotion and corporate sponsorships."

But how does this marketing campaign and the millions of dollars poured into the school's college sports program connect to the educational purpose of the university? How does going "head-to-head with the pro sports dollar" in Tampa, a city with professional sports franchises in all major sports and no tradition of supporting college sports, benefit the average undergraduate at USF?

Marketers appear unconcerned about these underlying questions of educational values and goals. Sadly, so do many university presidents and administrators who run the schools. Universities often allow their athletic departments to build expensive new facilities, mostly paid for by hidden taxes on undergraduates, and then sell the naming rights to the highest-bidding corporation. Universities also sell the floors of new basketball arenas and the sod of football stadiums to corporate sponsors, who place their names and logos in prominent places on the floor or the turf. In 2002, the University of Maryland opened a new basketball arena; and among the bidders for naming rights was the Enron Corporation. Fortunately for Maryland, Enron's bid fell short, sparing the school the need to explain an infamous name on its arena (*Baltimore [Md.] Sun,* 31 October 1998).

Universities have even sold the names of their traditional games. For example, the annual football match between the University of Oklahoma and the University of Texas at Austin, long known as the Red River Shootout, recently became the "Dr. Pepper Red River Shootout." The University of Oregon versus Oregon State rivalry, long known as the Civil War, is now officially the "Civil War Presented by Your Northwest Dodge Dealers." According to the *Minneapolis Tribune,* 1 February 2001, even the Hobey Baker Award for the best college hockey player, named for an outstanding amateur athlete at Princeton, who died heroically in World War I, recently became the "Hobey Baker Award Presented by American Express Brokerage."

In the *New York Times,* 14 October 2001, Robert Lipsyte's article "Stock Car Racing As Major College Sport? Why Not?" painted this picture of the future:

> Someday, when the beer gods are smiling, someone who looks like Brittany Spears will cry, "Student-athletes, start your engines!" and the first season of intercollegiate athletics NASCAR will roar into life. . . .
>
> Imagine the University of Michigan Cadillac with its Apple Computer, Nike, Heineken, and Victoria's Secret logos storming into a turn with the Michigan State Mercury, wearing the paint of Microsoft, Reebok, Coors, and the Gap, trying to slingshot past.
>
> Imagine the screaming in the skyboxes, the bingeing in the infield, the understanding professors working up NASCAR major courses on the anthropology of moonshining, the history of the carburetor, the denial of death.
>
> Education can't get higher than that.

College athletics has always run interference for College, Inc., and will continue to do so. There is no question that Lipsyte's image of a university race car plastered with the logos of corporate sponsors aptly epitomizes a future in which corporate sponsorship will penetrate into other parts of the university. I hope, however, that universities will remain unique places separated from the ordinary commerce of society. I hope that undergraduates will remain young men and women involved in intellectual exploration and who dream of changing the world. And I hope that a college education will not become a consumer item but will remain a meaningful experience that changes and shapes the future of individuals and the nation.

References

Quotations from the *Raleigh [N.C.] News and Observer* can be found at *http://www.uta.edu/depken/ugrad/sports/readings/athletes-as-billboards.pdf*. Quotations from all other cited newspapers can be found at *http://web.lexis-nexis.com*.

Bryant, Paul, and John Underwood. 1975. *Bear: The Hard Life and Good Times of Alabama's Coach Bryant*. Boston: Little, Brown.
Creamer, Robert W. *Babe: The Legend Comes to Life*. New York: Simon and Schuster.
Rader, Benjamin. 1983. *American Sports: From the Age of Folk Games to the Age of Spectators*. Englewood Cliffs, N.J.: Prentice Hall.
Savage, Howard, et al. 1929. "American College Athletics." Bulletin no. 23. New York: Carnegie Foundation.
Smith, Ronald A. 1988. *Sports and Freedom: The Rise of Big-Time College Athletics*. Oxford: Oxford University Press.
Smith, Ronald A., and John A. Lucas. 1978. *Saga of American Sport*. Philadelphia: Lea and Febiger.
Sperber, Murray. 1990. *College Sports, Inc.: The Athletic Department vs. the University*. New York: Holt.
———. 1993. *Shake down the Thunder: The Creation of Notre Dame Football*. Bloomington: Indiana University Press.
———. *Onward to Victory: The Crises That Shaped College Sports*. New York: Holt.
———. 2000. *Beer and Circus: How Big-Time College Sports Is Crippling Undergraduate Education*. New York: Holt.
Strasser, J. B., and Laurie Becklund. 1993. *Swoosh: The Unauthorized Story of Nike and the Men Who Played There*. New York: HarperBusiness.
Zimbalist, Andrew. 1999. *Unpaid Professionals: Commercialism and Conflict in Big-Time College Sports*. Princeton, N.J.: Princeton University Press.

Chapter 3

The Benefits and Costs of Commercialization of the Academy

DEREK BOK

COMMERCIALIZATION IN UNIVERSITIES—that is, making money from university activities—is not a new phenomenon in American higher education. In 1915, Yale University earned a surplus of more than $1 million (in current dollars) from its football team (Shulman and Bowen 2001). Columbia University and the University of Chicago sought to profit from correspondence courses (Flexner 1930). Such examples, however, occurred mainly at the periphery of the university and were far less common than they have become today.

In the past twenty-five years, the number and variety of commercial activities on the campuses of research universities have reached proportions never dreamed of in earlier periods. High-profile athletic programs have earned many millions of dollars each year for scores of institutions. Major efforts at technology transfer have resulted in thousands of patents issued every year with licensing revenues topping $1 billion in 2000 (Blumenstyk 2002). Corporations have signed multimillion-dollar research agreements with particular science departments, while parent universities have created venture capital organizations to invest in companies founded by their professors. Some business schools and medical schools are making millions of dollars from continuing education courses for business executives and practicing physicians. More recently, universities have begun to partner with venture capital companies to produce for-profit distance learning courses via the Internet.

The profusion of these commercial ventures reflects the critical importance of research and advanced education to contemporary society. In some cases, the prospect of profit has spurred universities to make much-needed contributions to technological progress and the training of executives and professionals. At the same time, the growth of commercial activity on campus has come with a cost. Big-time athletic programs have yielded a bumper crop of highly publicized scandals. Corporate sponsors have sometimes used their money to influence the results of university research (Bodenheimer 2001). Faculty investigators have acquired financial holdings that have exposed them to embarrassing conflicts of interest in carrying out their research (Porter and Malone 1992).

These misadventures hardly mean that all commercial activity by universities is unwise. They do suggest that these efforts are in need of careful reexamination. What benefits do commercial ventures bring to the academy, and how substantial are they likely to be? What are the risks, and what does experience teach us about the subtler costs that commercialization can entail?

Benefits of Commercial Ventures

To university sponsors, the immediate attraction of most commercial ventures is the prospect of bringing substantial new revenues to the university. In contrast to corporate profits, money made by academic institutions has the ennobling quality of being used not to line the pockets of private investors but to help fund scholarships, purchase library books, pay for new laboratory equipment, or support any one of a number of worthy educational purposes. Moreover, compared with many of the gifts, grants, and legislative appropriations that a university receives, commercial revenues have special value because they can generally be used for any purpose officials choose.

Commercial profits, however, are not always everything they seem. All too often, they fail to materialize in the anticipated amounts. The history of athletics shows clearly how rising costs can eat up anticipated gains, leaving most institutions with modest returns or even losses, along with millions of dollars squandered on stadiums and other expensive facilities that could have been better spent on education or research. Because of these costs, only a handful of universities make enough money from athletics to cover their expenses. Similar results have occurred in other commercial pursuits as well. Of an estimated two hundred or more patent licensing offices on American campuses, only 10 to 15 percent received more than $10 million in 2000; and a large majority failed to earn any appreciable profit (Blumenstyk 2002). Attempts to strike it rich by investing in companies started by members of the faculty have likewise produced disappointing returns in most cases. Although profit-making Internet ventures are too new for us to assess their ultimate profitability, early failures at institutions such as New York University and Temple University suggest that much the same pattern will prevail in this new field as well.

Even if universities do make a profit, they may not be able to retain it, at least in public institutions. Often, a visible surplus simply causes the state legislature to reduce appropriations, thereby nullifying any positive effect on the academic budget. Moreover, any profits that do remain may well end up being used for questionable purposes. For example, surpluses from football and basketball typically pay for scholarships given to athletes in other sports, such as track or tennis or swimming, that are not self-supporting. Far from promoting academic pursuits, therefore, athletic revenues compound the problem by helping to underwrite even more students who would not qualify for admission under the normal academic criteria.

The tone of this discussion may have ignored many of the greatest benefits of commercialization. After all, haven't big-time college sports brought entertainment to untold millions of Americans? Haven't patents and corporate collaborations greatly improved the process of turning scientific discoveries into useful products and processes, which is the principal reason why Americans allow billions of taxpayer dollars to flow from Washington each year into university laboratories? As for the Internet and the quickening interest of private investors in distance education, might not competition and the lure of profit be the only forces powerful enough to break through the thick crust of faculty inertia and bring about some real progress in university teaching and learning?

These are all fair questions. Without a doubt, apart from any money they bring, profits create incentives that can induce universities to behave in ways that benefit the public. Allowing universities to patent discoveries and license the patents for royalties has induced campus officials to work much harder than they previously did to identify scientific advances in their laboratories that might have valuable commercial uses. The lure of profits has likewise spurred many business schools to develop better educational programs for corporate executives. Again, however, one must be cautious in counting these advantages. Although they sometimes materialize, they often prove illusory. The history of athletics is full of brave assertions about gains that rarely turn out to be real—bigger gifts from alumni, improvements in the quality of the student body, important educational opportunities for minorities, to mention only a few. Even in the case of research, there are still critics who question whether the increased use of patents has enhanced or retarded scientific progress and its effects on productivity.

At times, moreover, when benefits to the public do emerge from entrepreneurial ventures, one can legitimately ask whether profit seeking by universities was truly necessary to bring about the positive results. For example, competition from rival institutions, including for-profit universities and other corporate providers, might be enough to make campus officials work harder to provide new and better Internet courses without the added incentive of making a profit. Similarly, much of the excitement that intercollegiate athletics brings to students and athletes also occurs at smaller colleges, where sports are conducted without the luxury boxes, the athletic scholarships, and the high pressure, all-consuming effort that big-time football and basketball now require. As for the public's entertainment, athletic clubs and professional teams have satisfied the popular demand for sports in other countries. It was not inevitable that the United States should become the only nation where universities use their students to present athletic spectacles for profit at the cost of compromising academic standards.

It also bears repeating that the incentives of commercial competition do not always produce a beneficial outcome; they merely yield what the market desires. Training courses will be cheap and of indifferent quality if employers seem to care only that their employees earn a certificate of completion. Profit making in supplying distance education via the Internet will bring optimal results only if students are discerning enough to prefer high-quality programs. As in commercial television, excellent programming rarely comes about unless the audience demands it.

Worse yet, competition for profit can sometimes produce deplorable behavior. Rivals can become so anxious to win that they resort to unsavory, even unlawful, methods. The constant cheating in athletic programs offers a depressing illustration. The periodic exposés of scientific fraud provide another.

These cautionary remarks may provoke a tart response from enterprising university presidents who are working hard to move their institutions into the higher reaches of the academic hierarchy. "Such high-minded arguments," they may declare, "are all very well for a former president of a university accustomed to a secure place in the academic firmament and buffered from misfortune by an endowment that approaches $20 billion. But how can other institutions without these assets hope to achieve greater eminence unless they can aggressively pursue every available opportunity to acquire the resources that excellence invariably requires?"

This is a valid question. In higher education, the cards are definitely stacked against any institution that lacks an established reputation and a large endowment. The best younger scholars and scientists usually move to institutions that already have strong faculties. Foundations and government funding agencies give the bulk of their money to support the universities with the best-known professors. The ablest students likewise flock to universities with established reputations, only to graduate eventually and transform themselves with uncommon frequency into financially successful alumni who support their alma mater with larger gifts than other institutions can normally obtain.

In all these ways the strongest universities tend to perpetuate themselves almost automatically. Success begets more success, which helps to explain why the list of top-rated universities in 2000 is remarkably like a similar list in 1950 or even in 1900. This process understandably frustrates university presidents who, in the best American tradition, want to lift their institutions to new heights and who chafe at watching the best-known universities continue to prosper even when their leadership seems stodgy and unimaginative.

With the odds seemingly stacked against them, enterprising university presidents may conclude that commercialization offers the best chance for a resourceful leader to break through the barriers of tradition and gain an advantage over more established rivals. Big-time athletics may hold many hazards, and the odds of success may be slim; but how else can a lesser-known university hope to acquire greater visibility, attract new donors, and lure talented students who might otherwise be unaware of the institution's existence? Perhaps only a few universities will make a substantial profit from the discoveries of their professors, but what better prospect exists for suddenly acquiring a big new pot of money to upgrade departments and attract outstanding professors? The Internet may not prove to be a bonanza, and other schools with more established reputations may have a brand-name advantage; but maybe, just maybe, these institutions will prove sufficiently sluggish to give a more aggressive university a head start that will mature into a lasting competitive advantage.

It is hard to argue against this line of reasoning. Although the rewards of commercialization are much more speculative than many enthusiasts acknowledge, the chances may still be good enough, compared with the alternatives, to make such a strategy seem attractive. The problem with the argument is that it is not complete. To make a full evaluation, one must consider the costs of commercialization as well as its potential benefits.

The Costs of Commercialization

The costs are, if anything, more speculative and intangible than the rewards. Seldom, if ever, can they be expressed in terms of money. More often, they have to do with the elusive world of values—specifically, with the principles that define the proper conduct of academic pursuits and thereby enhance their quality and meaning.

There are several important principles threatened by commercialism. Research universities are rarely, if ever, any better than their faculties. If they are to make their greatest contribution, therefore, it is imperative that they guard the integrity of their procedures for appointing and promoting professors. Those who are entrusted with such decisions should make them solely on the basis of the quality of the candidate's teaching, research, or other contributions to the academic purposes of the institution. They should not appoint professors because of their ability to attract corporate funding or their participation in a project of slight scientific interest that promises to yield large commercial rewards. If universities do not honor this principle, the quality of their academic work will suffer; and they will find it harder to recruit scientists and scholars of genuine distinction. Even the appearance of hiring professors on commercial grounds will lower the morale of the faculty and diminish the reputation of the university in the eyes of other scholars by suggesting that the institution is not committed to research and education of the highest quality.

Another important principle for selective universities is that all students should be admitted on grounds germane to the academic purposes of the institution: that is, on the basis of their capacity to benefit from the educational program, enhance the development of their fellow students, and serve the needs of society. If applicants can gain admission through their friendship with campus officials or for other reasons bearing no clear relation to the university's mission, the institution cannot make its greatest possible educational contribution. Once students are enrolled, any grades they receive for academic work should reflect an honest, objective evaluation of their performance in mastering the material of the course. Obviously, if grades can be bought or sold or altered for other reasons, the outside world can no longer rely on transcripts, some students can gain an unfair advantage over others, and confidence in the institution will suffer.

Athletics pose the most obvious threat to these principles. Large numbers of students are admitted to colleges every year with the expectation that they will play on varsity teams. Often, they are recruited by the coaching staff and would not gain entry were it not for their athletic prowess, a purpose having no evident connection with the true educational purposes of the institution. Such students frequently come to college for athletic rather than educational reasons, much like star quarterback Brian St. Pierre, who announced that he chose Boston College over Syracuse University not because he admired the reputation of the Boston College faculty for good teaching but because he preferred the football coach's offense.

Once admissions standards are lowered to accommodate large numbers of athletes with marginal academic qualifications, further dangers arise. Schools wishing to keep their best players eligible are often forced to create easier courses and simpler academic requirements. When especially talented athletes are at academic risk, pressures arise to find some way of keeping them in school, sometimes to the point of actually altering transcripts or ghostwriting their term papers. The awareness of such practices, of course, only adds to the cynicism of students and lowers the faculty's respect for the institution.

In addition to maintaining the integrity of the admissions process, universities should also make all other educational decisions to further the interests of students and society rather than to please a powerful trustee, suit the private convenience of faculty, or achieve other extraneous goals. This does not mean that educators have to shape their curricula to suit the wishes of their students or the views of public officials. The university, through its faculty, must make the final decisions about matters of teaching and curriculum. Still, the aim in forming such judgments should always be to meet the legitimate needs of students and society.

Commercialization threatens this educational principle because the profit motive shifts the focus from providing the best learning experience that available resources allow toward raising prices and cutting costs as much as possible without losing customers. Since most students are young and have great difficulty comparing how much they will benefit from the educational choices before them, universities may be able to capitalize on their reputation to offer inferior courses in order to make more money. Such practices violate a basic commitment owed by every educational institution to its students.

In similar fashion, profit seeking can lead universities to share their educational resources less widely than they should in order to earn a larger surplus for use elsewhere in the institution. For example, because continuing education programs are often used as profit centers, they rarely provide scholarships and hence are not accessible to many poor but worthy potential applicants. Business schools in search of profit may set such high tuitions for their executive education programs that managers from smaller companies cannot afford to attend. Technology transfer officers may needlessly grant exclusive licenses on important patents in order to share in the monopoly profits earned by the single licensee.

Another educational cost that commercialization can incur is the moral example such behavior provides to students and others in the academic community. Helping to develop virtue and build character has been a central aim of education since the time of Plato and Aristotle. After years of neglect, universities everywhere have rediscovered the need to prepare their students to grapple with the moral dilemmas they will face in their personal and professional lives. In colleges and professional schools, courses on practical ethics are now a common feature of the curriculum.

Although classes of this kind can serve a valuable purpose, students will be less inclined to take them seriously if they perceive that the institution offering the courses compromises its own moral principles in order to win at football, sign a lucrative research contract, or earn a profit from Internet courses. Undergraduates often learn more from the example of those in positions of authority than they do from lectures in a classroom. The most compelling moral examples any institution can give are ones that demonstrate a willingness to sacrifice immediate self-interest, if need be, for the sake of some higher principle. Conversely, the worst possible examples are those in which the institution, despite its high-minded pronouncements, does the reverse. The larger message of the liberal arts—that there is more to life than making money—is bound to ring hollow to many students in a university that repeatedly ignores its own values when they interfere with the search for more resources.

Commercialization also promises to touch the lives of college students in other ways that threaten to impair their educational experience. Two entering freshmen made news in 2001 by becoming the first to persuade a corporation to pay all their college expenses in return for spreading the company's message among their fellow undergraduates. Others will surely try to emulate this example, leaving campuses to contend with the prospect of an increasing number of students proselytizing for their corporate sponsors. Still other undergraduates have sold their lecture notes to one of the private companies that openly seeks materials of this kind for use in preparing course "guides" to sell to other students. Presumably, college authorities will wish to place restrictions on such behavior. But how can they do so convincingly if they themselves have accepted money in exchange for allowing companies to use the institution and its teaching to promote their corporate interests?

The last fundamental academic value is a fidelity to the basic canons of scholarly and scientific inquiry. To achieve the best intellectual results, investigators should be able to pursue the subject of their choice and to express their findings freely without being penalized for their opinions. In return, they should conduct their research openly and share their methods and findings freely with their fellow scholars in order to further the work of everyone concerned to the greatest possible extent. They should likewise try to express their views as truthfully and objectively as possible. Of course, human beings lack the power to eliminate all bias from their work. Every faculty will have members whose writing is influenced, perhaps unwittingly, by a desire for popular acclaim or a position of influence in the university or the outside world.

Nevertheless, in a community dedicated to the pursuit of truth and knowledge, professors must do their best to be accurate and objective; and the university should do what it can to minimize extraneous influences that could bias or distort their findings.

Commercialization can interfere with these canons of scientific inquiry in several important ways. Introducing opportunities for private gain threatens to divert some researchers from exploring more interesting and intellectually challenging problems. This possibility might conceivably be benign if the market were a reliable guide to the most promising subjects of research. It is theoretically possible for commercial motives to play a useful role in weaning first-rate intellects from a sterile preoccupation with scholastic puzzles like the players in Hermann Hesse's (1969) *The Glass Bead Game*. But profit does not play this role in the realm of basic research. Much commercially profitable research is trivial from a scientific point of view; witness the large sums spent trying to prove that one new drug is marginally different from existing substitutes. Conversely, the most important inquiries in science often involve questions no company will support because the answers will often be general laws of nature that do not hold any special rewards for the enterprise that funds the research.

Just as academic institutions will sometimes limit access to their educational programs in order to earn a profit, so also can they retard scientific progress in order to maximize their income. This is essentially what happens when universities delay sharing research materials with corporations in an effort to obtain a larger share of any profits that the corporations eventually earn. Similarly, zealous campus officials can slow commercial applications and drive up prices of valuable products by granting exclusive patent licenses where nonexclusive licenses would be feasible.

Corporate research support will also force the university to accept a certain amount of secrecy since corporations wish to avoid having valuable findings from the work they fund fall into the hands of competitors. From the standpoint of the university and of science itself, however, secrecy has several unfortunate results. It disrupts collegial relationships when professors cannot talk freely to other members of their department. It erodes trust as members of scientific conferences wonder whether other participants are withholding information for commercial reasons. It promotes waste as scientists needlessly duplicate the work that other investigators have already performed in secret for business reasons. Worst of all, secrecy may retard the course of science itself since progress depends upon every researcher's ability to build upon the findings of other investigators.

Apart from secrecy, academic scientists who enter into commercial ventures may also acquire financial interests that bias their work. Most research-ers are convinced that material considerations cannot possibly influence their judgment, despite a large body of evidence showing that such biases do occur (Rothman 1993). Thus, the norms of science do not discourage investigators from acquiring interests that threaten to influence their work. Without the university's intervention, these financial conflicts can easily multiply and create a significant risk for the objectivity of research.

Finally, industry funding will sometimes compromise the integrity of re-search because the stakes are so high. If the outcome of a researcher's inquiry can discredit a hugely valuable drug or cast doubt on the products or the pro-duction methods of entire industries, corporate sponsors will naturally be tempted to influence the outcome. Companies endangered in this way may try to cultivate and reward "friendly" academic experts or actually harass and intimidate academic scientists who threaten to publish results damaging to their products. In either event, the objectivity of university science will suf-fer in appearance if not in reality.

Commercialization can also harm the university community by creating divisions and conflicts that did not previously exist. Professors who work hard at their traditional academic tasks will resent the extra income earned by col-leagues who start a new business or spend a lot of time consulting. Humanists will feel devalued. Conflicts will arise between faculty and administration over the proper division of patent royalties or the management of a business founded by a professor but partly funded by the university. Graduate students may accuse their supervisor of taking their ideas to benefit a company in which the profes-sor has an interest. Scientists may bridle at the secrecy imposed by a colleague in their department who is funded by a corporation (Bodenheimer 2001).

The way in which entrepreneurial universities treat academic values will also have subtle effects on the commitment of the faculty to the work of the institution. Presidents and deans have little coercive authority; they cannot order professors to teach better courses or pay more attention to students or labor longer at their research. They can succeed only through persuasion, and their power to persuade depends on their ability to command the loyalty and respect of their faculty colleagues. Such respect is far more likely to come through example than from words alone. Academic leaders can hardly keep their professors from spending too much time earning money on the side if the university itself is trying to make a profit by investing in companies founded by its own scientists. Nor can presidents and deans expect their fac-ulty members to refrain from selling their teaching services to Internet com-panies once the administration has joined with private investors in a for-profit distance learning venture.

To be sure, money is not the root of all evil on university campuses. Professors were known to exploit graduate students, shirk their collegial duties, and even refuse to talk about their research long before opportunities arose to make a profit from such behavior. But money adds another reason, and an especially potent one at that, for putting selfish interests and private pursuits above responsibilities to students and colleagues.

Such self-serving tendencies are particularly corrosive in universities since faculty members enjoy such freedom and so many of their important activities cannot be prescribed in advance. Academic communities work well only when many professors voluntarily give generously of their time to help their institution, colleagues, and students. It is this willingness to do more for others than the job officially requires that is particularly at risk in an age when able scientists and scholars have so many opportunities to seek fame and fortune in the outside world.

If universities continue to behave more and more like corporations and turn increasingly to commercial ventures to enlarge their revenues, faculty members may reply in kind. Eventually, deans and presidents could find themselves discussing terms of employment not directly with their professors but with professional agents who use the reputation of their faculty clients to negotiate lower teaching loads, off-scale salaries, and greater freedom to pursue lucrative outside activities. In similar fashion, graduate students and faculty members who lack such power may feel compelled to protect their interests by forming unions and insisting on bargaining collectively with the administration.

Commercial activities can also damage the university's standing in the eyes of the public. Over the past forty years, confidence has declined sharply in the United States not only in government but in all kinds of institutions, including universities. Significantly, the organizations and groups that still command the greatest trust are invariably those, such as the Supreme Court or the military or the church, that are most devoted to goals that do not seem self-serving. Universities have traditionally been thought to fall within this category. Commercialization can eat away at this reputation, however, as word of its growing influence spreads from professional journals to congressional hearings, trade books, and even best-selling novels, such as John Le Carré's (2001) *The Constant Gardener*, which tells the tale, adapted from real life, of how a drug company corrupted the values of a research university in an effort to suppress damaging information.

Universities are more susceptible to public criticism now that they have become so important to the society. When college and professional schools are essential to coveted careers, students feel more resentful when they are denied admission or receive a failing grade. As universities grow richer, they begin to inspire envy more easily than affection. When campuses acquire more and more land, they arouse greater hostility from the surrounding community. Amid tensions such as these, evidence of aggressive commercialism, and of the scandals and misadventures that often come in its wake, can easily provoke strong disapproval and distrust.

As trust declines, the risk of government intervention increases. Newspaper stories about the conflicts of interest of scientists who are performing experiments on human subjects or the money that universities make on athletics through luxury boxes, television contracts, and advertising deals with clothing manufacturers create obvious opportunities for public officials to intervene. When Congress debates whether to act, universities that have openly indulged in entrepreneurial excess may find that the aura of public trust that once shielded them from hasty and unwise regulation is no longer available to protect them.

Of course, government intervention may be needed when there is no practical alternative. But regulation always comes at a cost, creating risks that unwise rules will result from political expediency, that red tape and needless delay will increase, that bureaucratic mistakes will proliferate. Already, officials are interfering much more in the affairs of universities than they did in generations past in an effort to increase their accountability and their responsiveness to various constituencies (Bok 1982). If the public comes to distrust universities more, and officials become even less inclined to respect academic autonomy, regulation may spread to such sensitive areas as admissions, faculty appointment procedures, curricular design, and other matters better left to academic discretion.

More important still, commercialization threatens to impair the university's reputation for objective, disinterested teaching and research. If medical schools are careless in stopping pharmaceutical firms from manipulating the results of clinical tests, if professors continue to write articles on controversial subjects without disclosing their ties to interested companies, if deans allow advertising to accompany their teaching materials, the public may come to question the independence and impartiality of the institution and its faculty.

The university's reputation for integrity could well be the most costly casualty of commercialization. A democratic society depends on having information on important subjects that people can rely on as reasonably objective and impartial. Universities have long been one of the principal sources of expert knowledge and informed opinion on a wide array of subjects ranging from science, technology, and medicine to economic policy, Supreme Court rulings, and environmental trends. This function has grown steadily more important now that so many issues that concern the public, such as biological warfare, global warming, nutrition, and genetic engineering, have become too technical for ordinary citizens to understand. Once the public begins to lose confidence in the objectivity of professors, the entire academic community suffers; but the consequences extend much further. At a time when cynicism is so prevalent and the need for reliable information is so important, any damage to the reputation of universities and to the integrity and objectivity of their scholars weakens not only the academy but the functioning of our democratic, self-governing society. That is quite a price to pay for the limited, often exaggerated, gains that commercialization brings to even the best-known institutions.

Evaluating Risks and Rewards

Looked at as a whole, the costs of increased commercialization seem greater than the benefits. Yet weighing the advantages and disadvantages on a case-by-case basis often leads university officials to embark on questionable money-making schemes. Looking back over the history of profit-seeking ventures, one quickly perceives a persistent tendency to exaggerate the benefits and minimize the dangers. Such a tendency is hardly surprising given the nature of the costs and benefits involved. The financial advantage to the institution will usually seem immediate, tangible, and extremely useful to help meet pressing needs. In contrast, the dangers to the conscientiousness of faculty or to the moral education of students or to the trust of the public are all intangible and remote. They may never materialize, making it all too easy for the officials involved to overlook them.

In contrast to the rewards, which accrue directly to the institution, many important costs seem further diluted by the fact that they are not unique to the university but threaten values that each institution shares with all of higher education, such as public confidence in the integrity of academic experts or the free exchange of ideas among scientists. Most of these costs do not result from any one commercial venture but only emerge through the cumulative effect of many similar activities. As a result, when officials consider profit-making opportunities one by one, they have a natural tendency to ignore these cumulative risks. They may give little or no weight to the possibility that their decision to proceed will contribute, however slightly, to an erosion of public trust or to a growing willingness of faculty members to neglect their academic duties in order to spend more time giving paid lectures or consulting or starting a new company. Officials know that any blame for turning down a potentially lucrative commercial proposal will rest squarely on them, while much of the cost that such a venture might entail will never be traced to any specific decision they make.

Not only is the usual method of evaluating commercial possibilities biased toward an affirmative outcome within the decision-making institution, but a parallel bias exists within the system of higher education as a whole. As a number of separate universities become aware of similar opportunities, for example, to accept commercial advertising in their Internet courses or to invest in companies started by their own professors, at least a few are likely to go ahead. Once these few move forward, others find it hard in such a competitive environment not to follow suit. Among a large number of independent institutions, each striving to better its position, the power of the minority to push other institutions into commercial activity is almost always greater than the majority's power to induce others to hold the line. Gradually, more and more universities will decide to commercialize; and as they alter their behavior, the standards for what is acceptable and unacceptable will begin to shift. Practices that were once universally condemned will now begin to seem acceptable. Another small step will have been taken in the steady advance of commercialization.

The record is filled with examples of this process. Because of its long history, athletics is especially rich in pertinent illustrations. In considering applicants capable of playing on revenue-producing teams, admissions officers in colleges with high-powered programs have gradually allowed the qualifications and academic performance of admitted athletes to fall further and further below the level of their classmates. Meanwhile, rules about giving athletic scholarships, scheduling games that interfere with classes, limiting the length of seasons, and prohibiting freshman eligibility have been slowly chipped away in the interest of fielding better teams and increasing net revenues.

The same process seems to be occurring in the field of scientific research, where norms about limiting the use of exclusive patent licenses, lending research materials, refusing to invest in faculty-sponsored businesses, and avoiding secrecy have all been eroded in the pursuit of money. In medical schools, pharmaceutical companies have gradually expanded their influence over the content of continuing education programs while gaining greater access to residents training in teaching hospitals. Experience with e-learning is much more limited, but there are early signs of a similar process. When Columbia Business School agreed to form a partnership with a for-profit company, U.Next, other leading universities quickly agreed to follow suit (Woody 1999).

Conclusion

Not all profit-making activities are unduly hazardous to the academic enterprise. Licensing patents appears to have been successful in causing universities to work much harder at identifying potentially useful discoveries and transferring them to industry for commercial development. The prospect of earning a profit has apparently spurred educators to provide more courses of higher quality for executives from for-profit companies and other organizations.

Notwithstanding these advances, university efforts to gain revenue from athletic teams, industry-funded research, and midcareer education have frequently resulted in unwise compromises with basic academic values. These tendencies suggest the need to consider the risks very carefully before deciding to proceed. Because of the biases inherent in the conventional methods for reviewing commercial ventures, universities need sturdier, more reliable safeguards than they have created heretofore if they are to avoid further erosion of basic values; and a few broad lessons can be drawn from past experience to indicate the contours of a workable solution.

First, universities need to look at the process of commercialization in its entirety, with all its benefits and risks, and try to develop clear rules and prohibitions that are widely publicized and conscientiously enforced. Without such guidelines, ad hoc decision making is bound to lead officials to succumb to the lure of money at the cost of academic principles not because it is the proper path to take but because it is the path of least resistance.

Second, universities should not rely on their presidents alone to enact and enforce appropriate rules. Presidents are under too much pressure to attract new revenue and to satisfy powerful professors to single-handedly undertake this responsibility. Without the active assistance of trustees and faculty, campus leaders will not be able to hold the line consistently against irresponsible commercial ventures.

Third, university leaders should also look for opportunities to make agreements with similarly situated institutions to create suitable limits on profit-making activities. In the absence of such agreements, competitive forces will exert intense pressure on individual universities to follow the lead of their least responsible sister institutions.

Fourth, reasonable and stable government funding is also essential to avoid undue commercialization. Despite the best intentions, survival will usually take precedence over other values. If traditional funding sources dry up, universities will resort to almost any money-making scheme to keep their programs going and stay competitive with their peer institutions. For this reason, government funding represents the ultimate defense against the decay of fundamental academic values.

Finally, useful limits on commercial activity are unlikely to emerge, let alone be effectively enforced, without the benefit of thoughtful discussion and public attention. The Sam Nunn/Bank of America Policy Forum's Conference on Commercialization of the Academy, which took place in April 2002 at Emory University and resulted in this book, exemplifies the kind of debate that the current situation requires.

References

Blumenstyk, Goldie. 2002. "Income from University Licenses on Patents Exceeded $1 Billion." *Chronicle of Higher Education*, 22 March, p. A31

Bodenheimer, Thomas. 2001. "Uneasy Alliance: Clinical Investigations and the Pharmaceutical Industry." *New England Journal of Medicine* 342, no. 20: 539.

Bok, Derek. 1982. *Beyond the Ivory Tower: Social Responsibilities of the Modern University*. Cambridge: Harvard University Press.

Flexner, Abraham. 1930. *Universities: American, English, German*. New York: Springer.

Hesse, Hermann. 1969. *The Glass Bead Game*. Translated by Richard Winston and Clara Winston. New York: Holt, Rinehart, and Winston.

Le Carré, John. 2001. *The Constant Gardener*. Sydney, Australia: Hodder and Stoughton.

Porter, Roger T., and Thomas E. Malone, eds. 1992. *Biomedical Research: Collaboration and Conflict of Interest*. Baltimore: Johns Hopkins University Press.

Rothman, Kenneth. 1993. "Conflict of Interest: The New McCarthyism in Science." *Journal of the American Medical Association* 269, no. 21: 2782.

Shulman, James L., and William G. Bowen. 2001. *The Game of Life: College Sports and Educational Values*. Princeton, N.J.: Princeton University Press.

Woody, Todd. 1999. "Ivy Online." *The Standard: Intelligence for the Internet Economy*. 22 October (*http://www.thestandard.com/article/display/0,1151,7122,00.html*).

Chapter 4

Increased Commercialization of the Academy following the Bayh-Dole Act of 1980

MARY L. GOOD

Many recent studies have indicated that the presence and participation of universities, especially research universities, is a major factor in the growth of economic clusters in the new knowledge-based economy (see Porter and van Opstal 2001; and Branscomb 1993, particularly the chapters by Brooks and Zinberg). Part of this new emphasis on the commercial contribution of the academy can be traced to the Bayh-Dole Act of 1980, which conveyed title to the intellectual property generated by federally funded university researchers to their universities. But the significance of Bayh-Dole becomes clearer after a review of earlier contributions of government-university partnerships to the economy and an examination of the political climate in 1980 that led to the Bayh-Dole legislation.

The Land-Grant Act

Perhaps the most important pre-twentieth century examples of government science policy came with the passage of the Morrill Act in 1862 and the establishment, by legislative action, of the National Academy of Sciences in 1863. The Morrill Act, also known as the Land-Grant Act, was a program to donate public lands to the states and territories to "provide colleges for the benefit of agriculture and the mechanical arts" (Dupree 1986, 150). It is perhaps surprising that these important legislative activities were carried out at the height of the Civil War. In both cases, the legislation provided the framework for important developments over the years. The impact of the National Academy of Sciences has been substantial; and its present form, especially its role as science advisor to the government, can be traced to the original bill.

The Land-Grant Act spawned the impressive network of state-supported agricultural and mechanical universities that today account for the majority of all engineering, agricultural, and technological colleges. It is not surprising that the academy is involved in commercial enterprises because the agricultural and mechanical universities were deliberately designed to foster the development of the agricultural and mechanical arts and to provide education for the working class. The impact on agriculture and the science and technology applied to U.S. agriculture was further promoted with the passage of the Hatch Act of 1887, which established the agricultural experiment stations attached to the land-grant institutions. The success of these institutions in the development of modern agriculture, including commercial enterprises, and their contribution to the quality, quantity, and cost of the U.S. food supply is unsurpassed anywhere in the world.

The National Advisory Committee for Aeronautics

There are many examples of university and faculty involvement in commercial interactions before 1980 (National Science and Technology Council, Committee on Civilian Industrial Technology 1996). The National Advisory Committee for Aeronautics (NACA) was established in 1915 and had a long history of aeronautical research at universities that became the foundation for commercial aviation. The role of Purdue University and other engineering schools was critical to this technology transfer. By 1939, the NACA had contracts for twelve special investigations at ten universities. By the mid–1920s, many industrial firms began to incorporate research departments in their organizations. By 1930, there were more than 1,600 industrial research laboratories in the United States that became the outlets for university research. In addition, the practice of using industrial consultants became standard: science and engineering faculty were hired by corporate laboratories to bring the newest scientific and engineering discoveries and provide a network for recruiting technical graduates to the laboratories. These engagements contributed to the faculty member's status, especially if the contract was with a major laboratory like DuPont or General Electric.

Many faculties, particularly in engineering and chemistry, were also engaged in helping local industry solve technical problems. One interesting case was the chemistry department at the University of Illinois. As chairman of the department, Roger Adams, one of the early giants of organic chemistry, used his graduate students during the Depression to synthesize industrial chemicals on demand for sale to industrial clients. He used the revenue to run the department and pay the students.

Government-Funded Defense Research

World War II saw the mobilization of the nation's scientists and engineers, and the results proved the value of government-funded research to the war effort. After the war, the need for a permanent, more robust federal research program became a priority. The result was the establishment of the National Science Foundation, the strengthening of the National Institutes of Health, the continuation of research efforts in support of the military, and later the establishment of the National Aeronautics and Space Agency (NASA).

The National Science Foundation was established to fund basic research, primarily in universities. However, major research grants were also made to universities from the "mission agencies," especially from the National Institutes of Health, the Naval Research Laboratory, NASA, the Air Force Office of Scientific Research, and the Atomic Energy Commission (later the Department of Energy). Federal support for research grew during the cold war era, and universities had so many opportunities for federal funding that their connection to industrial research declined significantly. In the 1950s and 1960s, this support included traineeships to help build a research work force and infrastructure resources to improve university capabilities in addition to individual research grants. Over time, the objectives of the government changed. Support became dependent on individual, peer-reviewed proposals; and the government procured research rather than provided general support for universities and students. Graduate-student stipends were paid from grants to a principal investigator, and university facilities were supported by overhead formulas monitored by government auditors. Under this regime and the overriding issue of national security, the physical sciences and engineering flourished.

The end of the cold war created new priorities. The lessened importance of the national security argument caused reductions in physical science and engineering research supported by the Department of Defense. Other mission agencies such as the Department of Energy, NASA, and the Environmental Protection Agency became more focused on applied science that could affect their agendas. The general interest of the public and breakthroughs in biomedical science made research for the National Institutes of Health a national priority. In all of these activities, any intellectual property discovered by government or by university scientists funded by the government was either the property of the government or put into the public domain by publication of research results. It was assumed that the public good would be served by an approach where private industry could use the ideas published and the government could control the science and technology for its own use. If patents were obtained, they belonged to the government, which provided nonexclusive licenses to potential product or process developers. Under this arrangement, licenses were few. The industry, outside of the defense arm, made little direct use of the intellectual property produced; and university-industry contacts were few, except for individual faculty consulting arrangements.

The Bayh-Dole Act of 1980

In the late 1970s and early 1980s the political climate in the United States changed in response to the rapid growth in electronic and automotive imports from Japan. Japan's economic vitality and the commercial success of Japanese manufacturing created real concern about U.S. economic competitiveness. In the debate about the role of government in economic development, the role of science and technology became a critical issue, particularly the value of federal investment in science and the need for technology transfer to the private sector. The result was government action designed to improve the competitive position of American business, particularly manufacturing. Patents and other intellectual property created from federally funded research were central to the discussion, as was the need for partnerships among government, industry, and university to provide more effective technology transfer. Among these players, one point seemed clear: if intellectual property were left in the public domain, corporate strategists would not move aggressively toward the development of new discoveries. The significant costs associated with developing a concept into a product or a process could not be recovered if the original intellectual property could be used by a "fast follower" who had benefited from the original development.

Originally, patents were seen as a way to give an inventor proprietary protection while publicizing the potential of the invention and limiting the time period for which the inventor could monopolize its value. Thus, while the value of intellectual property developed by industry could be captured by the subsequent development of products and processes, the value of nonexclusive licenses on government-generated intellectual property was much more difficult to capture. Debate on these issues culminated in a series of legislative acts created to stimulate U.S. economic competitiveness. Table 4–1 lists the individual acts (National Science and Technology Council, Committee on Civilian Industrial Technology 1996; Office of Technology Policy 2000). After 1989, other such "competitiveness" legislation was also passed; but the major policy changes were made in congressional acts of the 1980s.

For universities, the important piece of legislation was the Bayh-Dole Act of 1980. The act put universities in the business of technology transfer and

Table 4–1
Legislative acts created to stimulate U.S. economic competitiveness, 1980s

1980 *Stevenson–Wydler Technology Innovation Act.* Made tech transfer a specific mission of the federal labs and established tech transfer offices in each laboratory.

      Bayh-Dole University and Small Business Patent Procedures Act. Vested ownership of all intellectual property emanating from federal grants and contracts in the university or small businesses and contractors. Authorized federal agencies to patent their intellectual property (developed in house) and to grant licenses (including exclusive licenses).

1982 *Small Business Innovation Development Act.* Established small business innovative research and development grants for small businesses with a set-aside from agency research dollars.

1984 *National Cooperative Research Act.* Reduced antitrust barriers to cooperative industry research.

      Trademark Clarification Act. Amended the Bayh-Dole Act to expand scope of original legislation.

1986 *Japanese Technical Literature Act.* Required the Department of Commerce to collect, abstract, translate, and distribute declassified Japanese literature.

      Federal Technology Transfer Act. Amended the Stevenson-Wydler Act to allow government inventors to receive royalties from their inventions.

1987 *Malcolm Baldrige National Quality Improvement Act.* Instituted the Malcolm Baldrige Award to recognize quality improvement in U.S. firms.

1988 *Omnibus Trade and Competitive Act.* Made significant changes in U.S. trade policy and designated the metric system as the preferred system of weights and measures. Reorganized the technology functions of the Department of Commerce and renamed the National Bureau of Standards as the National Institute of Standards and Technology.

1989 *National Competitiveness Technology Transfer Act.* Amended the Stevenson-Wydler Act to make tech transfer a mission of government-owned and contractor-operated laboratories and clarified the execution of cooperative research agreements.

      National Institute of Standards and Technology Authorization Act. Made software development and innovation eligible for awards. Created the Technology Administration and transferred the oversight of the National Institute of Standards and Technology to that undersecretary in the Department of Commerce.

made them responsible for the management and disposal of intellectual property developed through their federal grants and contracts. According to Rebecca Zacks (2000), "Universities that would previously have let their intellectual property lie fallow began filing for—and getting—patents at unprecedented rates" (88). Zacks refers to the Bayh-Dole Act as "the Viagra for campus innovation" (88). Her analysis reports that campus intellectual property translated into 280,000 jobs and an estimated $33.5 billion in economic activity in 1998 alone. Table 4–2 shows the extent of university participation (Zacks 2000). A cursory review of these data indicates that the correlation between research expenditures and licensing income is not linear and that

Table 4–2
Comparison of Intellectual Property Production and Use, 1999

University	Rank in Technology Strength[a]	Number of Patents	Impact Index[b]	Licence Income (millions of dollars)	Research Expenditure (millions of dollars)
University of California	1	488	1.02	73.1	1,710
Massachusetts Institute of Technology	2	151	1.36	18	761
CalTech	3	103	1.20	5.5	151
University of Texas	4	115	1.00	≤4.3	?
Stanford	5	91	1.16	43.2	401
Columbia	11	59	1.17	61.6	261
Carnegie-Mellon	19	26	1.73	30.1	170
Michigan State	28	54	0.57	24.3	194
Yale	34	32	0.84	33.3	300
Florida State	below 50	?	?	46.6	112

SOURCE. Zacks (2000).
[a]Number of U.S. patents multiplied by the impact index.
[b]Frequency of patents citations, a 1.0 indicates average citation frequency.

what makes programs really substantial is an intellectual "home run." One example is the series of Taxol patents at Florida State University that drives the school's income; others are Lycos Internet technology at Carnegie-Mellon and the Cox–2 inhibitors at the University of Rochester. Older examples include the University of Wisconsin's discovery of Warfarin (coumadin), used initially for rodent eradication and now an important blood thinner, and the University of Florida's development of Gatorade. These discoveries, which have major commercial value, are unique; and most university tech transfer officers try to maximize the value of their complete intellectual property holdings.

The economic impact of these activities is now well understood, not just in terms of university return but in overall economic stimulus: the rapid conversion of science discoveries to new technologies and the creation of entirely new start-up businesses. This value has been noted; there have been many economic studies about the vibrant economic clusters that have grown up around university communities (Porter and van Opstal 2001). Significant examples include Silicon Valley, California (near Stanford University and the University of California at Berkeley); Cambridge, Massachusetts (near the Massachusetts Institute of Technology and Harvard University); and Research Triangle Park (near Duke University, the University of North Carolina, and North Carolina State University). A Bank of Boston study (2000) estimated that 4,000 graduates of the Massachusetts Institute of Technology had started companies with revenues of $230 billion and more than 1 million employees. In light of such results, state governments are focusing on the value of their universities and how they can help create economic clusters in their own states and regions. Many new state programs, such as the Kansas Institute of Technology (KTech), now support activities to leverage their university research programs and encourage new technology-based start-ups in their own areas. This commercialization of the academy is not just an American phenomenon. Cambridge University recently accepted $80 million from Microsoft for a computer science facility, Oxford University has a new business school funded by a Saudi multimillionaire, the Max Planck Society (the Munich Institute of Psychiatry) has a new genetic research center funded by Glaxo Smith Kline, and the Indian Institute of Science in Bangalore has attracted information technology companies from around the world as well as two new General Electric laboratories employing five hundred people each.

In the evolving knowledge-based global economy, this dependence on universities for cutting-edge, commercially viable science and technology as well as highly trained professional technologists is destined to increase. In the United States, the Bayh-Dole Act has been very successful in helping create the technological advancements its sponsors had hoped for. The results for both industry and the universities have been quite positive. As in all successful ventures, however, issues have surfaced that should be addressed. These concerns will be moderated by the changing political climate: economic competitiveness does not have the urgency it once had, while medical research has become a priority. The growth of biotechnology and the direct connection between university research and pharmaceutical products make this area of tech transfer an immediate concern. Universities license their patents but they also take equity interests. University researchers become principals in biotech start-up firms while continuing their work on federal grants. These activities have clarified the need for robust conflict of interest rules and drawn attention to the need for universities to assess their educational goals and objectives, particularly as they relate to original research and contributions to society at large.

Conclusion

Bayh-Dole has been a success. It has changed dramatically the way in which universities view their research portfolios and the potential intellectual property they contain. The result has been a major increase in university-industry interactions, most of which have greatly benefited the U.S. economy. The nation's immense lead in the biotechnology industry is a significant example.

The issue now is not to kill Bayh-Dole but to organize a mature, thoughtful discussion about how intellectual property should be managed to the benefit of all stakeholders.

References

Bank of Boston. 2000. Report (*http://web.mit.edu/newsoffice/founders/*).

Branscomb, Lewis M., ed. *Empowering Technology: Implementing a U.S. Strategy*. Cambridge, Mass.: MIT Press.

Dupree, A. Hunter. 1986. *Science in the Federal Government: A History of Policies and Activities*. Baltimore: Johns Hopkins University Press.

National Science and Technology Council, Committee on Civilian Industrial Technology. 1996. *Technology in the National Interest*. Washington, D.C.: Office of Technology Policy, U.S. Department of Commerce.

Office of Technology Policy. 2000. *Tech Transfer, 2000: Making Partnerships Work*. Washington, D.C.: Office of Technology Policy, U.S. Department of Commerce.

Porter, Michael, and Debra van Opstal. 2001. *U.S. Competitiveness, 2001*. Washington, D.C.: Council on Competitiveness.

Zacks, Rebecca. 2000. "The TR University Research Scorecard." *Technology Review* (July–August): 88–90.

Chapter 5

Delicate Balance

Market Forces versus the Public Interest

JAMES J. DUDERSTADT

Today, GOVERNMENT AND industry increasingly see universities not merely as centers of learning and basic research but as sources of commercially valuable knowledge. While university research and innovation are responsive to market demands and generate revenue, if they are not managed properly, they also are threats to many of the most fundamental values of the university, such as openness and academic freedom.

The efforts of universities and faculty members to capture and exploit the soaring commercial value of the intellectual property created by research and instructional activities create many opportunities and challenges for higher education. There are substantial financial benefits to those institutions and faculty members who strike it rich with technology transfer. In the 1980s, "red Ferrari in the parking lot" syndrome was the first sign of faculty wealth from technology transfer. In the booming days of the dot-coms, the more typical story mirrored this one: a young assistant professor of computer science told his department chair, "I'm going to take a one-year leave of absence to start up a company. If I'm successful, I probably won't return, but at least you may get a $1 million dollar gift from me. If I'm not successful, then I'll return and see if I can get tenure." Then there's another faculty member who informed his chair that he had set up a small foundation financed by his recent initial public offering (IPO), apologizing that his first gift would be only $10 million but expecting his contributions to rise rapidly.

Each of these stories is true. Nevertheless, for every positive gain from the commercialization of intellectual property, there are negative aspects of this balancing act between commercial and public interests. Scientists now sign agreements restricting both the methods and the results of their work. Stokstad notes that "more than one-quarter of U.S. geneticists say they cannot replicate published findings because other investigators will not give them relevant data or materials." (Stokstad, 2002) Further, there is growing evidence suggesting that industrial sponsorship actually influences the outcome of scientific work. Universities are encountering an increasing number of conflict of interest cases, stimulated by the exploding commercial value of intellectual property and threatening not only institutional integrity but even human life in conflicted clinical trials.

In recent years, many universities seem to have adopted the attitude that "what is good for General Motors [in this case, consistent with the Bayh-Dole Act] is good for the country." They recognize and exploit the increasing commercial value of the intellectual property developed in universities as an important part of their mission. This has infected the research university with the profit objectives of a business, as both institutions and individual faculty members attempt to profit from the commercial value of the products of their research and instructional activities. Universities have adopted aggressive commercialization policies and invested heavily in technology transfer offices to encourage the development and ownership of intellectual property rather than its traditional open sharing with the broader academic community. They have hired teams of lawyers to defend their ownership of the intellectual property derived from their research and instruction. On occasion, some institutions and faculty members have set aside the most fundamental values of the university, such as academic freedom and a willingness to challenge the status quo, to accommodate the growing commercial role of the research university (Press and Washburn 2000).

Where in such activites is the public interested? As Donald Kennedy (2001) has noted, "'Public interest' has two translations. In the more technical, political science sense, it refers to those attributes of a venture or an organization that supports the larger society, benefiting the welfare of all the people. More colloquially, it can also mean what the public cares about, what it is interested in" (2249).

It is certainly the case that many in both government and the corporate world have increasingly seen universities not merely as centers of learning and basic research but as sources of commercially valuable knowledge. But does this viewpoint take into account the public interest of a society that has created, supported, and depended upon the university as a place of learning, education, and unfettered scholarship? Is there a conflict between the commercial

demands of the marketplace and the broader roles of the university in our society? Perhaps the spirit of Bayh-Dole is not what should be driving university strategies for transferring the knowledge produced on their campuses to
benefit the public but rather principles more consistent with the history of
higher education in the United States and better aligned with the vision of the
university as a place of unconstrained scholarship and learning.

The Economics of Commercialization

The Association of University Technology Managers (2001) estimate that
during fiscal year (FY) 2000 universities and their faculties collected more than
$1 billion in royalties, created 368 spin-off companies, filed for 8,534 patents,
and executed 3,606 licenses and options. While this royalty figure is some 40
percent higher than in FY 1999, it includes several one-time events such as
$200 million paid by Genentech to the University of California—San Fran-
cisco to settle a patent dispute and the fact that several universities cashed in
their equity interest from earlier spin-off activities. Furthermore, while some
universities benefited greatly from these commercial activities, most received
less than $1 million in royalties, which was frequently not even sufficient to
cover the costs of their technology transfer activities. Actually, from the earliest days of the Bayh-Dole Act of 1980, only a few inventions and discoveries have struck it rich for universities (for example, recombinant DNA at the
University of California—San Francisco and Stanford; Lycos at Carnegie-
Mellon; carboplatin at Michigan State; and, of course, Gatorade at the University of Florida). In contrast, many individual faculty members have
benefited considerably from equity interest in spin-off companies through IPOs
and other financial events (Schmidt 2002).

    As Schmidt notes, "state lawmakers are sending public research universi-
ties a clear message: It's time to begin commercializing your discoveries to promote local economic development. Nearly a third of the nation's governors
have called on legislatures to pump money into public universities' research
and technology-transfer programs . . . . Several states also are considering, or
recently have passed, changes in their laws that eliminate barriers to collaboration between public-university faculty members and private companies. The
measures are intended to give for-profit companies unprecedented access to
public-university research facilites, while encouraging public universities and
their employees to hold a financial stake in companies making use of research
findings." (Schmidt, 2002)

    The desire of industry to keep pace with the rapid evolution of new tech-
nologies is reflected in the growth of industrial research and development activities to more than $200 billion in FY 2000. Industrial investment in basic

and applied research performed at universities is estimated to have increased by 20 percent (in constant dollars) between 1991 and 1997 as industry has shifted some of its research and development activities out of its laboratories and onto the campuses (Science and Engineering Indicators, 1998). Not only has the federal government invested heavily in areas such as biomedical sciences and information technology with strong commercial potential, but it has also rewritten patent and copyright laws to encourage licensing and developing the products of research. Universities and faculty researchers in many fields increasingly have come to think in terms of the commercial potential of their activities, the products and methods of their research, and their instruction as intellectual property to be developed and protected rather than shared. This is not surprising: we live in an age in which knowledge has become central to economic activities. As the source of much of that knowledge, universities are increasingly subject to powerful market forces.

Market Forces in an Age of Knowledge

Society is evolving rapidly into a postindustrial, knowledge-based society, a shift in culture and technology as profound as the social transformation that took place a century ago when an agrarian nation evolved into an industrial one (Drucker 1994). Industrial production is steadily shifting from material- and labor-intensive products and processes to knowledge-intensive products and services. A radically new system for creating wealth has evolved that depends upon the creation and application of new knowledge.

In a very real sense, we are entering a new age, an age of knowledge, in which the key strategic resource necessary for prosperity has become knowledge itself—that is, educated people and their ideas. Unlike natural resources, such as iron and oil, which have driven earlier economic transformations, knowledge is inexhaustible. The more it is used, the more it multiplies and expands. But knowledge is not available to all. It can be absorbed and applied only by the educated mind. As society becomes increasingly knowledge-intensive, it becomes increasingly dependent upon social institutions such as universities, which create knowledge and educate people as well as provide them with knowledge and learning resources throughout their lives (Bok 1990).

This expanding economic value of the university and its products, along with other factors such as changing social needs, economic realities, and rapidly advancing technology, have created powerful market forces acting upon and within higher education. Even within the traditional higher education enterprise, there is a sense that the arms race is escalating, as institutions compete ever more aggressively for better students, better faculty, government grants, private gifts, prestige, winning athletic programs, and commercial market dominance. Faculty members, as the key sources of intellectual content in both instruction and research, increasingly view themselves as independent contractors and entrepreneurs, seeking ownership and personal financial gain.

With the emergence of new competitive forces and the weakening influence of traditional regulations, the higher education enterprise is entering a period of restructuring similar to that experienced by other economic sectors, such as health care, communications, and energy. Higher education is breaking loose from the moorings of physical campuses, even as its credentialing monopoly begins to erode. It appears to be evolving from a loosely federated system of colleges and universities serving traditional students to, in effect, a global knowledge and learning industry driven by strong market forces.

As our society becomes ever more dependent upon new knowledge and educated people, upon knowledge workers, this global knowledge business must be viewed as clearly one of the most active growth industries of our times. Today, it is estimated that higher education represents roughly $225 billion of the $665 billion education market in the United States (Moe 2000). But even these markets are dwarfed by the size of the knowledge and learning marketplace—a convergence of education, communications, information technology and entertainment sectors estimated in excess of $2 trillion.

The perspective of a market-driven restructuring of higher education as an industry is perhaps both alien and distasteful to the academy yet is nevertheless an important framework for considering the future of the university. These social, economic, technological, and market forces are far more powerful than many within the higher education establishment realize. They are driving change at an unprecedented pace, perhaps even beyond the capacity of our colleges and universities to adapt. There are increasing signs that our current paradigms for higher education—the nature of our academic programs; the organizations of our colleges and universities; the way that we finance, conduct, and distribute the services of higher education—may not be able to adapt to the demands and realities of our times.

As each wave of transformation sweeps ever more rapidly through our economy and our society, the existing infrastructure of educational institutions, programs, and policies becomes more outdated and perhaps even obsolete. It is clear that no individual, institution, or government will be in control of the emergence and growth of the knowledge industry. It will respond to forces of the marketplace. Perhaps this is the most serious threat of the emerging competitive marketplace for knowledge and learning: the danger that it will not only distort but erode the most important values and purposes of the university. In a highly competitive market economy, short-term commercial opportunity and challenges usually win out over long-term public interests.

Concerns about Commercialization

In the past the public purposes of universities were determined primarily by public policy and public investment. Today, the marketplace may be redefining these roles. The ties between universities and the corporate world have proliferated and changed over recent decades. There has been a shift in the priorities of the university: away from the pursuit of knowledge and the education of the next generation toward the commercial lure of the marketplace.

While partnerships between universities and industry have existed for many years, in the past they tended to rely on traditional relationships such as the hiring of graduates, the use of faculty consultants, or the sponsorship of research. Financial associations with private industry were largely confined to grants awarded by companies to academic institutions for research in areas of mutual interest. Corporations played no part in designing or analyzing research studies, housing the data, writing the papers, or controlling the publications of results.

Things have changed dramatically in the past decade. Arm's length relationships are a thing of the past, and financial arrangements between corporations and researchers go far beyond simple grant support. In some research universities, the conflict of interest policies have been designed primarily to comply with federally funded research, while the increasing flow of privately funded research is eroding university-wide compliance with the spirit and letter of the federal guidelines. New forms of hybrid institutions have emerged to facilitate industry-university collaborations that are not formally covered by faculty policies. The increasing trend for students at the graduate and undergraduate levels to be involved in proprietary work with sponsoring corporations can create conflicts for which most university government committees have few policies and sometimes no oversight.

Of particular concern is the attention paid within the university research community to the commercialization of technology and discoveries, sometimes with the potential for very large financial rewards to individual faculty members under prevailing technology transfer policies and practices. The traditional belief of universities that proprietary claims were fundamentally at odds with their obligation to disseminate knowledge as broadly as possible fell by the wayside with the Bayh-Dole Act of 1980 (Press, et al., 2000). This legislation obliged those receiving federal funds for research to make strong efforts to promote the commercialization of their discoveries. From that time forward,

faculty researchers were expected to be aware of the potential commercial value
of their work; and their institutions were obliged to create the infrastructure
that would facilitate patenting, marketing, and licensing of their faculty's discoveries. It didn't take long for universities to realize that the Bayh-Dole mandate had the potential for becoming a cash cow for the institution and the faculty.
Universities invested heavily in technology transfer and licensing offices with
the missions of developing, protecting, and marketing intellectual properties.

Today, almost everything is viewed as having commercial value, be it a
reagent, a research method, a clone of cells, a molecule, or its sequence. Not
only the results but even the tools of science are now being restricted. In the
absence of standard policies, industry can demand greater control over the
research agenda, the release of research results, rewards to the institution and
the faculty, and the ownership of intellectual property, triggering competition
among universities for corporate support of faculty research on the basis of
customized conflict of interest agreements.

There is a certain irony in this increasing tendency for universities to ca-
ter to the commercial interests of industry and the marketplace. Despite the
increasing dependence of American industry on the research efforts of universities, public tax dollars and student tuition continue to pay the bills for
most campus-based research. It is true that industry research and development
have grown substantially over the past two decades to the point where today
the $200 billion that industry spends on research and development each year
forms almost two-thirds of the nation's total research and development effort.
Compare this change to the 1960s and 1970s, when the federal government
provided two-thirds of the support. Yet of this amount, less than $1 billion of
industry research and development expenditures go to support university research. In other words, industry today provides only 6.5 percent of the support for campus-based research, with the federal government and the
universities themselves picking up almost the entire tab. It is important to
realize that universities and the federal government are and probably always
will be, in effect, underwriting the industry-university research relationship.
This may be quite appropriate, but it needs to be recognized.

It is important to acknowledge that there are real costs associated with
the commercial exploitation of the intellectual property developed through
campus activities such as research and instruction. Despite the apparent opportunity for significant revenue from licensing and spin-offs, most universities will continue to heavily subsidize basic research, intellectual property
development, and technology transfer. Some faculty members may get rich
from spin-offs and IPOs, but many will be distracted from their primary responsibilities of teaching and scholarship. Still others will limit the dissemi-

nation of the results or methods of their research. Conflict of interest cases have become more frequent and complex, particularly when policies are reshaped or weakened to accommodate commercial activities. And perhaps most serious of all, unconstrained commercial forces are capable of distorting the academic roles and values of the university itself.

As Paul Berg (2000) noted in his testimony before a National Academies panel last year:

> What is ultimately most striking about today's academic industrial complex is not that large amounts of private capital are flowing into universities. It is that universities themselves are beginning to look and behave like for-profit companies. If we value unfettered basic research as the prime function of the academic setting, then it is fair to ask if the extent of current commercial interactions distorts that mission and promotes the public interest. In the short term the public benefits from products transferred from the campus to industry. But isn't the long term health and viability of the academic enterprise as the generator of basic untargeted knowledge and the innovator of ideas that challenge the zeitgeist also in the public interest? What is the right balance? I believe that the public interest extends beyond the immediate commercial benefits; it must be on guard against weakening the enterprise that we reply on to generate the knowledge and skills needed to sustain the effort in the long run.

How Can the University Control the Commercialization of Its Knowledge?

University administrations are increasingly pressured by external political and industrial interests and internal faculty demands to accelerate the transfer of intellectual property from the campus to the marketplace, even if this commercial effort runs counter to the traditional roles and values of the university. To be sure, the shortening time scale characterizing the transfer of knowledge from the lab to the marketplace demands a more intimate relationship between the university and private industry. But the issue is even more complex. Federal research support, channeled primarily through grants and contracts to individual faculty investigators, has created a culture on university campuses in which faculty members are expected to become independent research entrepreneurs capable of attracting the support necessary to sustain their research activities. The same culture extends to the disclosure, licensing, and commercialization of intellectual property, sustained by the substantial individual benefits associated with royalties and equity interest. This individualistic culture is perhaps best captured in the words of one university president who boasted, "Faculty at our university can do anything they wish—provided they can attract the money to support what they want to do!"

As a consequence, the modern research university functions as a loosely coupled adaptive system, evolving in a highly reactive fashion to its changing environment through the individual or small-group efforts of faculty entrepreneurs. While this has allowed the university to adapt quite successfully to the marketplace, it has also created an institution of growing size and complexity. The ever-growing, myriad activities of the university can sometimes distract from or even conflict with its core mission of learning, particularly when universities attempt to respond to the opportunities presented by the commercial marketplace.

Another more recent phenomenon is also driving the commercialization of the academy: the staggering funding available for biomedical research. During the past decade, a generous Congress, stimulated by an aging baby-boomer population, has doubled and then doubled again the budget for the National Institutes of Health so that in FY 2003 it is $27 billion, more than five times as large as the $5 billion budgeted for the National Science Foundation. As a result, more than 60 percent of every federal research dollar spent on the campuses today is for biomedical research. Little wonder, then, that the bottom line culture of biomedical investigators, long driven by the financial realities of academic medical centers and the product focus of the pharmaceutical industry, has infected the rest of the university.

It has become increasingly evident that the highly decentralized, entrepreneurial, bottom-line culture of the contemporary research university has simply outstripped the capacity of the traditional mechanisms and policies used to govern the university. Despite dramatic changes in the nature of scholarship, pedagogy, and service to society, the university today is organized, managed, and governed in a manner little different from the far simpler colleges of the early twentieth century. American universities have long embraced the concept of shared governance involving public oversight and trusteeship, collegial faculty governance, and experienced but generally short-term administrative leadership. While this system of shared governance engages a variety of stakeholders in the decisions concerning the university, it does so with awkwardness that tends to inhibit change and responsiveness. It further falls victim to powerful external forces such as market pressures and commercialization that challenge the core values and undermine the traditional academic roles of the university.

Because of their lay character, university governing boards face a serious challenge in their attempts to understand and govern the increasingly complex nature of the university and its relationships to society. This is made even more difficult by the politics of governing boards, particularly in public universities, that not only distract boards from their important responsibilities and stewardship but also discourage many of our most experienced, talented, and dedicated citizens from serving on these bodies. The increasing intrusion of state and federal government into the affairs of the university, in the name of performance and public accountability, can trample on academic values and micromanage institutions into mediocrity.

Efforts to include the faculty in shared governance also encounter obstacles. While faculty governance continues to be both effective and essential for academic matters such as faculty hiring and tenure evaluation, it is increasingly difficult to achieve true faculty participation in broader university matters such as policy concerned with technology transfer and conflict of interest policies. When faculty members do become involved in university governance and decision making, all too often they tend to become preoccupied with peripheral matters such as parking or intercollegiate athletics rather than strategic issues such as restrictions on the freedom to publish. The faculty traditions of debate and consensus building, along with the highly compartmentalized organization of academic departments and disciplines, seem incompatible with the breadth and rapid pace required to keep up with today's high-momentum, high-risk, university-wide decision environment.

There is yet another factor that mitigates against faculty governance. The fragmentation of the faculty into academic disciplines and professional schools, coupled with strong market pressures on faculty in many areas, has created an academic culture in which faculty loyalties are generally first to their scholarly discipline, then to their academic unit, and only last to their institution. Many faculty members move from institution to institution, swept along by market pressures and opportunities, unlike most nonacademic staff, who remain with a single university throughout their careers. Although faculty members decry the increased influence of administrative staff, it is their own academic culture, their preference for discipline loyalty rather than institution loyalty, coupled with the complexity of the contemporary university that has led to this situation.

The university president is all too frequently caught between the opposing forces of external pressures and internal campus politics and also between governing boards and faculty governance. Today, there is an increasing sense that neither the lay governing board nor elected faculty governance has the expertise, discipline, or accountability necessary to cope with the powerful social, economic, and technological forces driving change in our society and its institutions. The glacial pace of university decision making and academic change simply may not be sufficiently responsive or strategic enough to allow the university to control its own destiny. Academic values such as openness and academic freedom too often fall victim to opportunistic governing boards and university administrators who are seeking more immediate financial return from the commercial marketplace.

The complexity of the contemporary university and the power of the forces acting upon it have outstripped the ability of lay boards and elected faculty bodies to govern and have undermined the capacity of academic administrators to lead. It is time to consider replacing the existing paradigm of lay governing boards with true boards of directors comprised of experts experienced in the activities of higher education and held publicly, legally, and financially accountable. Beyond that, a new culture of faculty governance willing to accept responsibility along with authority is necessary. Further, academic leaders must be provided with adequate training in the profession of administration, management, and leadership, even as we delegate to them a degree of authority commensurate with their executive responsibilities. It is simply unrealistic to expect that the governance mechanisms developed decades or even centuries ago can serve well either the contemporary university or the society it aims to benefit.

Bayh-Dole Forever?

The federal government played a major role in stimulating and sustaining the American research university through the government-university research partnership first articulated in Vannevar Bush's (1945) report *Science—The Endless Frontier*. It has similarly triggered the explosion in campus activities designed to capture and exploit the commercial value of the intellectual property created by federally sponsored research through federal policies such as the Bayh-Dole Act of 1980. This legislation allows universities to retain the ownership of commercially valuable intellectual property produced in government-sponsored research. Universities have responded by providing strong incentives to their faculty and creating technology transfer offices to identify, protect, patent, license, and spin off commercially valuable products and companies. Before the Bayh-Dole Act, universities produced roughly 250 patents a year, most of which were never commercialized. In 2000 alone, universities filed for 8,534 patents and created 368 companies.

Technology transfer before 1980 occurred primarily through publication in scientific journals, technical consulting, continuing education and extension services, and the employment of trained graduates. To this array, Bayh-Dole added the transfer of a property right as the result of ownership of the intellectual property generated during the conduct of research, as manifested by patents, copyrights, trademarks, trade secrets, or a proprietary right in the tangible products of research. Fundamental to Bayh-Dole was the certainty that if universities were the owners of inventions from research, they could grant exclusive licenses, thus stimulating the private sector to invest in development.

The underlying tenet of the Bayh-Dole Act is that inventions resulting from federally funded research should be owned by universities and provided through exclusive licenses to industry for commercial development in the public interest. The act was based on the belief that a nonexclusive licensing policy simply is not effective in technology transfer. It is the incentive inherent in the right to exclude conferred upon the private owner of a patent that is the inducement to development efforts necessary to the marketing of new product. What is available to everyone is of interest to no one. Proponents of Bayh-Dole note that when the government held title to inventions under the policy that the inventions should be available to all (much the same as if the invention had been disclosed in a publication), the patent system could not operate as it was intended to.

But is this true? Although the recent increases in university patenting and licensing are widely assumed to be the direct consequences of Bayh-Dole, empirical evidence suggests that the impact of this activity on the content of academic research has been modest (Mowery et al. 1999). The growing importance of biomedical research, much of which relied on federal support that expanded significantly during the 1970s, was at least as important as Bayh-Dole in explaining increased university patenting and licensing after 1980. Other factors also encouraged the growth of university patenting in this and other areas, such as judicial decisions declaring that engineering molecules were patentable. It seems clear that an array of developments in research, technology, industry, and policy combined to increase universities' technology licensing. Bayh-Dole, while important, was not determinative.

Furthermore, the Bayh-Dole Act applies the linear model to science and technology policy: it assumes that if basic research results can be purchased by potential developers, thereby establishing clear potential for the commercial development of these results, commercial innovation will be accelerated. The earlier concept of a linear progression of basic research to applied research to commercial development to marketable products, a fundamental assumption of the *Science—The Endless Frontier* (Bush 1945) policies that have governed university research for the past half-century, has been replaced by a nonlinear process in which basic and applied research, development, and commercialization are mixed (Stokes 1997).

To quote Mowery et al., "the theory behind Bayh-Dole was that companies needed exclusive patent rights to develop and commercialize the results of university research, a theory that flies in the face of the position that patents tend to restrict use of scientific and technological information, and that open publication facilitates wider use and application of such inventions and knowledge. Are patents or restrictive licenses necessary to achieve application? Should such licenses be negotiated by universities, institutions not always known for their commercial expertise? Do a university-assigned patent and a licensing agreement delay or accelerate technology transfer? . . . [M]ore of what universities formerly would have placed in the public domain . . . now is patented and subject to administrative procedures that could restrict the diffusion of these research results. . . . These policies may raise the costs of use of these research results in both academic and nonacademic settings, as well as limiting the diffusion of these results."

Mowery, et al. note still other challenges to the conventional Bayh-Dole doctrine. The increasing emphasis on disclosing, patenting, and licensing much of what universities naturally would have once produced and placed in the public domain means that research is now subject to more complex administrative procedures. These policies may raise the costs of use of these research results in both academic and nonacademic settings as well as limit the diffusion of these results.

Donald Kennedy (2001) made an excellent further point in a recent editorial in *Science*. He suggests that, just as Bush's (1945) report "changed fundamental science from a venture dependent on small groups of privileged elites into a vast publicly owned enterprise, Bayh-Dole and related federal policies are driving university research toward the private sector, fueled by the mobilization of philanthropy and corporate risk capital." Continuing the frontier motif, he suggests we might regard the current framework characterizing technology transfer as the "great enclosure." "Just as the Homestead Act of 1882 transformed the American frontier from public land into a checkerboard of individually owned holdings by allocating land virtually free to those who would promise to live on and improve it, the largely public domain of basic research is now moving into private hands by yet another federal act, Bayh-Dole, which allows universities or individual scientists to claim ownership of the intellectual property created by federally sponsored research. Interestingly, these enclosure revolutions came about in the same way: both were implemented by purposeful government intervention and accomplished through statute."

Kennedy contends that while this has brought some major benefits, it has also been accompanied by significant costs. "New problems of conflict of interest, royalty distribution, and the propriety of commercial relationships have arisen for faculty members and university administrators alike. The contemporary enclosure of the Bush's *Endless Frontier* is replicating the history of the Homestead Act, yielding patent disputes, hostile encounters between public and private ventures, and faculty distress over corporate deals with their universities. Sometimes government action has unintended consequences, such as the recent executive order on stem cell research, which promises to transform a major public program into the proprietary sector. Many observers, noting these costs, advocate policies for reversing privatization."

The Need for New Paradigms

Transferring university-developed knowledge to the private sector fulfills a goal of federally funded research by bringing the fruits of research to the benefit of society. With this important technology transfer comes an increasingly close relationship between industry and the universities. While this benefits society, it also increases the risk that academic research will be compromised by constraining open publication of research methods and results while diverting faculty from more fundamental research topics not directly linked to commercial outcomes. Ironically, the freedom of universities from market constraints was precisely what allowed them in the past to nurture the kind of open-ended basic research that led to some of humankind's most important discoveries—for example, the solid-state physics undergirding unicrolectronics and the biological chemistry that revealed the structure of DNA.

There remains considerable uncertainty concerning just how universities should approach the commercialization of the intellectual property associated with campus-based research and instruction. Beyond the traditional triad of teaching, research, and service, it is useful to consider the products of the university as educated people, content, and knowledge services. Yet content— that is, intellectual property—cannot be bottled and marketed like other commercial products. It exists in the minds of people: the faculty, staff, and students of the university. As such, it can simply walk out the door.

Traditionally universities have handled content using the library model; that is, they have distributed knowledge freely through open publication. In the wake of Bayh-Dole, universities have swung to the other extreme by attempting to capture, patent, and license the intellectual property resulting from their scholarly and instructional activities, relying on armies of lawyers to defend this ownership. The past two decades have seen technology transfer shift from the library model toward the National College Athletics Association model, in which private profit has become a stronger motivating force than public interest.

Of course, although the federal government has encouraged and facilitated this shift through policies such as Bayh-Dole, it certainly does not require it. Indeed, the intellectual property policies of the National Institutes of Health state clearly that "Universities have no duty to return value to shareholders, and their principal obligation under the Bayh-Dole Act is to promote utilization, not to maximize financial returns. It hardly seems consistent with the purposes of the Bayh-Dole Act to impose proprietary restrictions on research tools that would be widely utilized if freely disseminated." (Press, et al., 2000) Furthermore, while disclosing, patenting, and licensing intellectual property may be appropriate for some areas (such as the product orientation of biomedical research), it may not be an effective mechanism for very rapidly evolving areas such as information technology or instructional content.

There are other models that universities might consider for technology transfer. One of the more interesting is provided by the open source movement in software development. In this model, a user community develops and shares publicly available intellectual property (such as a software source code), cooperating in its development and improvement and benefiting jointly from its use. Perhaps the leading example is the development of the Linux operating system, now evolving to pose a major competition to proprietary systems such as Microsoft Windows and UNIX. This gift economy is an emerging phenomenon: a community works together without any immediate form of compensation except for social capital intertwined with intellectual capital.

Of course, even this model can be taken to extremes, as evidenced by the Napster phenomenon, when enterprising students almost destroyed the commercial recording industry by creating a virtual commons in cyberspace for the swapping of digital recordings without compensation. Although this particular activity has been corralled by federal court decisions, it represents only an early example of the open source movement in which digital products such as the Linux operating system are created and distributed entirely in the public domain. Clearly there is a contradiction between the open source approach of Napster and Linux and the pay-for-it approach of most university intellectual property policies.

The Massachusetts Institute of Technology (MIT) has recently taken a major leadership step with its open courseware project, which aims at putting MIT course materials on the Internet for public use. As noted by the MIT's president Charles Vest (2001):

> The glory of American higher education is its democratizing reach. At MIT we plan to speed this process to Internet time, by making the primary materials for nearly all of our 2,000 courses available on the Internet for use by anyone anywhere in the world. We see this project as opening a new door to the powerful, democratizing, and transforming power of education. Almost our entire faculty sees this as a way to enhance our service to society and to improve education worldwide, goals they considered to be more important than revenue possibilities. (5)

It should be noted that Vest believes that the real key to learning at MIT is "the magic that occurs when bright, creative young people live and learn together in the company of highly dedicated faculty" (7). In this sense, the school views the open courseware project as a form of academic publishing rather than teaching because it puts materials into the hands of others to use as they see fit. From this perspective faculty members agree with many other members of the scholarly community that the spirit of open systems should prevail.

Although MIT has moved forward with this vision with the help of $10 million from private foundations, its course materials will be at the very high end of the science and engineering curriculum spectrum and aimed at only the most advanced students. Suppose, however, that a major public research university or, better yet, a small consortium of leading public universities were to extend this vision by providing in the public domain via the Internet not only the digital resources supporting their curriculum but also the open source middleware to actually use these resources. The result might well be the digital version of the land-grant extension role of the public university in the twenty-first century. The idea responds well not only to recent efforts such as the Kellogg Commission on the Future of the Land-Grant University (2000) but more broadly to the ongoing debate concerning just how public universities will serve our rapidly changing world.

Suppose that in return for strong public support, the nation's public universities could be persuaded to regard all intellectual property developed on the campus through research and intellectual property as in the public domain. They could encourage their faculty to work closely with commercial interests to enable these knowledge resources to serve society without direct control or financial benefit to the university, perhaps by setting up a commons environment adjacent to the campus, either geographically or virtually, where technology transfer is the primary mission. This might be just as effective a system for transferring technology as the current Bayh-Dole environment for many areas of research and instruction. Furthermore, such an unconstrained distribution of the knowledge produced on campuses into the public domain seems more closely aligned with the century-old spirit of the land-grant university movement.

Conclusion: What Is the Public Interest?

It is important to keep in mind the fundamental purposes and values of the university. The technology transfer policies of the University of Michigan begin with the statement: "The mission of the University is to generate and disseminate knowledge in the public interest. Essential to this mission is two fundamental principles: open scholarly exchange and academic freedom" (University of Michigan 1987, 26). The essential question comes down to determining the degree to which the increasing commercialization of the academy is threatening its most fundamental mission and values.

As Henry Rosovsky (2002) put it at a recent meeting of American and European educators, the marriage between universities and industry is "against nature." It represents a symbiotic relationship between two unlike organisms with vastly different characteristics and objectives. The values of the university involve freedom of inquiry, the open sharing of knowledge, a commitment to rigorous study, and a love of learning. The goals of the marketplace are return on investment and shareholder value.

The questions that remain before us and the issues that should be addressed through further dialogue both on the campuses and with those who are served by the university are many. What is the public interest in the transfer of knowledge from the campus to society through commercial avenues? How are the rules and expectations characterizing the interaction between the university and the commercial marketplace changing? Is there an appropriate balance of public and private interests in today's universities? How are policies, practices, and dialogue concerning the relationship between the university and industry affecting the traditional scholarly mission and sense of community on the campuses? Do universities and faculty have the necessary tools to manage the complexity of new relationships with industry?

The market forces driven by the increasing commercial value of the knowledge produced on our campuses are powerful indeed. Yet if they are allowed to dominate and reshape the higher education enterprise without constraint, some of the most important values and traditions of the university will likely fall by the wayside. As we assess these market-driven emerging learning structures, we must bear in mind the importance of preserving the ability of the university to serve a broader public purpose.

The American university has been seen as an important social institution created by, supported by, and accountable to society at large. The key social principle sustaining the university has been the perception of education as a public good. In other words, the university was established to benefit all of society. As in other institutions, such as parks and police forces, individual choice alone cannot sustain its usefulness in serving the broad range of society's education needs. Hence, public policy dictated that the university merited broad support by all of society, rather than just by the individuals benefiting from its particular educational programs.

Yet even as the need of our society for postsecondary education intensifies, we also find erosion in the perception of education as a public good deserving of strong societal support (Zemsky 2003). State and federal programs have shifted from investment in the higher education enterprise in the form of appropriations to institutions or students to investment in the marketplace for higher education services in the form of tax benefits to students and parents. Whether a deliberate or an involuntary response to the tightening constraints and changing priorities for public funds, the new message is that education has become a private good that should be paid for by the individuals who benefit most directly: the students. Government policies that not only enable but intensify the capacity of universities to capture and market the commercial value of the intellectual products of research and instruction represent additional steps down this slippery slope.

Education and scholarship are the primary functions of a university, its primary contributions to society, and the most significant roles of its faculty. When universities become overly distracted by other activities, they not only compromise these core missions but also erode their priorities within our society. The shifting perspective of higher education from that of a social institution shaped by the values and priorities of broader society to, in effect, an industry that is increasingly responsive to the marketplace only intensifies this concern. While it is important that the university accept its responsibility to transfer the knowledge produced on its campus to serve society, it should do so in such a way as to preserve its core missions, characteristics, and values. In particular, the nature of higher education as a public good rather than simply a market commodity needs to be recognized by higher education and reestablished by strong public policy and public investment at the federal, state, and community levels because the future of the university in an ever more knowledge-driven society is clearly a national concern.

References

Association of University Technology Managers. 2001. *Annual Survey of Technology Licensing Activity, FY 2000*. Washington, D.C.: Association of University Technology Managers.

Berg, Paul (2000). Testimony at hearings of the Committee on Science, Engineering, and Public Policy of the National Academies, Stanford University, March.

Bok, Derek. 1990. *Universities and the Future of America*. Durham, N.C.: Duke University Press.

Bush, Vannevar. 1945. *Science—The Endless Frontier*. Washington, D.C.: National Science Foundation.

Drucker, Peter F. 1994. "The Age of Social Transformation." *Atlantic Monthly* (November): 53–80.

Kellogg Commission on the Future of State and Land-Grant Universities. 2000. *Renewing the Covenant*. Washington, D.C.: National Association of State Universities and Land-Grant Colleges.

Kennedy, Donald. 2001. "Editorial: Enclosing the Research Commons." *Science*, 14 December, p. 2249.

Moe, Michael T. 2000. *The Knowledge Web*. New York: Merrill-Lynch.

Mowery, David C., Richard R. Nelson, Bhaven N. Sampat, and Arvids A. Ziedonis. 1999. "The Effects of the Bayh-Dole Act on U.S. University Research and Technology Transfer." In *Industrializing Knowledge*, edited by Lewis Branscomb, Fumio Kodama, and Richard Florida, 269–306. Cambridge, Mass.: MIT Press.

Press, Eyal, and Jennifer Washburn. 2000. "The Kept University." *Atlantic Monthly* (March): 39–54.

Rosovsky, Henry. 2002. "And the Walls Come Tumbling Down." In *The Glion III Symposium*, edited by Luc Weber and Werner Hirsch, 13–30. Paris: Economica.

Science and Engineering Indicators, 1998, National Science Board NSB98-1. Washington D.C.: National Science Foundation.

Schmidt, Peter. 2002. "States Push Public Universities to Commercialize Research." *Chronicle of Higher Education*, 29 March, p. A26.

Stokes, Donald E. 1997. *Pasteur's Quadrant: Basic Science and Technological Innovation*. Washington, D.C.: Brookings Institution Press.

Stokstad, Erik. 2002. "Data Hoarding Blocks Progress in Genetics." *Science*, 25 January, p. 599.

University of Michigan. 1987. *Standard Practice Guide, Intellectual Property*. Ann Arbor: University of Michigan.

Vest, Charles M. 2001. *Disturbing the Educational University: Universities in the Digital Age: Dinosaurs or Prometheans?* Cambridge, Mass.: MIT Press.

Zemsky, Robert. 2003. "Have We Lost the 'Public' in Higher Education?" *Chronicle of Higher Education*, 30 May, pp. B7–B9.

Chapter 6

Pushing the Envelope in University Involvement with Commercialization

RONALD A. BOHLANDER

JUST AS UNIVERSITIES are being applauded for taking up catalytic roles in economic development, many are questioning whether increasing university involvement in the commercialization of technology will lead to a decline in traditional academic values. Conflicts are inevitable. For example, the need to protect information of proprietary value to a company may conflict, in principle, with universities' usual desire to publish new knowledge openly.

While the growth of economic activity and jobs in communities around universities is generally seen as a good thing in itself, such progress necessarily happens through the accumulated success of individual private interests. Knowledge developed at a university has special value to a given company if it provides that company with an edge. There is a saying popular in entrepreneurial circles that intellectual property that belongs to all belongs to no one. Investors reward those with technological advantage. One measure of whether new knowledge has vitality is whether it gets into practice and products, not just into the library; and this necessarily involves engagement with specific interests.

Despite the tensions, universities often feel driven to stay engaged in commercialization, for several reasons:

1. Faculty want to ensure the relevance of their work.
2. There is increasing competition for research funding and a recognition that industrial research and development coffers are deeper than federal sources (National Science Board 2000).
3. Community stakeholders reward universities who adopt a constructive

role in developing new products, new companies, and ultimately job growth.

But let's set aside questions about whether or not universities should be involved in commercialization and instead consider how that involvement should be structured. How can universities better manage conflicts that arise between their great purpose to create and disseminate knowledge for use by all, on the one hand, and the possible opportunity, on the other, to help individual companies realize private benefits through the acquisition of specific technology, and in the aggregate, to stimulate growth? It is important to focus on the quality of the management we can bring to bear and on our ability to make the difficult choices to engage in some kinds of activities and not others.

This chapter explores what we have learned about meeting these challenges and ameliorating such conflicts based on experiences in aggressive programs of technology commercialization in the Georgia Tech Research Institute (GTRI). This contract research and development organization is an uncommon sort of institute and is mirrored in only a few research universities across the country. In the chapter, I detail GTRI's origins, describe how the institute operates as a whole, and briefly cover some highlights of its work in commercial product realization. Although a client-oriented contract research and development organization like GTRI may get out in front of the mainstream in experiencing certain kinds of commercialization challenges, a number of the lessons learned can be adapted to conventional university research and development.

GTRI and Its Place in the University

Founded by the Georgia legislature in 1919 and located within Georgia Tech, the organization actually began operation in 1934 (when it received its first state appropriations) under the name "Engineering Experiment Station (EES)." As the name suggests, the legislature created the organization as an analogue of agricultural experiment stations and extension services that commonly promoted farm economic development in rural communities. Many such stations and services were also centered in universities.

From the outset, EES (and later GTRI) were chartered to do the following:

- Promote scientific, engineering, and industrial research
- Encourage industrial and economic development
- Promote the general welfare of Georgia and its natural resources through science, engineering, and industrial research
- Assist national programs of science, technology, and defense

In the early years, EES researchers solved problems important to traditional industries largely rooted in rural areas. For example, "They were first to demonstrate successfully the feasibility of producing viscose rayon from Southern pine pulp. With funding from the Textile Foundation, they developed cotton roving and spinning processes that were three to five times faster than those used by industry at the time" (Rogers 2002, 1). During World War II, EES researchers were recognized for valuable electronics research applicable to the defense effort; and federal defense funding started to flow. In the cold war build-up in defense electronics in the 1970s and early 1980s, EES played a pivotal role; and defense contracts peaked at 80 to 90 percent of the institution's budget. On the fiftieth anniversary of operations, the organization was given a new, more modern name: the Georgia Tech Research Institute. Throughout its history, GTRI has remained a corporate part of the Georgia Institute of Technology and is seen as a prime place within the university for applying engineering research and development. GTRI's director is a vice president of the university and reports to the provost.

Even though the mix of work has evolved over time, GTRI has nevertheless remained faithful to its full legislative charter. With the downturn in defense spending in the late 1980s and heightened interest in global competitiveness, GTRI's leaders have naturally reemphasized the importance of work with industry. Today, the organization has a work force of close to 1,000 employees, about half of whom are degreed professionals and members of the general faculty of Georgia Tech. The remaining half consists of support staff and student employees. The research volume has held steady at about $100 million for several years and represents more than 35 percent of the university total. Currently, the work conducted at GTRI is comprised of Department of Defense research (roughly 75 percent), industry research (10 percent), and research for the state or other federal agencies (15 percent). The recession has affected industry research and development spending; in previous years GTRI had a higher volume of industrial work (see figure 6–1).

With its overall portfolio of research and design, GTRI is strongest in these topics:

- Acoustics and aerodynamic performance
- Advanced electronics
- Controls
- Display technologies
- Embedded software
- Environmental management
- Fuel cells

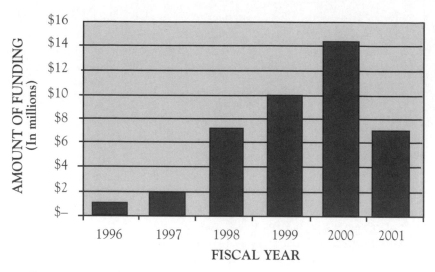

Figure 6–1. Trends in industry's research and development funding to GTRI.

- Information technology
- Knowledge management
- Logistics and manufacturing automation
- Modeling and simulation
- Photonic, electro-optical, and solid-state devices and materials
- Radar and other sensors
- Telecommunications
- Test and evaluation
- Transportation

The institute places great emphasis on service to its clients, both because it is consistently committed to quality but also for other practical reasons. More than 90 percent of GTRI's budget is in contracts, or "soft money." Faculty members are not tenured and depend for their continued employment on success in satisfying an ongoing stream of clients. Only a few members of the GTRI faculty teach for-credit courses; this is not a normal requirement of employment. For the most part GTRI operates according to its clients' schedules. Some have likened the situation to having a research and development service business located within the university.

Inherent in the founding legislative intent was the sense that a modern university must expand its purposes to include services to the state in vital areas, such as economic development. These functions are to be consistent with, but not necessarily identical to, traditional roles of teaching and research.

Practice what
you preach

Teach what
you research

Research what
you practice

Figure 6–2. White's university work cycle
SOURCE: J.A. White, "A Tribute to NSF's I/UCRC Program." Keynote address, twentieth
anniversary of the National Science Foundation Industry/University Cooperative Research
Centers Program, Washington, D.C., January 1994

As in the precedent agricultural service programs, there is a presumption that
such an institute will offer educational programs for practitioners that help
them do their jobs better. In keeping with this intent, GTRI is one of the
largest contributors to Georgia Tech's offerings in continuing education.

GTRI is also somewhat analogous to another kind of affiliated university
institution, the teaching hospital. In both, activities take place that are found
in some measure outside of universities; interns gain invaluable experiences
that enhance their education; the state of the art is advanced in the respective fields and leads to published work; and individuals are served, patients
are healed in the hospital, and clients receive research and development results from the research institute. An institute like GTRI has a special place
in a university and may become increasingly important to people coping with
a drastically accelerating generation of new knowledge. Continuing education
and knowledge management, linked with cutting-edge research, are rising in
importance and may transform the university.

In the early 1990s, John White, Jr., then dean of engineering at Georgia
Tech and now chancellor of the University of Arkansas, articulated a cyclical view of university activities (see figure 6–2). According to White, these
activities don't just coexist in the university; they feed each other. While GTRI
operates in a niche, it nevertheless participates in each part of this cycle in
varying degrees.

Figure 6–3 illustrates some of the important inputs and outputs of a
research institute such as GTRI. Clearly, university research generates not just
tangible results and reports; the people who have been through the learning
experience are its most important output. Because people are transformed by

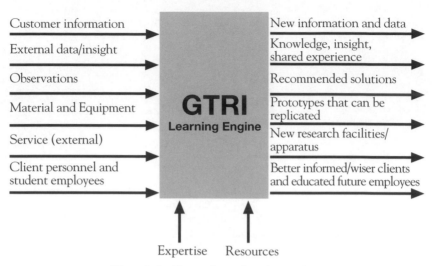

Figure 6–3. Research as a learning engine

the process, research and development, even in the arena of commercialization, are part of the fundamental educational process of the university.

Commercial Product Realization

In 1994, a graduate-level course was created at Georgia Tech that focused on techniques for rapid product development involving collaboration in the development cycle among multiple business partners or virtual corporations formed through cooperation between start-up and established companies, suppliers, and even customers. The course covered topics in management issues as well as hands-on experience in new technologies supporting design, product visualization and simulation, design collaboration, and e-business. Following the cycle shown in figure 6–2, the course drew on GTRI's research for the air force's air logistics command, the army's aviation and missile command, and associated defense contractors. Then in 1997, GTRI responded to requests from several companies for assistance in product development, which created an opportunity for firsthand collaboration in the application of product development techniques that the institute faculty had been researching and teaching. To date, a number of similar project relationships have been consummated, amounting to an aggregate approaching $20 million in research and development.

Many of GTRI's product developments have been in the realm of telecommunications, including products in digital television transmission, digital telephony, and high-speed optical fiber switches and multiplexing equipment. Until the first quarter of 2001, these markets attracted vigorous investment and competition. Similar kinds of product developments are currently getting underway in medical engineering technology and transportation sectors.

Work in the commercial arena is technically challenging and intense. A government sponsor may be too busy to correspond with researchers more often than once a quarter. But product realization research and development matter intensely to the client companies, and researchers may receive daily e-mail messages and telephone calls. Considerable value—even the fate of the client company—can rest on the outcome of the research. The knowledge front that must be covered is also wider than in academic research because one must know what is happening in the marketplace as well as in the technical literature. Cutting-edge electronic products must often incorporate just-introduced components that turn out to have defects, and ways must be found to compensate for these, adding to the complexity of product development. Global or national technical standards, which can be a real friend to entrepreneurial product development, are also not always settled or rigorously followed in emerging product areas. Work done to advance a specific product often spurs many others in the industry toward better products and standards.

GTRI has drawn together a staff of as many as fifty research faculty, technicians, and student employees from multiple departments within GTRI, creating a virtual division of the organization with staff located in at least three buildings who are connected by fiber networks. By necessity GTRI has used networked design tools that foster and support collaborative engineering. This has enabled researchers to more easily exchange information with clients with operations in several other states as well as with their suppliers and customers around the world. GTRI has worked out practical techniques for data interchange and security across a variety of software platforms.

To keep ahead of client needs, GTRI has vigorously pursued internal intellectual property creation and development and, as a result, has been able to license seven patents and patents pending under royalty-bearing licenses in connection with these projects. It is too early to say whether the licensees and their products will be successful or whether the royalties will amount to a significant income stream. But contract research and development typically exist in a pricing structure that make them a low-margin business. Thus, royalties could help significantly in seeding exploratory work that will lead to future research avenues.

In addition to licenses and development contracts between the parties, there are typically multiple mutual nondisclosure agreements covering proprietary technology important to the new products at the center of these products. The university does not yet hold equity in any of the client companies involved in projects, but such an arrangement would not be out of the question in appropriate circumstances and with the appropriate management. Typically, equity might be held if the university were to help faculty spin off from research and start new businesses themselves, but the activities described here are not of that kind. The decisions to spin off are usually taken by individual faculty on their own initiative, and there have been notable successes arising from GTRI over the years—for example, Scientific Atlanta and Digital Furnace, currently a division of Broadcom. Such activity has not yet matured to the point at which GTRI itself has encouraged and facilitated the decision to form a spin-off company, but such eventualities are being discussed in coordination with the staff of Georgia Tech's incubator programs.

Products that have been the subject of GTRI projects are now entering the marketplace and experiencing some success. Some are consumer products, and GTRI is working with clients and their manufacturers to assist in production and product testing. Here, GTRI draws on substantial Georgia Tech investments in manufacturing engineering expertise and related laboratories built up over the past two decades. The work, which involves much more than just design development, has spawned the term *product realization*.

Critical Management Issues

GTRI learned early on that, to meet the intense expectations of clients depending on help in product realization, core project staff for each account must be dedicated to that client for the duration of a project. In this manner, staff can proceed with project work expeditiously and remain available to respond when special needs or questions arise, as they inevitably do. This is somewhat different from the common practice in staffing government-funded research, where staff members are typically involved in two or more projects at a time. The burn rate with dedicated staff can be substantially higher, but the high value of product development is generally acknowledged to warrant it. Nevertheless, managing to have enough talented staff to effect dedicated assignments yet avoid too much idle time between assignments is a delicate balance. It helps to be able to buffer this work by drawing staff for expanding or new efforts from a larger practice for government clients. The converse is also true: when industry funding goes down, it is good to have a large government client base to which the staff may return. GTRI has involved academic faculty colleagues in specialized assignments in product realization projects, but generally it is difficult for academic faculty to fit into a dedicated assignment in view of the time pressures of teaching and student interaction.

Research universities and their research staff have, by and large, grown up in a culture shaped by performing research and development under government contracts and grants. Both university personnel and government contract officers know the well-laid-out procedures required by the Department of Defense, the National Science Foundation, and the National Institutes of Health that make the process predictable and organized. When GTRI decided to increase industry-funded research, it recognized that it needed to familiarize its faculty and support staff with the very different culture of contracting and interacting with industry. Internal staff courses were developed for this purpose.

In parallel, GTRI recognized that it often had problems working out contracts on terms acceptable to industry; negotiations were uncomfortably long and awkward, which detracted from the likelihood of creating long-term client relationships. Working closely with its contracting office, the Georgia Tech Applied Research Corporation, GTRI talked with a number of its industrial clients to get a better feeling for their needs and worked with them to find better common ground. In many cases, GTRI simply became better focused about what it needed to have in contract terms so that terms could be better articulated. The institute also found that it helped to negotiate master agreements with its clients that laid out basic terms and conditions. Specific projects were then implemented with task orders under these agreements that set out all the project-specific details. Thus, parties settled terms and conditions up front and streamlined subsequent contracting to meet evolving client needs. Working to refine this process in concert with refining internal staff training has been very effective. Whenever GTRI senses that it might be awkward to teach a particular process, the institute has taken that sense as a sign that the process might need to be improved.

GTRI has maintained a center for leadership over these processes in its industry business development office as well as in the commercial product realization office. The latter is focused on research and development operations but is knowledgeable about what works well in relations with clients. The two offices have worked closely together to improve processes and disseminate best practices.

After a few years of operations, GTRI recognized that all of the research and development staff members involved in product realization work were gaining important familiarity with the quicker pace of work necessary to help clients respond to the volatile world in which they were introducing new products. Needing a specific answer by the end of a given day instead of four weeks from now was no longer necessarily an occasion for "You want it when?!" Most GTRI researchers enjoy the excitement of this pace, and even prefer it, because they feel a great sense of accomplishment when technology becomes tangible in products that make it to the marketplace.

Avoiding Conflict of Interest or Commitment

There are really two kinds of such conflict: organizational and individual. On the organization's part, the university tries to avoid making exclusive commitments to work in a specific field only for one research and development sponsor. This is a matter of both principle and practicality, for the university as a whole spans thousands of faculty members with diverse interests and interactions with the public. An exclusive relationship would be impractical to manage, even if it were desired. Yet a specific research and development group is clearly limited in its ability to do identical work for multiple clients if separate proprietary issues are involved. Occasionally opportunities must be declined if they would create a conflict of interest. By keeping commitments to its clients as narrowly defined as possible, GTRI has managed to keep the frequency of such declined relationships negligible.

Individuals in GTRI are subject to and supportive of a strict discipline in which they must declare any outside commercial interests or consulting arrangements and have them approved before becoming involved in such opportunities. It is an accepted part of the culture that strict integrity is managed and maintained. For example, a GTRI employee cannot generally do outside consulting for one of the institute's contract research and development clients or even do outside consulting of a similar nature to that which is done inside the organization. GTRI has also advised its staff that making significant private investments in client companies represents a conflict of interest. While this requirement has been respected, during boom years it has occasioned some angst about why staff would want to stay involved in product realization as part of a university team if they receive no big payoffs of stock options, as industry development teams often do.

Protecting University Integrity

Interestingly, one of the most salient and helpful developments to reinforce university values and integrity has come from the Internal Revenue Service. Under IRS revenue procedure 97–14 (1997), restrictions are imposed on universities' interactions with commercial interests, which, if not followed, result in penalties that include loss of tax exemptions both for the institutions and for bonds that may have been used to build some university buildings. Gradually, the nation's major research universities have come to understand and attend to the implications of the revenue procedure: basically, a university shall not become captive to private commercial interests, and the essential test indicator is that university-developed intellectual property must not be presold.

A great deal of attention has been given to the impact of the Bayh-Dole Act, which assigns rights to universities to patent and license technology they develop under federal funding (Council on Governmental Relations 1999). But not all inventions arise from federal sponsorship. Not so long ago, there was a common assumption that, if a company funded work at a university, that company would want to own all the intellectual property arising from the work. While this often seems reasonable on the surface, it puts universities in a work-for-hire mode that raises questions about the integrity of the institution. Some universities, such as the Massachusetts Institute of Technology, have held the line rigorously against that assumption and asserted ownership themselves in every case. Universities who wished to be more flexible had few guidelines to follow. The IRS has now established a regulation that clarifies the agency's view that work for hire is unacceptable in view of the corporate purpose of a tax-exempt university. Under revenue procedure 97–14, an agreement to license or otherwise convey exclusive access to intellectual property may be entered into only after the intellectual property is developed sufficiently that its value may be assessed; and it can only be transferred then at a fair market cost. It is not possible to include in a research agreement the sale or exclusive license of intellectual property to be developed through the agreement, under risk of penalty from the IRS. As a result, it is now common practice for universities to retain ownership of the intellectual property they develop, whether or not it was produced under sponsorship agreements. At Georgia Tech, clients may be granted a first right of refusal to negotiate an exclusive license on fair and reasonable terms to intellectual property first conceived under sponsorship agreements, once it is far enough along to be available and able to be evaluated (see figure 6–4). At GTRI, this subject has been carefully handled in staff training so that faculty leaders are prepared to discuss ownership of intellectual property with prospective clients. Thus, GTRI can set a tone with clients; and both sides are better able to understand the unique benefits and restrictions involved when a company engages a university group to assist it in product realization.

While intellectual property terms are pivotal in contract negotiations, other issues must also be protected. Among them are mutual limitations on and review of publicity to avoid inappropriately implied exclusive endorsement. Conversely, the university must also insist on the right to publish generic findings arising out of industry-funded work while maintaining careful restrictions on the disclosure of proprietary information. Again, these points

For Inventions First Conceived or First Reduced to Practice in the Course of Georgia Tech Research:

The Georgia Tech Research Corporation (GTRC) will claim title to the technology.

GTRC will seek appropriate patent and copyright protection and will seek licensees to commercialize the technology. GTRC may elect not to pursue such protection and commercialization. In such instances, the technology may be placed in the public domain or assigned to the inventor under certain terms.

GTRC will retain the right to practice the technology at Georgia Tech in research and for educational purposes.

GTRC will retain its background Intellectual Property.

GTRC will comply with the Bayh-Dole Act including, among other things, reporting inventions to federal government sponsors, licensing technology to United States companies, and the use of due diligence provisions in license agreements.

GTRC will provide the United States government with appropriate nonexclusive licenses for inventions that result from federally funded research. GTRC will respect the intellectual property rights of others.

GTRC will share net royalties for Intellectual Property with inventors and their units according to the policies in the Faculty Handbook. GTRC's share of the royalties will be used to partially offset the costs of the technology transfer program and to further the research and education programs of Georgia Tech.

GTRC may offer the sponsor of a research project a non-exclusive, nontransferable right to use resulting Intellectual Property for internal, noncommercial purposes.

GTRC may offer the sponsor of a research project a limited right of first refusal to an exclusive license to resulting technology on fair and reasonable terms to be negotiated when the technology is available.

GTRC will avoid obligating the intellectual property rights of present and future students.

Potential conflicts of interest for those responsible for the design, conduct, or reporting of research must be disclosed and managed, reduced or eliminated.

Figure 6–4. Georgia Tech policy in 2002–2003 on intellectual property rights in sponsored research agreements. *Note:* The board of regents has given the Georgia Tech Research Corporation the responsibility for managing all Georgia Tech intellectual property including that arising in GTRI. Quoted with permission by GTRC.

are vital to preserving the essential character of a university while helping it play a role in meaningful economic development and service to industry.

Getting Paid

The reality is that getting paid requires significantly more proactive attention with commercial clients than it does in government contracting. The latter may involve significant exercises in bureaucracy; but in the end, regulations keep the process on track in a fairly predictable and reliable way. Companies, even Fortune 500 ones, run into tight times in particular budgets. Moreover, company staff members often feel free to contest bills or use to their advantage loopholes arising from any contract performance irregularities. In good times, things often go smoothly; but motivations for nonpayment can arise suddenly, and watchfulness is required. Therefore, GTRI has trained its faculty and staff to avoid issues that may provide excuses for nonpayment down the road. Complete protection is impossible, however; and litigation as recourse is expensive in several respects.

Dedicated product development sometimes proceeds with high rates of expenditure that can expose the university to the risk of holding large receivables. Therefore, this concern must be proactively managed up front, first by performing adequate due diligence regarding credit history and other factors, then by setting terms for prepayment as appropriate. Due diligence and watchfulness must continue over the life of the relationship. By taking such steps, the university can stay out of financial difficulty and maintain the financial solvency expected of a public institution.

Conclusion

Building a program of product realization with industry has been a rewarding adventure, albeit one that has stretched GTRI a great deal. GTRI remains committed to expanding its involvement in research and development for industry, and the biggest opportunities seem to be those closest to value origination: the product realization area I have discussed in this chapter. Growth will be possible only if GTRI continues to respond to client needs and deliver excellent engineering of critical value. The institute is fulfilling a significant part of the GTRI charter, consistent with important stakeholder expectations. Success also requires proactive management to ensure that conflicts are minimized and managed and that academic values are not only respected but nurtured. For example, such programs must promote the learning experiences of clients, student interns, and the research community itself, and thus lead to expanded future effectiveness. GTRI has shown that a university research and development group can be an effective agent in helping industry bring products to market. Such experiences serve as a virtual laboratory that builds at least vicarious familiarity and can make necessary techniques more accessible to new groups entering into such work.

References

Council on Governmental Relations. 1999. "The Bayh-Dole Act: A Guide to the Law and Implementing Regulations" (*http://www.cogr.edu/bayh-dole.htm*).

Internal Revenue Service. 1997. Revenue procedure 97–14. *IR Bulletin* 1997–05 (*http://www.unclefed.com/Tax-Bulls/IndexDigest/Bonds.html*).

National Science Board. 2000. *Science and Engineering Indicators, 2000*. NSB–00–1 and 2. Arlington, Va.: National Science Foundation.

Rogers, Janice. 2002. "The Georgia Research Institute: Creating Solutions through Innovation Since 1934." Internal GTRI publication.

Chapter 7

Conflicting Goals and Values

When Commercialization Enters into Tenure and Promotion Decisions

KAREN A. HOLBROOK

ERIC C. DAHL

UNIVERSITIES ARE INCREASINGLY asked to broaden their role in economic development and undertake activities that connect them with the private sector in efforts to derive economic value from commercializing their research and educational outcomes. It is widely recognized that there are many potential conflicts between commercialization goals and traditional academic values. To counter them, universities have evolved a range of mechanisms to preserve scientific impartiality, academic freedom, and ethical behavior and to guard against conflicts of interest. There is also increasing awareness that a conflict of interest exists between traditional values embedded in the tenure and promotion process of universities and the social and institutional expectation that some faculty members will play important roles in economic development activities. Universities are beginning to recognize and respond to this conflict of interest.

The Bayh-Dole Act and the Rise of Technology Transfer at Universities

More than two decades ago, Congress recognized that the federal government could not oversee the daily commercial management of the intellectual property that was being created at universities as an outcome of federal investments in research. At the time, the government held title to about 28,000 patents that had resulted from federally funded research, but fewer than 5 percent of these patents were licensed to industry for the development of products. Because there was no government policy regarding the ownership of these inventions, the ability of industry to adopt and develop the new technology was limited. The Bayh-Dole Act of 1980 transferred ownership from the federal government to American universities and thereby gave responsibility to the universities for managing and commercializing intellectual property from federally funded research. Thus began the expansion of the university technology transfer enterprise, with enhanced enthusiasm and even more mandates for partnerships among universities, industry, and the government. The act also opened the door to new revenue streams for institutions and their faculty. Only about thirty universities were actively involved in technology transfer when Bayh-Dole was enacted in 1980. Today the total is more than two hundred.

Technology transfer activities are firmly embedded in the culture of the modern university. They are seen as a vital component of the research enterprise and are endorsed at the highest levels of university administration. According to Steven Sample (2001), president of the University of Southern California:

> We need to incorporate technology transfer as part of the basic mission of the university. We need to integrate it with the rest of what we do.
>
> It must be a university-wide mandate. Universities can and should do more to instill a climate on campus which will enhance their ability to do tech transfer. That approach begins with the university's top leadership. If the president and the provost aren't enthusiastically supportive, tech transfer will never take hold. (http://uscnews.usc.edu/presidential/2001_InnovationAndTech.html)

Technology transfer is often cited as an example of the relevance and impact of university research in modern society. It has resulted in a wide range of consumer products, new drugs, medical treatments, new processes, and new curricula and has motivated faculty and students to become entrepreneurs. The entire biotechnology industry has come into existence because the federal government has made it possible for universities to transfer technology effectively.

The positive economic impact of the Bayh-Dole legislation is readily demonstrated. In the late 1970s and early 1980s, roughly two hundred licenses and options were negotiated between universities and industry each year. For fiscal year 2000 alone, more than 4,300 licenses were executed and $1.26 billion in licensing and options revenue was generated among the 190 institutions that responded to the Association of University Technology Managers'

(2002) annual survey. Compare those figures with the $200 million in total annual licensing income recorded in the same survey ten years earlier. In addition, a total of 3,376 start-up companies based on university technology have been formed since 1980; of these, 2,309 were still in operation ten years later.

The Role of the Research University in Economic Development

Economic development has long been a goal for research institutions, especially public land-grant universities, which "were to support the infant republic, help citizens, and promote economic development as well as train minds and improve manners" (Moos 1981, 2). Today, both public and private universities have embraced the role of economic development and have established an extensive infrastructure to support wealth re-creation through the transfer of technology, products, expertise, and copyrights generated by research and educational programs. Some have even created their own seed and venture capital funds to invest in faculty-initiated start-up companies. These activities support numerous interactions, cooperation, and collaborations with other institutions, industries, organizations, and governments that help to build the reputation of the university. They also underpin and create incentives for research on campus across all programs. States recognize the value of these university activities and design initiatives to invest in them to support the partnerships. They also have changed laws and universities have revised policies to liberalize faculty ownership in the companies they create (Schmidt 2002). Moreover, states, regions, and the cities in which universities are located periodically complete economic impact studies using a variety of metrics and inflation-adjusted multipliers to calculate and track the effect of research funding on local economies.

For most institutions, economic development is incorporated in both the mission and strategic goals of the university. The university system of Georgia (2000), for example, emphasizes the relationship between the preparation of students and the health of the state's economy in its sixth strategic goal: "accelerating economic development by providing, when feasible, needed graduates, appropriate academic programs, and expanding marketing of the system and its institutions as an economic asset of the state" (*http://www.usg.edu/admin/regents/statements/html*).

Universities are firmly entrenched in these industry relationships and continually seek to develop new ones while using the relationships and the dollars that flow from them as benchmarks of their success (University System of Georgia 2000, Waugaman and Tornatzky 2001). In measuring university performance, states value what can be quantified. Criteria such as the number of patent applications per $10 million in research and development funding, the number of patents awarded, the amount of licensing income, and the number of start-up companies formed can be used as cross-sectional and longitudinal measures of one aspect of university effectiveness (Waugaman and Tornatzky 2001).

Ongoing Innovation

The record of achievement in innovation does have flaws. With two hundred institutions experimenting with commercialization over the past twenty years, critics in the press have had an easy job aggregating the negative outcomes. They have blamed universities for selling out, losing their commitment to impartiality, forgoing unfettered discovery for directed and financially rewarding applied research, and shifting the culture of academia away from intellectual exploration. Sample (2001) addresses this criticism:

> We all know that the values and goals of a university are fundamentally different from those of a profit-seeking business, as well they should be. That is . . . why there is such concern about universities abandoning their academic integrity in an effort to court businesses and capitalize on university research. . . . "Chasing profits" is not the intent and we must constantly guard against undermining the basic purpose of the academy. (*http://uscnews.usc.edu/presidential/ 2001_InnovationAndTech.html*)

Universities have made good-faith efforts to limit conflicts of interest and commitment on the part of individuals and institutions by crafting and revising policies to meet the changing features of the research environment. The technology transfer system, even with its overall statistical successes, is still a work in progress.

In terms of the broader issues of university intellectual culture, academic freedom, and the traditional values of university research, institutions have made some astute decisions that deserve to be more widely emulated. The effort of universities to form partnerships with the private sector in commercializing intellectual property benefits not only the American economy but also the long-term health of the universities themselves as centers of intellectual exploration.

The Wisconsin Alumni Research Foundation (WARF) is one example. Established in 1925 by alumni of the University of Wisconsin, its original goal was to capture the commercial opportunities of vitamin D. After this goal was reached, WARF became the template for many university commercialization efforts. At present, more than $1 billion worth of products are sold under license from WARF each year, resulting in royalty payments from the foundation's share of the proceeds to more than three hundred researchers at the Madison campus and providing funds to the university to be used for research, graduate education, the purchase of land and equipment, and investment in new buildings (Culbrandsen 2002).

A less well known example is the University of Washington Royalty Research Fund. In the mid–1980s, some university leaders advocated the idea of putting a significant portion of the university's royalty revenue into a research fund to support peer-reviewed research grants throughout the entire university, even in departments that made no contribution to the university's fund through license and royalty income. While this practice is more widely accepted today, it was controversial when it was proposed. Some faculty felt strongly that royalty revenues should be returned only to the programs that generated them. Nevertheless, the university's Royalty Research Fund was created in 1992; and annual grants of $10,000 to $40,000 began to be awarded to faculty through a peer-reviewed process to support the research of beginning or established faculty members from departments as diverse as science, engineering, linguistics, anthropology, art, history, dance, painting, and many others. During the fund's first five years, $3.6 million in seed awards generated more than $38 million in additional funding. By 2000, $11 million had been awarded for more than 550 projects throughout the university. One award allowed a young professor in the Department of Asian Languages to travel to India to study religious manuscripts in ancient Indian dialects. Subsequent to his travel, eighty fragments of Buddhist literature written on scraps of birchbark in the first century A.D. were discovered in clay jars in India and acquired by the British Library. They are the oldest Indian manuscripts of any type and are as important to Buddhism as the Dead Sea scrolls are to Judaism and early Christianity. The most qualified expert in the world to transcribe and interpret these fragments was the University of Washington professor who had been studying examples of obscure early Indian dialects since visiting India a few years previously on a research trip funded by the University of Washington Royalty Research Fund (Illman and Kwiram 1997). This is an interesting story of the diversity of intellect and the range of exploration in research universities. The relevant point, however, is that the use of licensing revenue to send a linguist to India validates, in a very real sense, the university's involvement in commercialization for the enhancement of scholarship within the university.

Promotion and Tenure in the Academy

Significant economic and academic value is derived from the commercial activities of universities, which is used to support the longstanding aims of institutions. But productivity of faculty in this arena is often excluded as a criterion for professional advancement. Entrepreneurial activities of any sort are largely ignored by promotion and tenure review committees. Because incentives and rewards to promote such activities are typically external to the tenure process, tenured senior faculty generally engage in entrepreneurial activities and commercialization more readily.

The promotion and tenure process is a time-honored construct in American academic life. Tenure decisions are among the most important ones made at research universities, perhaps *the* most important. The quality of the faculty lies at the heart of an institution's reputation and future. Ownership of the promotion and tenure process rightly rests with the faculty. But because these decisions affect all aspects of the university, updated policies and practices are essential to underpin success for the future and to recognize and reward the productive accomplishments of faculty.

Traditional Factors in the Promotion and Tenure Process

At most institutions, research productivity is the primary factor in the tenure decision, typically measured in books in print or the quality of papers published in distinguished journals. In some disciplines, grant support also may be a positive factor in evaluating research productivity and is especially valued if it is federal and awarded through a peer-reviewed process. Industry research support may be viewed less favorably because it may be thought to support private-sector projects rather than basic research.

Intellectual stature is essential for both tenure and promotion. Advancement from assistant to associate to full professor is sometimes correlated with achieving a scholarly reputation that grows from regional to national to international prominence. Letters of recommendation are important in determining stature, as are affiliations with national and international scholarly organizations and service on national review panels, editorial boards, and advisory boards.

Excellence in teaching is a requirement for promotion and tenure and is assessed through student and peer evaluations. In most institutions, the weight given to teaching has increased, although good teaching is not likely to save a faculty member with a mediocre research record. Intellectual stature is characteristically tied to recognition through research accomplishment rather than teaching prowess. Tenure committees at most institutions also consider public service, but this is almost always a secondary consideration except in a few specific service and training fields.

Today, the roles, responsibilities, and expectations of faculty have expanded to include many other activities that, for the most part, have not been incorporated into the criteria for promotion and tenure used by departmental, college, university promotion, and tenure review committees. These expectations include innovation and entrepreneurship; the use of technology in teaching and scholarship; working in a global environment; providing experiences for students through internships, cooperative experiences, and service-learning opportunities; supervising undergraduate research; strengthening interdisciplinary collaborations; and demonstrating accountability to stakeholders defined broadly across many public sectors.

Faculty members receive conflicting messages when these new expectations are ignored in promotion and tenure decisions. The result is a failure to truly appreciate the faculty member who is engaged in patent development, consulting with outside companies, or productive activities such as establishing a start-up company. Students are now required to be technologically savvy, yet faculty members who create educational software are regarded less favorably than faculty members who restrict their activities to traditional scholarship and publication. Similarly, faculty time spent directing undergraduate students in research is not counted favorably toward promotion and tenure. Although there is little question that academia places high value on the first author, the principal investigator, the thesis supervisor, and the lead instructor, universities must also recognize the collaborative nature of scholarship and develop an expanded set of essential contributions in assessing a faculty member's work for promotion and tenure.

Information Technology and Tenure

A recent article in the *Chronicle of Higher Education* describes a growing recognition in tenure decisions of the importance of technology development for effective research and teaching (Young 2002). Most universities seek to improve the quality of their instructional technology by developing educational software, Internet applications, and distance learning tools. They encourage faculty to engage in these efforts and offer competitive grants to promote such activities yet give mixed signals to junior faculty. For instance, institutions may provide funding or release time so that these young professors can learn about or develop technology to support research or instruction but then fail to consider these activities as a valid measure of productivity in promotion and tenure deliberations. This kind of work may be viewed as tangential or even detrimental to personal advancement.

Young (2002) relates the story of a psychology professor whose expertise and considerable commitment of time allowed him to create a respected online resource to teach introductory psychology students. He was later told by a member of his tenure review committee that his efforts were viewed as "not being a research project—it counts sort of like service, but it's also sort of a hobby" (A26). The message was "Don't waste time teaching online or laboring over electronic course enhancements unless you've already climbed to the top of the tenure and promotion ladder. Review committees may not take technology work seriously, so stick to traditional academic activities like publishing journal articles" (A25). It is still risky for junior faculty members to devote serious effort to these types of activities in lieu of adding more publications to their dossiers. As a consequence, the university does not benefit from the very activities it seeks to promote.

An informal comparison of online promotion and tenure policies at twenty-three American universities viewed to be peers by the University of Georgia revealed that only six included instructional technology development as a valid criterion and only two referenced applications of commercialization of this technology. This underscores the suspicion that, at many universities, novel applications of information technology or the development of digital instructional materials are not valued by committees at all. At best, they might be seen as a minor component of teaching. The conflict between goals and values is similarly apparent when the percentage of universities investing in technology resource centers and development is compared with the percentage that includes information technology development in faculty review and promotion guidelines.

It is possible that information technology development activities are not included as a criterion in promotion and tenure decisions because it is difficult to assess their merit and quality as well as the broad impact of the work. Moreover, anyone can publish instructional materials online. Promotion and tenure committees rely primarily upon peer-reviewed products when assessing quality and relevance. But peer review for courseware development may be on the horizon. A new national group known as the Multimedia Educational Resource for Learning and Online Teaching (MERLOT) has assembled a directory of such materials and developed a program to evaluate them (Young 2002, A26). If MERLOT succeeds, professors will review course materials on the Internet as part of their professional duties, just as they judge and edit journal articles. Developers of online courseware will have peer evaluations of their online instructional contributions to include in their promotion and tenure dossiers. It has also been suggested that promotion and tenure committees should include members with enough personal expertise to understand digital courseware development; that online publications be evaluated online, not as printouts; and that the relationship between courseware creation and the tenure process be spelled out in the initial contracts of newly hired faculty.

There is movement within the academic community to begin to resolve conflicts between new goals and traditional values. Institutions do revise their value structures to accommodate new academic need. Instructional technology development is beginning to receive recognition commensurate with its importance to the institution and the university's teaching mission.

Commercialization and Tenure: Goals versus Values

Clearly, universities have invested significantly in support mechanisms and research investment strategies to exploit the commercial potential of intellectual property. They also encourage faculty to help in this process; and in doing so, faculty are caught in an apparent conflict between traditional academic values and those commercialization goals that increasingly benefit both the academy and the economy. Faculty contributions in this sphere are often ignored or devalued when their productivity is evaluated in the promotion and tenure process. This situation is even more problematic than the previous example because activities such as consulting with industry, prototype development, product refinement, or involvement with start-up companies are even more distant from traditional measures for promotion and tenure.

Such faculty efforts have traditionally been viewed as occurring outside the context of academic promotion and tenure decisions. Because of the potential for faculty to derive income from this type of activity, technology transfer is often viewed more as a matter of personal business, a perquisite, to be undertaken only after the primary obligations of faculty have been met. The reward system for technology transfer is monetary and is not viewed as a step in professional development. Success in this area can also generate resentment from deans, department heads, and other faculty members, who may believe they are bearing the traditional academic burdens while their entrepreneurial colleagues are filling their pockets, abusing students, and advancing industrial research and development. Collegiality may be threatened by engagement of only some faculty of a unit in this less traditional activity: "Greed and suspicion lead to a breakdown in the ability to create a win-win relationship between the entrepreneur and university" (University System of Georgia 2002, vi).

Activity by Professional Level

If technology commercialization is not counted toward tenure, we should not be surprised that junior faculty members are reluctant to commit the required time and energy to this kind of activity. At the University of Georgia, a list of 190 faculty members who recently disclosed technologies includes only nineteen assistant professors—10 percent of total disclosures. A broader survey would probably find similar proportions at other institutions; in fact, a similar study undertaken at the University of Florida a few years ago also revealed the dominance of the senior faculty in this domain, with 75 percent of the disclosures. Younger faculty are implicitly discouraged from engaging in commercialization because the promotion and tenure guidelines of their institutions do not recognize this activity; they are explicitly warned by senior colleagues and departmental chairs that establishing research directions not influenced by industrial goals is the best way to assure future academic success.

Other factors also affect who is involved in technology transfer activities. Senior faculty have more research experience and wider contacts to draw on for industrial sponsorship in the commercialization of technologies. Creating a start-up company has come to be viewed by some as a capstone accomplishment to round off their conventional research careers.

A recent publication prepared on behalf of the Southern Growth Policies Board (Tornatzky, Waugaman, and Gray 2002) surveyed twelve research universities selected because they understand the value of engagement and external partnerships as well as how to connect with their partners to promote economic development. One of ten measures of assessment, "faculty culture and rewards," reveals the extent to which each of these universities provides symbolic support: through entrepreneurial training, mission statements that avow enthusiasm for applied research and economic development, adoption of flexible policies permitting faculty engagement in commercialization of technology, and the rewarding of faculty success with awards, luncheons, banquets, or monetary prizes. Only a few, however, have explicitly included such activities in promotion and tenure guidelines.

The recently revised promotion and tenure guidelines at North Carolina State University include statements regarding "realms of faculty responsibility" to include extension and engagement with constituencies outside the university, managerial support and technology innovation, and applied research that produces "practices and technologies useful to society." The Ohio State University believes that "attracting top faculty and students is based on the notion that academic research and technology partnerships are not an either or proposition." Guidelines for promotion and tenure in the College of Food, Agriculture, and Environmental Science at Ohio State were recently revised to include entrepreneurship and economic development activities. Faculty members at Pennsylvania State University have engaged in conversations to define scholarship and have included activities related to patents and licenses within the definition of research scholarship. Outreach activities are some of the criteria now being used to evaluate faculty for promotion and tenure at the University of Wisconsin. Outreach may include technology transfer, and factors used to evaluate faculty may include patents awarded and copyrighted materials prepared. Similarly, Virginia Polytechnic Institute and State University has acknowledged explicitly the value of outreach, external partnerships, and a role in economic development (Tornatzky, Waugaman, and Gray 2002, n.p.). Other universities among the twelve have not gone so far as to modify promotion and tenure documents, although other overt mechanisms of support demonstrate a favorable culture for entrepreneurial activities. Nonetheless, there is clear evidence that research universities value these activities and are slowly coming around to rewarding faculty who engage in them.

There are always advocates of the status quo. No doubt, to many it seems sensible to protect junior faculty from commercialization by keeping the tenure policy taut and inflexible in the belief that the unfamiliar and perilous machinations of the private sector will disappear if ignored. According to this logic, close interactions with industry should be reserved for the grizzled veterans. This outlook, however, is unrealistic. It assumes that nothing has really changed in the twenty years since the passage of the Bayh-Dole Act, and it fails to acknowledge that many of the newly hired faculty will come from graduate programs with strong commercial capabilities integrated with their research laboratories. These faculty members will seek programs that support their continued interactions with industry at the level they have already experienced in graduate school. Graduate students are looking for this kind of research support within their institutions. Promotion and tenure policies will have to take this new dynamic into account if institutions hope to remain competitive for the best new faculty and graduate students.

It would be destructive to academic values to grant promotion and tenure based on licensing revenue, industry contracts, or start-up participation alone. But promotion and tenure procedures should be brought into alignment with a modern world in which universities and the private sector support each other in commercial collaborations. The value of these accomplishments can be incorporated into the traditional measures by devising means to analyze and critique these discoveries and partnerships as we do research publications. Faculty should be encouraged to incorporate their discoveries and expertise into instructional content and be recognized for their public-service contributions in helping to create new companies, jobs, tax revenues, and products. In professional advancement, one size does not fit all. In all cases, however, the ultimate requirement for tenure is that faculty members be scholars. Yet academia must find new and better ways to recognize and encourage scholars who are also entrepreneurs.

The scholar-entrepreneur is not a new phenomenon. These are scholars of unimpeachable integrity with an abiding interest in research and a gift for recognizing product-related applications of new intellectual property, who also are superior teachers. They derive satisfaction from seeing the impact of their research in the marketplace, and they inspire trust and creativity in collaborations as they move from the classroom to the laboratory to the company boardroom. These professors are important role models for the kind of college graduates this country will increasingly need: the intentional learners—those integrative thinkers who readily adopt skills and identify the problems and solutions needed in a rapidly changing, technology-based world (Sample 2001, *http://uscnews.usc.edu/presidential/2001_InnovationAndTech.html*).

True scholar-entrepreneurs are vital to the current environment, but their numbers will certainly not increase if academia continues to tell them that they will not be rewarded professionally—that they will even be penalized—for any commercial activities undertaken in the first five to seven years of their professorial career. Academia must, as Sample (2001) points out, distinguish between professional and market values. But it must do more:

> [Academia must] get beyond the idea that commercialization of
> university research is inherently inimical to the role of the university.
> . . . There is simply too much at stake not to pursue tech transfer more
> vigorously. Not only for what it can do for universities, but even more
> for what it can do for society as a whole. It can add new dimensions to
> university research, while at the same time providing new educational
> opportunities for faculty and students. (*http://uscnews.usc.edu/*
> *presidential/2001_InnovationAndTech.html*)

Conclusion

Senator Sam Nunn of Georgia once commented about technology: "Bridges must be built between the world of science and the world of human relations, bridges which can give shape and purpose to our technology and breathe heart and soul into our knowledge" (Terrazas 1996, *http://gtalumni.org/StayInformed/techtopics/win96/nunn.html*).

Tenure is an arcane and sometimes puzzling aspect of the world of academia. The university is a vastly different institution today, and the promotion and tenure process needs to continue evolving if universities are to attract and protect the caliber of faculty members needed to harness commercial opportunities as well as support the longstanding values of the academy. This will require careful thought, comparing of notes, and the devising and sharing of best practices among the nation's institutions.

Adapting promotion and tenure policies and processes to reward and attract scholar-entrepreneurs should not be viewed as revolutionary but as a synthesis. Yet when accepting this challenge, we must also take precautions. With change in an entrepreneurial direction, universities must still maintain their traditional identity and value systems. Academic freedom, open inquiry and shared results, peer review, and even the promotion and tenure process itself are cornerstones of scholarly endeavors and continuing contributions to the long-term benefit of society. It is time, however, that the nation's academic institutions adapt intelligently and acknowledge in the promotion and tenure process the increasing synergy between American business and academic culture. We need "to learn from each other about the innovations implemented to take advantage of the relationships created by the merging cultures of business and education, the connection between research and economic development, the entrepreneurial attitude of many faculty . . . and the new partnerships among universities and with private enterprise and government" (Holbrook 1998, *http://www.nasulgc.org/publications/crpge/letter.html*).

References

Association of University Technology Managers. 2002. "FY 2000 Survey Summary." Northbrook, IL: Association of University Technology Managers.

Gulbrandsen, C. E. 2002. "Creative Management of Technology Transfer and Patenting: The How and Why of the University of Wisconsin Madison Approach." Paper presented at the NACUBO/KPMG Twentieth-Century Executive Symposium, 3–5 March.

Holbrook, Karen. 1998. "University Research and Technology Transfer in a Changing World." Summary of a workshop of the Council on Research Policy and Graduate Education of the National Association of State Universities and Land-Grant Colleges, 5–7 April.

Illman, D., and A. Kwiram. 1997. "UW Showcase: A Century of Excellence in the Arts, Humanities, and Professional Schools at the University of Washington." Seattle: University of Washington, Office of Research.

Moos, M. 1981. *The Post Land-Grant University: The University of Maryland Report.* College Park: University of Maryland Press.

Sample, Steven B. 2001. "Innovation and Technology Transfer in Universities." Paper presented at the California Public Affairs Forum of the California Council on Science and Technology, Stanford Research Institute, Menlo Park, 3 December.

Schmidt, P. 2002. "States Push Public Universities to Commercialize Research." *Chronicle of Higher Education*, 29 March, p. A26.

Tornatzky, Louis G., Paul G. Waugaman, and Denis O. Gray. 2002. "Attracting Top Faculty . . . Not Either Or" (*http://www.southern.org/pubs/innovationU/osu.pdf*).

University System of Georgia. 2000. *Project Scope I: Benchmarking Study: Final Report* (*http://www.usg.edu/admin/regents/statements.html*).

———. 2002. "University System of Georgia Commercialization Research Study" (*http://www.usg.edu/admin/regents/statements.html*).

Waugaman, Paul G., and Louis G. Tornatzky. 2001. "Benchmarking University-Industry Technology Transfer in the South and EPSCOR States: 1997–1998 Data." *STCV Report* 6 (April).

Young, J. R. 2002. "Ever So Slowly, Colleges Start to Count Work with Technology in Tenure Decisions." *Chronicle of Higher Education,* 22 December, pp. A25–A27.

Chapter 8

Buyer and Seller Views of University-Industry Licensing

JERRY G. THURSBY
MARIE C. THURSBY

U<small>NIVERSITY-INDUSTRY LICENSING</small> has been one of the most rapidly changing areas in the licensing of new inventions. According to the Association of University Technology Managers (1998), the number of universities with technology transfer offices grew from twenty in 1980 to more than two hundred in 1990. Based on information provided by the eighty-four American institutions that reported in each of the years 1991 and 2000, the number of licenses executed grew 161 percent.

This growth has been controversial enough to be the subject of a cover story in *Atlantic Monthly* (March 2000) and for the National Academy's Committee on Science, Technology, and Economic Policy to ask whether licensing has gone too far in diverting faculty from their primary duties in education and basic research. Issues range from the practical (such as "what's different about licensing from universities?") to the more abstract (such as "does increased license activity reflect changes in the conduct of science?"). Understanding this phenomenon is increasingly important because universities are considered to be critical to industrial innovation, with state as well as federal governments looking toward them for economic development benefits.

Two recent surveys attempted to capture objectives, characteristics, and issues in university-to-industry licensing of university technologies. The first was designed to be answered by university technology transfer office licensing professionals.[1] These university personnel are responsible for finding and executing licenses. The second, directed toward industry licensing executives, was sent to those who actively license in from universities as well as those who actively license in technologies but do not do so from universities.[2] This

chapter combines the results from both surveys in a manner that character-
izes the nature, objectives, characteristics, and issues from the perspectives of
the seller (university) and the buyer (industry). It presents evidence about the
level of licensing activity and its distribution across universities, fields, and
technologies and addresses five aspects of the licensing process:

- University objectives in licensing
- Stage of development, failure rate and faculty involvement
- Reasons firms do not license in from universities
- Reasons firms do license in from universities
- Marketing and identification of university inventions

An Overview of the Licensing Process and Its Current State

For the eighty-four American institutions responding to the Association of
University Technology Managers' (1993, 2002) survey in both 1991 and 2000,
the number of inventions disclosed by faculty increased 84 percent, the number of new patent applications filed increased 238 percent, the number of license and option agreements executed rose 161 percent, and royalties increased
more than 520 percent (in real terms). In 2000, 166 American institutions
reported 12,015 invention disclosures, 4,049 licenses executed, and 6,098 new
patent applications. In addition, 157 institutions reported $169 million in
cashed-in equity and $1.2 billion in income.[3] These magnitudes are widely
cited as evidence of university success in technology transfer and have been
partly responsible for rising public policy concerns. But they may paint a mis-
leading picture, given that there is substantial variation in licensing success
across universities, across fields within universities, and (as regards income)
across technologies.

If we exclude survey respondents that answer for multiple universities
(such as the University of California system), there remain 160 U.S. institutions in 2000 for which we can look closely at the distribution of licensing
activity. Table 8–1 summarizes the range, mean (average), and median for disclosures, licenses executed, new patent applications, and royalty income.[4] Note
that, in each case, there is a substantial range in reported results; and half of
all respondents report figures far below the average for all institutions. For example, while the average number of licenses executed in 2000 for these 160
institutions was twenty-two, half of the institutions reported ten or fewer licenses in that year. Licensing activity tends to be concentrated among a few
large successful institutions. This is particularly apparent from the income figures. Half of all institutions earned less than $1.1 million in 2000, and about

Table 8–1
University Licensing Activity

	Range	Mean	Median
Disclosures	1–425	64	36
Licenses executed	0–218	22	10
New patent applications	1–259	33	20
Royalty income			
(in millions of dollars)	0–148	5.8	0.99

SOURCE: Association of University Technology Managers (2002).

80 percent earned less than $5 million. On average, 1.5 technology licensing professionals and 1.1 clerical staff work at the institutions with licensing incomes below the median. Given the low licensing income of these institutions, it is easy to make a case that most spent more on the operations of their offices than they received in royalty income.[5]

Technology transfer offices were asked for the percent of disclosures in various fields. Not surprisingly, disclosures tended to be concentrated in science (22 percent on average), engineering (29 percent), and medicine (33 percent). As recently as 1997, the association collected information on royalty income from licenses in the life sciences and the physical sciences. In that year, about 87 percent of all royalty income was generated by the life sciences.

Very few licenses generate revenues. In the association's 2000 survey, 161 institutions reported 19,320 active licenses; of these, only 8,521 (44 percent) had generated licensing income in that year. Technology transfer professionals were asked for the percentage of total licensing income generated by the top five income-generating licenses. The average for the fifty-three responding institutions was 76 percent. Fewer than half of all active licenses generate income, and only a few generate the bulk of licensing income.

University Objectives in Licensing

Is this dramatic growth primarily policy-driven (that is, to promote industrial application of university inventions under Bayh-Dole), or is it the universities' response to tight research budgets (that is, to raise revenue)? In other words, to what extent are the motives behind licensing purely profit-driven? Before evaluating the university-industry technology transfer process and questions such as these, it is important to understand university objectives in licensing.

Technology transfer professionals were asked about their objectives and,

Table 8–2
Measures of Success: "Extremely Important" Objectives (according to % of respondents)

Objective	Technology Transfer Office	Faculty	Central Administration
Royalties/license fees generated	70.5	41.0	69.4
Sponsored research funds	34.4	75.4	48.4
Number of licenses/options signed	49.2	11.5	24.2
Number of patents awarded	16.4	16.7	14.5
Number of inventions commercialized	60.7	36.1	32.8

SOURCE: Authors' university survey.

from the perspective of their office, the objectives of the central administration and faculty. Table 8–2 shows the percentage of respondents who indicated that each of five different objectives was "extremely important" as a measure of success.[6] Note that each objective's importance to the central administration and the faculty is based on the perceptions of the technology transfer office.

Licensing income is the most important objective for the technology transfer office and the central administration, while sponsored research funds are the most important objective for the faculty, although such funds are also an important objective for the technology office and the central administration. Note the importance the office attaches to the number of inventions commercialized. University licensing professionals reported that they view the commercialization of inventions as a measure of compliance with the Bayh-Dole Act. It is clear that, while income is important, it is only one of multiple university objectives in licensing.[7]

Stage of Development, Failure Rate, and Faculty Involvement

Universities are generally selling early-stage technologies, and a key to understanding the licensing of university technologies is appreciating this fact. These generally embryonic technologies are risky due to their high failure rate, and faculty inventors are frequently involved in further development of the technology after the license is signed (see table 8–3). The early stage of development explains why many firms do not license university inventions. Here we explore the relation between stage of development, the performance of inventions that businesses do license, and the frequent need for faculty input in development after a license is signed.[8]

Table 8–3
Stage of Development

Stage	Technology Transfer Office	Industry
Proof of concept (no prototype)	45	38
Prototype (only lab scale)	37	36
Preclinical stage	26	15
Clinical stage	10	5
Manufacturing feasibility known	15	9
Ready for practical or commercial use	12	7

SOURCE: Authors' university and industry surveys.

Both surveys asked respondents to indicate the percentage of time that licensed-in technologies were in various stages of development at the time the license was executed. The combined results show that few licensed-in technologies were deemed ready for practical (that is, commercial) use, and a substantial number were simply a proof of concept (the earliest listed stage of development).

In part because of their early stage of development, these inventions have a high failure rate. Forty-two percent of industry respondents indicated that university inventions had a higher failure rate than nonuniversity licensed-in technologies, while only 11 percent reported a lower rate.[9] Those who noted a higher failure rate reported, on average, that 48 percent of their university licenses were for technologies that were only a proof of concept; all others reported that only 31 percent were in a proof-of-concept stage. Further, the correlation between the reported failure rate and the fraction of licenses that are in a proof-of-concept stage is 0.31, while the correlation with the fraction that are ready for practical or commercial use is –0.23. Industry respondents reported a greater failure rate for early- (72 percent) versus late- (43 percent) stage technologies. Not surprisingly, failure is closely related to the stage of development of the licensed technology.

Overall, industry respondents indicated that about 40 percent of all licenses require faculty involvement. The comparable figure from the university survey is 71 percent. To examine whether faculty involvement in further development varies with the stage of development at the time of the license, we asked a question regarding faculty cooperation in development and stage of development. As one might expect, we found an inverse relationship between faculty involvement and stage of development. For technologies in the earliest stages of development (proof of concept, prototype, and preclinical), industry respondents indicated that faculty were involved in further develop-ment more than 40 percent of the time, whereas faculty were involved only about 25 percent of the time for the latest-stage technologies ready for use.

Industry respondents were asked why faculty input is important for fur-ther development. The most important reason is faculty's specialized knowl-edge, indicated by 67 percent of the respondents. By contrast, only 17 percent indicated that faculty development was cheaper than in-house development.

Finally, we asked for reasons behind the failure of university technolo-gies. Forty-seven percent indicated a failure of the technology, 26 percent noted that the lag time to market application was longer than expected, and 13 percent indicated that the technology would infringe on the intellectual property of others. Eighteen percent of the time, failure of a technology was related to the failure of a faculty member to deliver know-how or cooperate in further development. Because 46 percent of licenses are considered fail-ures and 18 percent of failures are associated with failure of faculty involve-ment, it follows that about 8 percent of all university licenses will fail as a direct result of the failure of faculty involvement. According to the industry survey, faculty are involved in further development about 40 percent of the time. Thus, the 8 percent failure rate is concentrated in the 40 percent of li-censes that involve further faculty efforts. Richard Jensen and Marie Thursby (2001) discuss the moral hazard problem associated with needed faculty ef-forts in further development of licensed technologies. Whether or not one considers an 8 percent faculty "failure" to be high, it is clear that the moral hazard problem is not insignificant.[10]

Why Firms Do Not License in from Universities

There were three hundred respondents to the industry survey. Of these, 188 had not licensed in from universities during the five years before the survey, although many had sponsored research at universities. Respondents in this lat-ter group were asked why they had not licensed in university technologies dur-ing this period. A yes-no response was permitted for each of the seven reasons listed in table 8–4, which gives the percent of respondents who indicated yes for each reason. Aside from the fact that firms rarely license in, the dominant reasons pertain to the nature of university research: either the research is at too early a stage, or it is not relevant to the firm's line of business.

Industry respondents were then asked to indicate the most important rea-son for not licensing in from universities. Because a large fraction of respon-dents indicated that the most important reason for not licensing in from universities was that they rarely did any licensing, only the percentages asso-

Table 8–4

Reasons for Not Licensing in from Universities (% of respondents)

Survey Statement	"Yes" Response
We rarely license-in research from any source.	57.7
University research is generally at too early a stage of development.	48.9
Universities rarely engage in research in our line of business.	37.4
University policies regarding delay of publication are too strict.	20.3
Universities refuse to transfer ownership to our company.	31.3
We are concerned about obtaining faculty cooperation for further development.	15.9
Other	28.0

SOURCE: Authors' industry survey.

ciated with the "most important reason" after excluding the respondents who rarely license in are presented. For example, excluding those who rarely license in and who list this as the most important reason, 33 percent of respondents list the early stage of university technologies as the most important reason for not licensing in from universities. For 22 percent of the respondents, the dominant reason was that university research isn't relevant for the firm's line of business. Setting aside "rarely license-in," the most important reasons for not licensing in university technologies is associated with the nature of university research. These two reasons alone account for more than half of the "most important reason" responses. Reasons associated with either university policies (delay of publication and ownership) or behaviors (faculty cooperation) are strikingly less important.

Many of the respondents who did not actively license in from universities nonetheless sponsored research; in fact, for a number of those who list the early stage of development as a reason for not licensing university technologies, the amount of sponsored research is substantial. This raises an interesting question: why do they sponsor research while finding university research to be typically at too early a stage of development to be useful? There are several points worth noting. First, the sponsored research might well be "contract work." That is, money is paid for a clearly specified deliverable rather than being directed at a general research question. Second, in interviews, industry licensing executives reported that there are ancillary benefits to licensing university technologies, such as access to faculty for consulting purposes or graduate students for positions in the firm's research and development laboratory.[11] It is also the case that those who actively license from universities cite as important the establishment of contacts and access to university labs. Twenty-three percent of respondents who license in from universities cite the establishment of a working research relationship with faculty as an important motivation in seeking faculty input in further development of the licensed technology. One licensing executive went so far as to claim that the sole purpose of licensing university technologies was to establish a relationship with the faculty inventor.

It is common for a firm to examine a university technology but then choose not to license in the technology. When asked about problems significant enough to convince a firm not to license in early-stage technologies, the most important reason cited by industry licensing executives relates to the firm's market niche. Of industry licensing executives surveyed, 51 percent cited market niche as their primary reason for not licensing in. Another 39 percent cited problems in obtaining either internal or external funds, and internal funding problems are cited as being of greater importance than are external funding problems. The final choices relate to necessary scientific expertise from either in-house staff or faculty. Neither issue was of particular importance to respondents; only 16 percent cited a lack of necessary in-house expertise, and only 10 percent cited a lack of faculty cooperation.

Why Firms Do License from Universities

When evaluating why firms license from universities, it helps first to look at the purpose of licensed-in technologies and then at the importance of university technologies. Forty-three percent reported that the purpose of licensed-in technologies was new product development, and only 14 percent mentioned process improvement. Nineteen percent of licenses were for a research tool, and 24 percent were for a platform (or core) technology. Interestingly, only 4 percent indicated that the licenses were to prevent a rival company from licensing the technology. This last figure follows, we believe, from the fact that university technologies are embryonic; so few firms show interest in a given technology. University technology transfer offices were asked about the frequency of bidding on a technology by more than one firm. Forty-four percent said this occurred rarely or never, and 51 percent indicated that it only occurred sometimes. Because it is rare that more than one firm shows an interest in a particular technology, it should follow that few firms license to prevent a rival from licensing that technology.

Regarding the importance of university technologies, respondents were asked for the percentage of the time that universities had been critical to the development of new products or processes. By critical we mean that the product or process could not have been developed without substantial delay. The average response for patents licensed in from universities was 24 percent; for nonpatentable technology it was 8 percent, and sponsored research was 14 percent. By way of comparison, in-house patents were critical 49 percent of the time. When weighted by the number of executed licenses with universities, these percentages change substantially for in-house patents, which fall to 35 percent, and for nonpatentable university technology, which rises from 8 percent to 29 percent. How might one interpret these results? It is our view that, because in-house research and development is directed toward the needs of the market and hence the needs of the firm, it should be the case that in-house patents are more important generally than are university patents. It is striking that the importance of university patents is so close to that of in-house patents. This possibly follows from the more basic nature of university research, meaning that university inventions may be more fundamental and less incremental than industry inventions are. Hence, while the firm's research and development are generally directed at the firm's needs, university research, when applicable to the needs of the firm, is more fundamental.

To understand reasons behind increased licensing activity at American universities, we divided respondents into those who had increased their contractual activity with universities between 1993 and 1997 and those who had decreased their activities or had made no change in activities. Half of the sample had increased contractual contacts, while only 16 percent had decreased such contacts. Because so few respondents had decreased contractual relationships, we need only consider those with increasing contracts. Before turning to the results, it is instructive to note the magnitude of the increases reported. For those noting an increase in agreements, the number of licenses grew by 86 percent in 1997, compared to the average of the preceding four years; and their research funding to universities doubled. On average, each of these firms executed thirteen licenses per year and provided $13.2 million in sponsored research with American universities.

Respondents were given five reasons for increasing contracts (in addition to an "other" category) and were asked to indicate importance using a five-point Likert scale. Table 8–5 shows the relative frequency of each response; note that a "don't know" category was included in the survey but excluded from the table. The first three reasons relate to university costs and changes in environment regarding licensing, while the last two relate to changes in corporate research and development. What stands out is the greater importance attached to university receptivity than either costs or faculty research orientation; three times as many respondents recorded a 1 (extremely important) for

Table 8–5
Most Important Reason for Not Licensing In (% of respondents)

Survey Statement	"Yes" Response
University research is generally at too early a stage of development.	32.8
Universities rarely engage in research in our line of business.	21.9
University policies regarding delay of publication are too strict.	1.6
Universities refuse to transfer ownership to our company.	14.8
We are concerned about obtaining faculty cooperation for further development.	0.8
Other	28.1

SOURCE: Authors' industry survey.

"universities' receptivity" as recorded a 1 for "costs" or "faculty orientation."[12] Further, a change in "reliance on external research and development" is more important then either "costs" or "faculty orientation." Note that the reason for a change in "reliance on external research and development" could come about because of reasons associated with universities. Therefore, we computed the simple correlation between individual respondent answers to the "reliance on external research and development" question and the "costs," "faculty orientation," and "universities' receptivity" responses. The only significant correlation is between research and development and "costs"; the correlation is 0.49, suggesting that, to the extent that reliance on external research and development is related to university characteristics, it is the cost of university research that is important.

As we have noted, there are growing concerns that the increase in licensing activity indicates that faculty are moving more toward applied research (that is, research of direct importance to the current needs of industry and consumers) and away from their traditional focus on basic research. While the most important reason for increasing contacts is "university receptivity," 11 percent of respondents noted that a change in the orientation of faculty toward the needs of business was extremely important. Those concerned with this issue may well regard that figure as alarming. Clearly, more research is necessary on the effects of licensing on faculty behavior. The bulk of licenses, however, are based on research funded by the federal government, which is generally regarded as basic research. In the survey of university technology transfer offices, respondents indicated that 67 percent of inventions disclosed

Table 8–6
Reasons for Increased Contacts (% of respondents)

	Extremely Important 1	2	3	4	Not Important 5
Cost of university research	10.9	19.6	30.4	10.9	28.3
Faculty research more oriented toward the needs of business	10.6	21.3	27.7	19.1	21.3
A change in universities' receptivity to licensing and/or research agreements	29.2	27.1	20.8	10.4	12.5
A change in our unit's reliance on external research and development	20.8	37.5	10.4	14.6	16.7
A change in the amount of basic research conducted by our unit	18.4	22.4	20.4	14.3	24.5

SOURCE: Authors' industry survey.

were the result of federally sponsored research, while only 19 percent came from industry-sponsored research.

Marketing and Identification of University Inventions

It is uncommon for more than one firm to show interest in a university technology. This appears to follow from the embryonic nature of most university technologies. The market on the buyer side is said to be "thin," so mechanisms for bringing together firms and university technologies take on great importance. In both surveys, respondents were asked about methods used by universities to market technologies and methods used by firms to identify technologies to license.

In the university survey, technology transfer offices were asked to list the procedures they used to market technologies. Table 8–6 depicts the percentage of respondents who noted different procedures. Note the importance of inventor and personal (some of which are undoubtedly inventor) contacts. In a study of 1,100 licenses by universities and national labs, Christiana Jansen and Harrison Dillon (1999) found that 56 percent of the primary leads for licenses came from faculty.

Table 8–7 depicts the importance of six mechanisms for finding university licenses as reported by industry licensing executives surveyed. Based on similarity in responses, it is clear that the mechanisms for identifying technologies fall into three categories: (1) journal publications, patent searches,

Table 8–7
Technology Transfer Office Marketing Efforts

	% of Respondents
Website	37.5
Personal contacts	75.0
Direct mailing/fax	52.5
Trade shows	18.8
Meetings	20.8
Inventor contacts	58.3

SOURCE: Authors' university survey.

and presentations, which are indirect efforts in that they do not involve any direct contact with university personnel; (2) general indirect efforts by either the university technology transfer office via marketing efforts or the firm via routine canvassing; (3) one-on-one approaches based on personnel contacts. These last efforts are the most important, with indirect efforts second in importance.

What stands out in table 8–8 is the extreme importance of personal contacts between the firm's research and development staff and university personnel. Because the most likely university contacts are faculty inventors, this result underscores the central role that faculty, who are the ones most familiar with the technology, play in the transfer of technology after an invention is made.

Conclusion

In the public debates over policies that govern university patent licensing, university administrators and politicians alike tend to focus on aggregate statistics and growth rates in licensing activity. University administrators do so to advocate the university role in economic development, while politicians express alarm at the money-making role of licensing. These snapshots of licensing, however, mask much of what is going on in the technology transfer process. Our purpose here is to present survey evidence from both universities and the firms that license from them to provide a more balanced, in-depth view.

From the business survey, it is clear that licensed university inventions are often critical for the firms that license them. At the same time, these inventions have a high failure rate because of their early stage of development at the time they are licensed. Both the business and university surveys indicate that, without incentives for faculty to cooperate in further development,

Table 8–8
Industry Sources for University Licenses (% of respondents)

	Extremely Important 1	2	3	4	Not Important 5
Journal publications	19.6	31.4	31.4	13.7	3.9
Patent searches	24.0	33.0	24.0	10.0	9.0
Presentations at professional meetings	13.1	37.4	31.3	16.2	2.0
Marketing efforts by the university's technology transfer office	12.0	15.0	23.0	26.0	24.0
Personal contacts between our research and development staff and university personnel	45.7	31.4	14.3	2.9	5.7
Our licensing staff routinely canvass universities	9.3	19.6	16.5	24.7	29.9

SOURCE: Authors' industry survey.

invention failure rates would be greater than observed. The high failure rate and need for faculty cooperation have several important implications for license contracts. To the extent that firms or universities are averse to risk, it is important for contracts to allow risk sharing. For inventions that require faculty involvement in further development, it is important for contracts to include payments tied to ultimate commercial success, such as equity or royalties (Jensen and Thursby 2001). Finally, even for those inventions that are successful, few have substantial monetary returns. In addition, monetary returns are not the sole objective of university central administrations, faculty, and university technology licensing professionals.

Notes

We gratefully acknowledge financial support provided by the National Science Foundation (SES 0094573), the Alan and Mildred Peterson Foundation, and the Sloan Foundation and National Bureau of Economic Research through the NBER Project on Industrial Technology and Productivity.

1. We conducted our university survey jointly with Richard Jensen. For details on survey design and response rates, see Jensen and Thursby (2001); Thursby, Jensen, and Thursby (2001); and Thursby and Thursby (2002a).
2. For details, see Thursby and Thursby (2002a, 2002c).
3. This does not include sponsored research money tied to an executed license, which is usually about 20 percent of the amount that is paid directly as license income.
4. We exclude sponsored research tied to a license because this goes directly into research. We also exclude cashed-in equity because such income tends to be highly irregular through time.

5. This is not to say that these institutions have failing technology transfer offices. These are only current figures and do not address potential future revenues, and they ignore spillover effects such as the ability to attract faculty if there is a licensing office in place.

6. For an analysis of these objectives, see Jensen and Thursby (2001); Thursby, Jensen, and Thursby (2001); and Jensen, Thursby, and Thursby (2002).

7. For more on the objectives of universities, see Thursby and Kemp (2002).

8. For a detailed analysis of faculty involvement in university licensing, see Thursby and Thursby (2002a).

9. We asked for the percent of licensed-in agreements with universities that were not successful; by not successful we mean that the technology did not fit the need anticipated at the time of the license. For example, it did not reach the royalty stage.

10. It is, of course, the case that some of this failure to deliver on the part of faculty relates not to moral hazard but to the fact that the needed development was simply not possible on scientific grounds.

11. For more on this issue, see, for example, Sander (2000).

12. For more on the sources of growth in university licensing, see Thursby and Thursby (2002c).

References

Association of University Technology Managers. 1998. *AUTM Licensing Survey*. Northbrook, Il: Association of University Technology Managers.

———. 1998. *AUTM Licensing Survey*. Northbrook, Il: Association of University Technology Managers.

———. 2002. *AUTM Licensing Survey*. Northbrook, Il: Association of University Technology Managers.

Jansen, Christiana, and Harrison Dillon. 1999. "Where Do the Leads Come From? Source Data from Six Institutions." *Journal of the Association of University Technology Managers* 11, no. 1: 51–66.

Jensen, Richard, Jerry Thursby, and Marie Thursby. 2002. "The Disclosure and Licensing of University Inventions: "The Best We Can Do with the S**t We Get to Work With." Unpublished manuscript.

Jensen, Richard, and Marie Thursby. 2001. "Proofs and Prototypes for Sale: The Licensing of University Inventions." *American Economic Review* 91, no. 1: 240–59.

Sander, Erik. 2000. "Industrial Collaboration and Technology Transfer through University/Industry Research Centers." Paper presented at meetings of the Technology Transfer Society, July.

Thursby, Jerry G., Richard Jensen, and Marie Thursby. 2001. "Objectives, Characteristics, and Outcomes of University Licensing: A Survey of Major U.S. Universities." *Journal of Technology Transfer* 26, no. 1: 59–72.

Thursby, Jerry, and Sukanya Kemp. 2002. "Growth and Productive Efficiency of University Intellectual Property Licensing." *Research Policy* 31, no. 1: 109–24.

Thursby, Jerry, and Marie Thursby. 2002a. "Are Faculty Critical? Their Role in University-Industry Licensing." Unpublished manuscript.

———. 2002b. "Industry/University Licensing: Characteristics, Concerns, and Issues from the Perspective of the Buyer." *Journal of Technology Transfer*. Forthcoming.

———. 2002c. "Who Is Selling the Ivory Tower? Sources of Growth in University Licensing." *Management Science* 48, no. 1: 90–104.

Chapter 9

The Increasingly Proprietary Nature of Publicly Funded Biomedical Research

Benefits and Threats

ARTI K. RAI

DURING THE PAST several decades, basic biomedical research has become the subject of a truly formidable number of proprietary claims.[1] To some extent, this shift toward property rights reflects a shift of the underlying scientific landscape. At one time, basic biomedical research did not have substantial commercial value. Today, however, such research is the foundation of the lucrative pharmaceutical industry, which has long been dominated by proprietary claims, particularly patents.

But the rise of proprietary biomedical research cannot be explained solely by science and economics; the legal system has also done its part to encourage the patenting of basic research. The U.S. Court of Appeals for the Federal Circuit, which has jurisdiction over all patent case appeals, has lowered the so-called utility standard so that even inventions that are useful only for further research can be patentable. The Federal Circuit has also significantly lowered the patent law's "nonobviousness" standard, which holds that an invention is not patentable if, at the time it was made, it would have been obvious to a person with ordinary skill in the relevant field of scientific endeavor. Additionally, the court has opened up the area of information technology to patents. This expansion is significant because biopharmaceutical research is increasingly being conducted using patentable software and data structures.

In this new era of patents, private firms have been quick to seize advantage. In the past ten years, these firms have filed patent applications on subject matter ranging from gene fragments of unknown function to proteins embodied not in their biological form but as data structures on a chip (Marshall 1996).

Trends in University Assertion of Proprietary Rights

Notably, however, private-sector increases in patenting have been outstripped by increases in patenting by institutions that receive public funding to do basic research. Between 1979 and 2000, the number of patents issued to universities on an annual basis grew by 1,325 percent—from 264 to 3,764 (Association of University Technology Managers 2001). The increase in patents issued to institutions of higher learning substantially exceeded the 220 percent increase in overall patenting during the same period.[2] Patents now bring universities more than $1 billion annually in licensing revenues. In 2000, the University of California system alone received more than $250 million dollars in such revenues, while Columbia University received almost $150 million (North Carolina State University 2002).

The driving force behind this growth in university patent applications has been the 1980 law known as the Bayh-Dole Act. Bayh-Dole explicitly encourages universities to patent publicly funded research, based on the theory that such patenting, followed by exclusive licensing to private firms, is necessary to achieve commercial development. The lion's share of these patents, in terms of both numbers and the revenue they bring to universities, goes to biomedical research. The Association of University Technology Managers (2001), for example, estimates that about 70 percent of licensing revenues are generated by biomedical patents.

Apparently constrained by traditional norms of academic science, universities have not gone as far as the private sector has in search of biomedical patents. For example, schools have not tried to patent gene sequences and protein structures of unknown function. Likewise, they have tended not to engage in "defensive" patenting: that is, patenting merely for the sake of protection from infringement suits or to prevent others from patenting (Rai 1999). Some, however, have patented fundamental, broadly enabling research. To cite one prominent example, the Wisconsin Alumni Research Foundation (WARF), the technology transfer arm of the University of Wisconsin, has a broad patent on primate embryonic stem cells. Because human beings are, of course, primates, this patent covers all human embryonic stem cell lines, no matter how such lines are derived. In addition, despite the political controversies surrounding human embryonic stem cells, much of the research necessary to get the primate patent was publicly funded.[3]

Moreover, although the University of Wisconsin has thus far been relatively circumspect in making legal claims based on its patent, some universities, or at least their exclusive licensees, are asserting their basic research patents in a manner that hinders rather than facilitates commercial development. For example, Harvard University, the Massachusetts Institute of Technology (MIT), and the Whitehead Institute for Biomedical Research have a patent on federally funded research involving a basic biochemical pathway known as the NF-kB cell signaling pathway. This patent claims all drugs that work by inhibiting NF-kB signaling. Because the NF-kB pathway has been implicated in a variety of common diseases, including cancer, osteoporosis, rheumatoid arthritis, and atherosclerosis, the patent may cover treatments for all of those diseases. Indeed, the exclusive licensee of the NF-kB patent is Ariad Pharmaceuticals, now suing or threatening to sue dozens of companies that have chosen to develop commercial products even without exclusive rights on the upstream research. Notably, Ariad Pharmaceuticals itself has yet to make a commercial product based on the NF-kB pathway.

Proprietary activity in academic science now extends not just to patented research but also to unpatented research tools, such as reagents and data bases. Private firms often impose strict restrictions on the tools they provide to universities. Universities return the favor by imposing restrictions on the tools they provide to private firms. Even transfers of tools between universities may be difficult. For example, in a recent survey, 47 percent of geneticists reported that they had, within the past three years, been denied additional data or materials regarding research published by other academics. This figure is significantly higher than the 34 percent who had reported such denials in a prior survey conducted in the mid-1990s. The reasons cited by geneticists for such denials included the need to honor the requirements of an industrial sponsor and the need to protect the commercial value of results (Campbell and Blumenthal 2002).

Reasons for Concern

There are many reasons why the public should be concerned about the increasingly proprietary nature of academic research. The availability of property rights can create conflicts of interest that damage patients' faith in the medical enterprise. Further, undue emphasis on immediate commercial benefit may distort the educational experience of graduate students.

Even from a strictly economic standpoint, moreover, there is reason for concern. The most obvious economic problem created by patent rights is deadweight loss, which occurs when those who could have afforded the invention at a competitive price lose access because they cannot afford to pay the monopoly price. Deadweight loss concerns are particularly acute for publicly funded research. In the case of such research, the conventional incentive arguments for allowing patent rights simply don't apply. When research is publicly funded, and doing such research is the basis for career advancement, no other incentives for doing research are necessary. In addition, the argument that motivated Bayh-Dole (that university patents and exclusive licensing agreements are necessary to stimulate subsequent commercial development) does not apply to discoveries that can be disseminated without exclusive licenses (and associated inventor involvement) and that can serve as the basis for patents further downstream. For example, two of the technologies central to the recombinant DNA revolution—Stanford's Cohen-Boyer technology and similar technology created at Columbia by Richard Axel—were adopted and developed rapidly without the need for an exclusive license (Colyvas et al. 2002). Although the universities in these two cases did, in fact, take out patents, they licensed the patents nonexclusively to a wide variety of researchers. In such cases of nonexclusive licensing, the university patent merely serves as a tax on commercial development, the opposite of what Bayh-Dole intended.

Given that the purpose of Bayh-Dole was to stimulate commercialization rather than to raise revenue for universities, nonexclusive licenses can be problematic. But there are reasons to be concerned about the monopoly or quasi-monopoly control of basic research platforms that can result through exclusive licensing to a private firm. A monopolist is unlikely to see the myriad applications of a research platform such as a cell signaling pathway or stem cells. Many argue that the profit-maximizing monopolist will readily extend the license to follow-on researchers, who will improve upon the research. Unfortunately, this theory is belied by history. These types of licensing negotiations often break down due to inadequate information and strategic behavior. For example, progress in the electrical lighting, automobile, and aircraft industries was impeded because holders of broad pioneer patents in these industries could not conclude satisfactory licensing agreements with potential improvers (Merges and Nelson 1990). Breakdowns in negotiations are particularly problematic in the biological area because scientific realities preclude "inventing around" certain research platforms. Indeed, there are documented cases of biomedical inventions exclusively licensed by universities where the exclusive licensee appears to be preventing the exploration of alternative research paths by other firms (Colyvas et al. 2002).

Moreover, in certain cases, the exclusive licensee may be more interested in extracting revenue from a commercial developer than in developing a commercial product itself. For example, as noted previously, Ariad Pharmaceuticals, the exclusive licensee of the NF-kB patent, has yet to develop a product itself. This type of strategic behavior may explain the results of a recent study of 805 inventions licensed exclusively by MIT between 1980 and 1996. The study determined that the relationship between the strength of patent protection acquired by the exclusive licensee and the speed of commercialization was far from unequivocally positive (Dechenaux et al. 2003).

Possible Responses

The most obvious response to concern over proprietary research would be making appropriate changes in patent law. To some extent, these changes have already occurred. In response to pressure from the National Institutes of Health and members of the academic community, the U.S. Patent and Trademark Office's recent guidelines on the utility standard make it clear that inventions with only speculative research functions are no longer patentable. Related guidelines indicate that the scope of patents on early-stage biotechnology research may be relatively narrow.

But there is reason to be wary of going too far with reform of patentability standards. Patents on end-product drugs have always been vital to the biopharmaceutical industry (Cohen, Nelson, and Walsh 2000). However, biotechnology entrepreneurs insist that they need patents even on their research platforms to create these platforms and to attract risk capital for further development (Golden 2001). There is some reason to take these claims at face value. Although biopharmacology is becoming an information industry based on data, downstream development will, for the foreseeable future, require more than just low-cost data generation and manipulation. Rather, it will require considerable capital investment, primarily in the form of actual animal and human testing. Such investment is unlikely to occur without either public funding or some type of proprietary right. Thus, while commons-based approaches have successfully produced commercial products in the software and computer industries, such approaches are likely to have more limited application in biopharmacology. Indeed, biopharmaceutical companies may feel compelled to assert proprietary rights even in upstream data, notwithstanding the fact that subsequent development will probably proceed more quickly without such rights. These companies might argue that even the initial generation of biological data can be costly and will not occur without patent rights.

When research is publicly funded, however, patents are less critical. Obviously, they are not necessary to produce the research itself. Bayh-Dole assumes that patenting and exclusive licensing are necessary for dissemination and development. But this assumption is not always valid. As noted, the Cohen-Boyer recombinant DNA technology and discoveries such as embryonic stem cell lines can be, and have been, widely disseminated without exclusive licenses and associated inventor involvement. Monetary incentives to develop the discoveries can be created by the prospect of downstream patents. Certainly, in some contexts, patenting and exclusive licensing will be necessary. For example, publicly funded machines for DNA sequencing required additional private investment before they could be turned into commercially reliable equipment. Patents on those machines were necessary to attract such investment, particularly because investors were unlikely to be able to secure downstream patents. Similarly, patents on promising therapeutic compounds are necessary to get these compounds ready for commercial distribution.

The policy challenge is to distinguish publicly funded invention that is best developed through patents or other proprietary claims from invention that is best developed in the public domain, unencumbered by proprietary rights. In an area as complicated as biomedical research, this is a formidable task. The decision makers who establish the boundaries should be not only extremely knowledgeable about such research but also motivated to act in the overall public interest.

In many respects, overall public interest should align with the self-interest of universities. Universities reap the rewards of proprietary restrictions on research, but they must also pay the cost of circumventing the restrictions imposed by other universities. Thus, universities should have some incentive to resist property rights. Unfortunately, however, they face a significant collective action problem. The hope of commercial gain from property rights can be very enticing. University administrators will be reluctant to disavow these gains, particularly if they think other universities are going to continue to act in proprietary ways. The collective action problem is exacerbated by the reality that the university is far from monolithic. On the contrary, it has different constituencies with divergent interests. While the financial costs and time delays associated with proprietary restrictions are salient to university scientists, only the financial gains from such restrictions are likely to be salient to university technology transfer officials. Similarly, while research scientists may adhere to open science norms, these norms are likely to have less influence over university administrators. Indeed, one recent survey of sixty-two technology transfer offices determined that generating licensing revenue was viewed as the most important goal, with 71 percent rating revenue generation as "extremely important" (Thursby, Jensen, and Thursby 2001).

These difficulties notwithstanding, open science norms have been of some help in solving the collective action problem. For example, as noted previously, universities have been somewhat more restrained in their patenting activities than the private sector has. In addition, in 1996, leading academic scientists signed a pledge—the so-called Bermuda rules—to make human genome data publicly available. Despite objections from technology transfer officials and pressure to compromise open access so as to facilitate collaboration with the for-profit genome sequencing venture led by Craig Venter, this pledge has been kept.[4] In this case, however, the researchers in question were a tight-knit group with power in their respective academic communities. Other efforts, particularly those in which leading scientists have not played a central role, have been less successful. For example, we have seen repeated violations of the 1995 Uniform Biological Material Transfer Act, a voluntary agreement among university technology transfer offices that was intended to simplify the exchange of unpatented research tools among universities (Eisenberg 2001, Campbell and Blumenthal 2002). The primary violators appear to be the technology transfer officers who draft these agreements. As noted, these officers are not likely to be as committed to open science norms as scientists themselves.

The lesson to be drawn is that universities, and particularly university administrators, cannot necessarily be trusted to take sustained collective action in the public interest. By contrast, research sponsors such as the National Institutes of Health, which both benefit from proprietary restrictions (through their own intramural patenting and licensing programs) and incur their costs (because grantee research grants must cover the cost of licensing), can act without having to overcome the collective action problem. In addition, actions by research sponsors oriented toward the public domain fortify the position of those in the academy who continue to adhere to open exchange standards.

Acting in conjunction with members of the academic community oriented toward the public domain, the National Institutes of Health (NIH) has already taken some important actions to fortify that domain. Early on in the genome project, NIH supported the Bermuda rules by declaring that researchers who received grants for large-scale genome sequencing must not seek proprietary rights and must make their findings immediately available. NIH did something similar with SNP research, although the need for NIH-funded research in this area was ultimately obviated by a public SNP data base created by various pharmaceutical companies and academic centers working in conjunction with the Wellcome Institute, a British charity that is part of the public Human Genome Project.

More recently, NIH has published guidelines urging universities that patenting and exclusive licensing are not necessarily the best way to promote the development of invention. These guidelines also urge universities to refrain from imposing proprietary restrictions on the exchange of unpatented research tools. NIH has also published draft guidelines recommending that grantees adopt a presumption in favor of open sharing of data generated from its funded projects.

Although NIH has some authority to limit assertions of proprietary rights on unpatented research materials, the agency's power to enforce a no-patenting regime is quite limited. Moreover, to the extent that NIH pressure on universities to disseminate unpatented materials widely simply leads these universities to patent more extensively, such federal pressure may be counterproductive.

Under Bayh-Dole, a sponsoring agency can restrict a grantee's right to patent only by declaring that, because of "exceptional circumstances," patenting does not serve the interests of commercialization (35 U.S.C., sec. 202[a][i]–[ii]). This declaration of exceptional circumstances is subject to extensive administrative appeal. It must also be reported to the U.S. Department of Commerce, which is the primary agency responsible for administering Bayh-Dole. Therefore, perhaps not surprisingly, NIH has almost never used this authority.

The only other legal authority that Bayh-Dole confers on NIH is the power to mandate licensing if the agency determines that a grantee is not taking active steps to commercialize a particular invention. Actually using this power, however, is even more cumbersome than declaring exceptional circumstances. Any use of the power is subject to administrative appeal; in addition, any action by the agency is stayed pending determination of the appeal. NIH has never used this particular power.

Thus far, NIH efforts have succeeded because universities appear to have felt constrained by residual norms of open access. But growing evidence of university norm violations, particularly in the area of unpatented research tools, suggests that purely hortatory efforts may no longer be sufficient. For this reason, we should consider giving agencies such as NIH that sponsor research somewhat greater discretion to require that the results of their sponsorship be left in the public domain.

A recent article by Arti Rai and Rebecca Eisenberg (2003) offers two suggestions in this regard. First, the "exceptional circumstances" language could be deleted from Bayh-Dole so that agencies are permitted to impose a no-patenting regime in all situations in which patenting is not likely to contribute to utilization and development. Second, the process of judicial review necessary before an agency mandates compulsory licensing could be streamlined.

Potential Objections

It could be argued that academic researchers might chafe at these restrictions and defect to private-sector funding. But NIH funding is the coin of the realm for academic promotion and success. It is unlikely that university researchers will openly alienate the agency. In any event, NIH is unlikely to use its authority in a manner that is fundamentally at odds with the goals of academic researchers. Agency leadership is, after all, drawn from this very community of researchers. Indeed, in several cases involving the Human Genome Project, agency action has merely fortified efforts that grantee researchers were already making.

Moreover, as noted previously, NIH itself now reaps considerable financial benefits from patenting and licensing its own intramural research. In fiscal years 1993 to 1999, the agency executed more than 1,000 licenses based on its own and U.S. Food and Drug Administration intramural invention portfolios. During this period, NIH royalties accounted for 70 percent of all federal royalties from technology transfer. Thus, NIH is unlikely to underestimate the benefits of patenting.

Conclusion

In sum, contemporary biomedical research requires both property rights and a public domain. The challenge lies in determining where, in any given case, the boundary between public and private should be drawn. NIH, acting in conjunction with grantee scientists, is likely to be well positioned to make this determination.

Notes

1. Portions of this chapter are based on Rai and Eisenberg (2003).
2. Between 1979 and 2000, the number of utility patents issued annually by the U.S. Patent and Trademark Office increased from 48,854 to 157,495.
3. At the time that Wisconsin filed for the primate patent, stem cell researcher James Thomson had not actually derived human embryonic stem cell lines. Because of the federal moratorium then in place on funding for human embryonic stem cell research, this next step in the research process was funded by a private biotechnology firm, Geron.
4. For an interesting first-person account of the discussions that led to the Bermuda rules and the tensions created by Venter's proposal, see Sulston and Ferry (2002).

References

Association of University Technology Managers. 2001. "AUTM Licensing Survey: FY 2000" (*http://www.autm.net/index_ie.html*).
Bayh-Dole Act. 1980. 35 U.S.C. sec., 202(a)(i)-(ii).

Campbell, Eric G., and David Blumenthal. 2002. "Data Withholding in Academic Genetics: Data from a National Survey." *Journal of the American Medical Association* 287: 473.

Cohen, Wesley, Richard R. Nelson, and John P. Walsh. 2000. "Protecting Their Intellectual Assets: Appropriability Conditions and Why U.S. Manufacturing Firms Patent (or Not)." Working paper no. 7552. Cambridge, Mass.: National Bureau of Economic Research.

Colyvas, Jeannette, Michael Crow, Annette Geljins, Robert Mazzoleni, Richard Nelson, Nathan Rosenberg, and Bhaven N. Sampat. 2002. "How Do University Inventions Get Into Practice?" *Management Science* 48: 61.

Dechenaux, Emmanuel, Brent Goldfarb, Scott A. Shane, and Marie C. Thursby. 2003. "Appropriability and Timing of Innovation: Evidence from MIT Inventions." Working paper no. 9735. Cambridge, Mass.: National Bureau of Economic Research.

Eisenberg, Rebecca S. 2001. "Bargaining over the Transfer of Proprietary Research Tools: Is This Market Failing or Emerging?" In *Expanding the Boundaries of Intellectual Property: Innovation Policy for the Information Society*, ed. Rochelle Dreyfuss, 223–50. Oxford: Oxford University Press.

Golden, John M. 2001. "Biotechnology, Technology Policy, and Patentability: Natural Products and Invention in the American System." *Emory Law Journal* 50: 101.

Marshall, Eliot. 1996. "Patent Office Faces 90-Year Backlog." *Science* 272: 643.

Merges, Robert P., and Richard R. Nelson. 1990. "On the Complex Economics of Patent Scope." *Columbia Law Review* 90: 839.

North Carolina State University. 2002. "University Licensing Revenues and Patent Activity for Fiscal 2000" (*http://www2.acs.ncsu.edu/UPA/peers/current/research_intensive/lice_pant_res.htm*).

Rai, Arti K. 1999. "Regulating Scientific Research: Intellectual Property Rights and the Norms of Science." *Northwestern University Law Review* 94, no. 1: 77.

Rai, Arti K., and Rebecca S. Eisenberg. 2003. "Bayh-Dole Reform and the Progress of Biomedicine." Law and Contemporary Problems 66: 289.

Sulston, John, and Georgina Ferry. 2002. *The Common Thread: A Story of Science, Politics, Ethics, and the Human Genome.* New York: Bantam.

Thursby, Jerry G., Richard Jensen, and Marie C. Thursby. 2001. "Objectives, Characteristics, and Outcomes of University Licensing: A Survey of Major U.S. Universities." *Journal of Technology Transfer* 26: 59.

Chapter 10

The Clinical Trials Business

Who Gains?

MARCIA ANGELL

THERE IS NO BETTER, or more troubling, example of the commercialization of the academy than changes in how clinical trials are conducted at academic medical centers. Clinical trials of drugs and other medical treatments in human subjects have always been part of the mission of academic medical centers; but in recent years clinical trials have grown into a multibillion dollar business, and the stakes for the medical centers are enormous.

According to Center Watch, a Boston-based firm that collects and publishes data on the clinical trials industry, there are now some 80,000 clinical trials underway in the United States involving about 50,000 researchers and 8.3 million human subjects. The lion's share of these studies are sponsored by the pharmaceutical industry, which is required to test its new drugs on human subjects before applying for U.S. Food and Drug Administration (FDA) approval to market them. In addition, pharmaceutical companies conduct trials on drugs that are already on the market to buttress promotional claims and extend exclusive marketing rights.

Because pharmaceutical companies do not have direct access to human subjects, they have traditionally contracted with academic researchers to conduct trials on patients in teaching hospitals. This practice has changed dramatically over the past decade. The changes reflect the relative financial positions of the pharmaceutical industry and the academic medical centers. The big drug companies are now hugely profitable; and as a result, the pharmaceutical industry has acquired enormous power and influence. In contrast, the academic medical centers have suffered shrinking reimbursements for their educational and clinical missions. To a remarkable extent, the academic medical centers have become supplicants to drug companies, deferring to them in ways that were unheard of just a few short years ago.

The Loss of Scientific Objectivity

Until the 1990s, industry sponsors simply awarded grants to researchers to test their products and then waited for the results. The drug companies had no part in designing or analyzing the studies, they did not claim to own the data, and they certainly did not write the papers or control whether they were submitted for publication. But as the power of the pharmaceutical industry grew, drug companies began designing studies to be carried out by academic researchers who do little more than supply the human subjects for clinical trials and collect data. Often, the sponsors maintain control of the data, analyze it, and control publication. In multicenter trials, researchers may not even have access to all of the data. In fall 2001, the editors of thirteen medical journals wrote a joint editorial urging that authors be given access to their own data and be responsible for their own conclusions (Davidoff 2001). That was an extraordinary admission of how far things have come.

In addition to grant support, researchers now may have a variety of other financial ties to the sponsors of their work. Researchers sometimes serve as consultants to the same companies whose products they are testing, join advisory boards and speakers' bureaus for sponsors, enter into patent and royalty arrangements, agree to be the listed authors of articles ghostwritten by interested companies, promote drugs and devices at company-sponsored symposia, and accept expensive gifts and trips to luxurious settings. Many researchers also have equity interest in their corporate sponsors. Certain institutional conflict of interest rules preclude some of these activities, but the rules are generally extremely lenient (Lo, Wolf, and Berkeley 2002).

These types of relationships between academic researchers and corporate sponsors are troubling for several reasons. Increasingly, the pharmaceutical industry is setting the research agenda, which has more to do with the industry's mission than with the mission of academic medical centers. Sponsors may contract with academic researchers to carry out studies for almost entirely commercial purposes. For example, pharmaceutical companies often sponsor trials of new drugs that are really no different from existing drugs. In addition, they may sponsor tests of drugs to supplant virtually identical drugs that are going off patent.

There is now strong evidence that the studies themselves are biased by drug-company influence. Industry-supported research is far more likely to be favorable to the sponsors' products than is National Institutes of Health–supported research. There are many ways to bias studies, and they are by no means always obvious. Bias is not always intentional. Investigators may naturally favor their sponsors when the collaboration is close and profitable. There have also been several widely publicized cases of sponsors who tried to prevent the publication of unfavorable results (Bodenheimer 2000).

There are growing concerns about the protection of human subjects when researchers have financial ties to drug companies that gain from the research. The issue became public in 1999, when teenager Jesse Gelsinger died in a University of Pennsylvania trial in which the principal researcher had a large financial interest in the outcome. Similar concerns were raised about two studies at the Fred Hutchinson Cancer Center. There's no way of knowing, of course, whether the financial interests played any part in the researchers' decisions in these cases. That is the problem. Further, human subjects may not receive adequate information for informed consent about the risks of clinical trials or the merit of them. Would a human subject willingly agree to participate in a clinical trial, with its inherent risks and inconveniences, if the trial clearly had only commercial interest?

Collaborations between academic medical centers and the pharmaceutical industry have the potential to benefit both medical science and industry. But the current terms and conditions of those collaborations pose real threats to the independence and impartiality that should mark medical research. The following reforms would safeguard the integrity of research in commercial/academic collaborations:

- *Limited financial ties between researchers and sponsors.* Researchers who receive grant support from industry should have no other financial ties to those companies. Nor should they expect to in the future. For any given company, researchers must decide whether they want either to be consultants or to accept grants, but they should not do both. Consulting arrangements are virtually ubiquitous in academic medicine and are often more about supplementing income than about transferring technology.
- *Researcher control of study design, analysis, and publication.* Researchers should not accept grants with strings attached. They should insist on designing and analyzing their own studies, writing their own papers, and deciding about publication. The data should reside with the researchers and be fully available to them.
- *Selection of studies based on scientific merit.* Researchers should

undertake industry studies only if they have scientific merit. Often, for example, industry-sponsored trials compare a new drug with a placebo when the scientifically relevant question is whether the new drug is more effective than an existing drug. The study may win FDA approval for the new drug, but it offers no useful information to doctors in the treatment of patients.

The Marriage of Medical Centers and Industry

Like individual faculty members, academic medical centers are joining with industry in multiple deals that may compromise their independence and impartiality. Even though income from industry-sponsored research is still relatively small (about 15 percent of the total), it is disproportionately concentrated on clinical trials. Academic medical centers do not want to lose that business, but they are now facing competition from a new private research industry. This new industry currently conducts about half of all clinical trials. Because of the competition stemming from this new industry, academic medical centers have become extremely accommodating to the pharmaceutical industry. For example, most academic medical centers now have special clinical research offices or institutes that offer companies quick soup-to-nuts service. The Harvard Clinical Research Institute (HCRI), for example, originally advertised itself on its website (*http://hcri.harvard.edu*) as being led by people whose "experience gives HCRI an intimate understanding of industry's needs, and knowledge of how best to meet them." (That sentence was later dropped.) Is that really the purpose of an academic institution like Harvard Medical School?

Academic medical centers have many other ties to industry as well. The Bayh-Dole Act permits medical centers to patent drugs discovered with National Institutes of Health funding and later license them to industry in return for royalties. In this way, both industry and academia benefit from taxpayer subsidies. Increasingly, institutions and researchers license their discoveries to small biotechnology companies set up for this purpose. Both institutions and researchers are part owners. If things go well, the smaller company then licenses the discovery to a large one.

Finally, industry also finances part of the education and training of medical students and house officers. Drug companies set up educational programs even within the best medical schools and teaching hospitals and are given virtually unfettered access to young doctors, plying them with gifts and promoting their products. But if the drug companies were really providing education, they would be paid for their services. In fact, the money flows not from teaching institution to educational program provider but in the opposite direction. Industry clearly is paying academia for access. It is, in fact, self-evidently absurd to look to companies for education about the products they are selling.

The boundaries between academic medical centers and industry are dissolving, and their missions are becoming fused. More precisely, the medical centers are increasingly adopting the mission of industry. They see themselves as partners, and junior partners at that. But is this new relationship true to the traditional missions of academia and industry?

Academic medical centers are charged with educating the next generation of doctors, conducting scientifically important research, and taking care of the sickest and neediest patients. These are the missions which justify their tax-exempt status. In contrast, investor-owned businesses are charged with increasing the value of their shareholders' stock. That is their fiduciary responsibility, and they would be remiss if they did not do it. All other activities are merely means to that end. In the case of drug companies, the point is to sell profitable drugs, not necessarily important ones; and they sponsor clinical research as a means to that end. Further, drug companies are not in the education business, except as a means to the primary end of selling drugs. The difference in missions is often deliberately obscured: by industry because it is good public relations for companies to portray themselves as research institutions; by academia because it enables involved parties to avoid examining their consciences too closely.

So what is the outcome of all this? In the past five years, the number of drugs tested has increased dramatically, but the number approved annually by the FDA has remained constant at about one hundred. The number of innovative drugs—that is, new molecular entities—has been declining steadily since a high of fifty-three in 1996. In 2001, only twenty-four drugs approved by the FDA were new molecular entities. The remaining new drugs were mainly new formulations and combinations of old drugs. Of the twenty-four new drugs, only seven were classified by the FDA as showing a significant improvement over other drugs already on the market. That trend continued in 2002, when only seventeen new molecular entities were approved, of which seven were improvements over existing drugs. Instead of important new drugs, there has been an onslaught of copycat drugs directed toward chronic, often minor, ailments in affluent people. The great majority of new cancer and AIDS drugs are the result of National Institutes of Health–funded research. Often these are licensed or transferred to the drug companies. Taxol, for example, was developed by the National Cancer Institute and then given to Bristol-Myers-Squibb, which sells it at many times the cost of manufacturing it.

Medical centers bow to industry not only for the financial rewards but also to appease their faculties. Like Hollywood, academic medical centers run on a star system; and faculty stars are now accustomed to supplementing their income with pharmaceutical industry money. The academic medical centers are afraid that strictly enforcing conflict of interest rules will cause them to lose their stars to rival institutions. Further, they are not in a strong moral position to enforce conflict of interest rules when they themselves often have equity in the same companies whose products their faculties are studying.

Reforms for Institutions

Institutions should not become outposts for industry by allowing investor-owned companies to set up teaching or research centers in their hospitals or providing drug companies with access to their students, house officers, and patients. They and their senior officials should also not hold investments in health care industries. The editors of the *New England Journal of Medicine* established such a rule, and it did not create a hardship. Among other problems, when researchers or institutions invest in drug and device companies, those transactions can look like insider trading.

Most important, institutions must collaborate to develop a common policy on conflicts of interest for themselves and their faculty. As it now stands, researchers may threaten to leave institutions with stringent policies and go to more lenient ones. Only by working together can institutions stop further erosion of the scientific integrity of research conducted in our academic medical centers. Our institutions are now so immersed in the ideology of the marketplace that any resistance to further commercialization is considered quixotic. But medical research is special. Patients should not have to wonder whether researchers are motivated by financial gain, and the public should not have to wonder whether medical research is credible. Academic medical centers are shortsighted indeed if they continue down the path of selling out their scientific integrity in favor of commercial interests.

References

Bodenheimer, Thomas. 2000. "Uneasy Alliance—Clinical Investigations and the Pharmaceutical Industry." *New England Journal of Medicine* 342, no. 20: 1539–44.

Davidoff, Frank 2001. "Sponsorship, Authorship, and Accountability." *New England Journal of Medicine* 345, no. 11: 825–27.

Lo, Bernard, Leslie E. Wolf, and Abiona Berkeley. 2002. "Conflict of Interest Policies for Investigators in Clinical Trials." *New England Journal of Medicine* 343, no. 22: 1616–20.

Chapter 11

Reforming Research Ethics in an Age of Multivested Science

SHELDON KRIMSKY

Universities and their faculty have embraced a new role for science that combines its classical mission ("knowledge is virtue") with postindustrial goals rooted in the Baconian tradition ("knowledge is productivity"). The new symbiosis between academia and commerce, amply nurtured by public policies, is forcing a critical reexamination of research ethics on issues such as sharing of information, commodification of knowledge, conflicts of interest held by scientists and their institutions, and the mingling of medicine and business in clinical trials. Government agencies, universities, journal editors, and professional societies are beginning to reexamine the norms under which academic science has functioned for more than one hundred years. At stake is public trust in the autonomy of university research and the extent to which, in the words of Columbia University historian Richard Hofstadter, [the pursuit of knowledge] "is esteemed not as a necessary instrument of external ends, but as an end in itself" (Press and Washburn 2000, 54). This chapter explores the indicators of changing patterns of research support at universities; the connection between these patterns and the current trends in university entrepreneurship; and the new ethical norms under consideration by professional groups, research institutions, journal editors, and government agencies in response to the growth in conflicts of interest in academic science and medicine.

The changing patterns of funding for university research indicate the growth of university entrepreneurship. Research universities and their faculty have become more dependent on and accepting of private funding and, along with such funding, a business model of research. The rapid development of university entrepreneurship in the past twenty years—what Sheila Slaughter and Larry Leslie (1997) term *academic capitalism*—has effected changes in the traditional norms of science. New guidelines in research ethics, mostly focused on transparency of interests and disclosure, are a response to the conflicts of interest and the growth of public mistrust of science arising from the mixture of pure and profit-oriented research that has become endemic within major academic institutions.

Indicators of Change

To understand the emergence of the new entrepreneurial university, we can examine five factors that characterize the changes taking place in academic institutions:

- Private funding of research
- Faculty consulting and service on company advisory boards
- Faculty equity and personal involvement in companies
- University-industry partnership
- Intellectual property held by faculty and universities

For several of the indicators the trends have been quantified. Other trends, such as increases in faculty consulting and personal involvement in new companies, are revealed through indirect measures as well as national and site-specific surveys.

The incentives for university-industry collaborations, created largely by federal legislation passed in the 1980s, began to produce effects during the 1990s. According to statistics compiled by the National Science Foundation, American research universities are obtaining more of their research and development funds from industry. Research and development expenditures in universities and colleges rose from $18.8 billion in 1992 to $27.5 billion in 1999, a 46 percent change. In that same period industry contributions to the research and development budget of the academic institutions rose 60 percent from $1.3 billion to $2.1 billion. Industry contributions to the research and development budgets of colleges and universities amounted to 4.1 percent in 1980, 6.8 percent in 1992, and about 8 percent in 2001.

Still, the vast expenditure of university research comes from federal and foundation sources. These figures, however, do not tell the whole story. A smaller percentage of trend-setting research universities have quite a different profile of funding. Over a seven-year period, industry funding at Duke University increased 280 percent while total research and development rose 85 percent. At the University of Texas in Austin there was a 725 percent in-

Table 11–1
Top Ten Industry-Funded Universities in the United States, 1999

Institution	Industry-Funded Research and Development	Percent Change, in Industry-Funded Research Development 1992–99	Total Research and Development	Percent Change, in Total Research and Development 1992–99	Industry-Funded Research and Development as a Proportion of Total
Duke University	121,630,000	280	348,274,000	84.6	34.9
Massachusetts Institute of Technology	75,444,000	51.4	420,306,000	25.9	17.9
Pennsylvania State University	65,698,000	53.9	379,402,000	36.3	17.3
Georgia Institute of Technology	62,752,000	163.9	263,725,000	46.3	23.8
Ohio State University	52,034,000	271.8	322,810,000	58.8	16.1
University of Washington	51,319,000	101.6	482,659,000	54.0	10.6
University of Texas— Austin	39,729,000	725.3	258,122,000	12.9	15.4
University of California— San Francisco	36,830,000	490.8	417,095,000	40.5	8.8
Texas A&M	34,722,000	30.1	402,203,000	31.7	8.6
University of Michigan	34,432,000	37.8	508,619,000	29.4	6.8

SOURCE: National Science Foundation. 1999. Science and Engineering Indicators—Academic Research and Development Expenditures: FY 1999. NSF-01-329. Washington, D.C.: National Science Foundation, table B-38.

crease in industry research and development funding while total research and development increased by 13 percent. Also, a review of industry funding as a proportion of total research and development for the top ten industry-funded universities reveals that Duke University heads the list at 35 percent followed by the Georgia Institute of Technology at 24 percent, the Massachusetts Institute of Technology at 18 percent, Pennsylvania State University at 17 percent, and the University of Texas at 15 percent. A decade ago, 15 percent of university research and development coming from industry was considered an upper limit (see table 11–1.) Now, as universities have become more aggressive in seeking private funding sources, it is no longer unusual to see industry-funded research and development exceed 15 percent of their total research and development budget. For example, in 2000 the industry support in the research budgets of Alfred University, the University of Tulsa, Eastern Virginia Medical School, and Lehigh University was 48 percent, 32 percent, 24 percent, and 22 percent, respectively. As university research and development funding begins to reach these levels, it brings with it changes in the culture of scientific research that make academic traditionalists uneasy.

The federal legislation and executive policies that created incentives for private investment in academic research were based on two assumptions. First, American competitiveness in the global marketplace would improve by stimulating technology transfer of discoveries at universities. Second, new efforts to balance the federal budget would mean declining support for university research. Corporations saw an opportunity to shift resources from investments in internal research and development to collaborations with academic institutions. The number of university industry research centers has risen dramatically in the past decade. By 1990 there were close to 1,000 at more than two hundred American universities and colleges, and more than half of the number were established in the 1980s. Meanwhile, during the past two decades, the federal share of support for universities and colleges has declined, accounting for 5.8 percent of the total federal research and development budget, the lowest share since the end of the 1950s. In *Academic Capitalism,* Slaughter and Leslie (1997) observe that "U.S. public research universities are attempting to maximize revenues from external sources as the several state governments decrease their shares of support" (238).

A confluence of events, including the 1980 U.S. Supreme Court Decision on the patenting of living organisms (which opened the door for gene patents); the Bayh-Dole Act (which gave universities the intellectual property rights to federally funded discoveries); and the Human Genome Project (which infused large sums of research dollars into university-industry collaborations), has created a patent frenzy in academia. According to Slaughter and

Leslie, "the Bayh-Dole Act of 1980 signaled the inclusion of universities in profit making" (45). In the twenty-five years from 1974 to 1999, the patent awards among the top-hundred research universities rose from 177 to more than 3,000 (Association of University Technology Managers 2000).

Other indicators of the commercialization of university research can be found in the rise in trade secrets and self-imposed restrictions on the sharing of scientific data. A series of studies reveal these trends in the biomedical sciences. One study, which surveyed more than one hundred faculty members in the forty universities that receive the largest share of federal research in the United States, reported that biotechnology faculty with industry support were four times as likely as other biotechnology faculty to report that trade secrets had resulted from their university research. The number of trade secrets was directly related to the amount of university support (Blumenthal et al. 1986).

A survey of senior executives in life-sciences companies found that the majority of companies supporting academic research require scientists to hold information confidential for more than six months, a period many professional societies view as dangerously long (Blumenthal 1986). In another survey of geneticists, nearly 50 percent responded that their requests for scientific information from other scientists were denied; more than one-third indicated that data withholding is increasing among members of their community (Campbell et al. 2002). Finally, a study of fourteen high-profile science and medical journals revealed that one-third of the articles published in 1992 had at least one lead author with a personal financial interest in the subject matter of the work (Krimsky and Rothenberg 1996).

The intense commercialization of the academy, a phenomenon that is now widely acknowledged, has created a need for new ethical guidelines in universities, government, scientific and medical journals, and professional societies to protect the integrity of science and to secure its trust within the broader society. Litigation and fear of litigation are forcing some changes. In *The Research University in a Time of Discontent*, Jonathan Cole observes, "universities must balance their dedication to a neutral position regarding the outcome of scientific experiments against their efforts to support entrepreneurial efforts of their talented faculty" (Cole, Barber, and Graubard 1994, 32). But the balance point is precisely what is being contested.

There are signals that the pendulum has swung too far, that disclosure will not be accepted as the universal antidote for the condition, and that some restraints are being considered. The ethical limits of research and publication integrity are being tested. Some efforts are underway to reset the academic sector's moral compass. Five major institutional stakeholders are beginning to respond to the public's concerns about conflicts of interest in science and medicine: the journals, professional societies, governmental agencies, universities, and nonprofit research institutes.

Scientific Publications

Scientific journal editors have become more sensitive to the appearance of conflict of interest by contributors and editorial staffs. During the 1990s many of the leading medical journals adopted conflict of interest policies. Most policies added financial disclosure requirements for authors. Some journals took a tougher stance and sought to prevent authors from contributing editorials or reviews if they had a direct conflict of interest with the subject matter. Medical journals are far ahead of basic science journals in establishing author guidelines on conflict of interest. Issues of ghostwriting, prestige authorship, and authors who do not have full control of their data trouble some journal editors. The International Committee of Medical Journal Editors took a bold step in recommending that their member journals require a signed statement affirming that the author alone has made the decision to publish the data and that the individuals listed as authors have made a worthy contribution to the article.

Compliance with the conflict of interest policies of academic journals is based on the honor system. Most journals do not have the personnel or the time to assess the level of compliance. When a colleague and I published a study of the rates of author disclosure in nearly two hundred peer-reviewed journals with conflict of interest policies, a number of editors were surprised that their journals did not have a single disclosure of personal financial interest for the entire test year (Krimsky and Rothenberg 2001). In the current climate of academic commerce, it seemed unlikely that so many authors had nothing to disclose. This raises the question of compliance when a policy has no sanctions against violators.

Except for a small number of internationally acclaimed journals that do well economically, many operate under tight financial constraints. Electronic access to journals has reduced subscribers to hard copies, putting some journals in even greater economic peril. If editors place too much emphasis on author conflicts of interest, they may lose potential contributors who would rather publish in a journal that doesn't require disclosure of their personal income or equity holdings. Journals are making some effort to respond to the rising tide of scientific conflict of interest, but they cannot do it alone. A few journals proscribe authors with conflicts of interest from publishing editorials or reviews; most can only offer their readers voluntary disclosure. To be fully effective, the response to author conflict of interest must be systematic and include all players in the research community.

Professional Societies

Several professional associations in science and medicine have begun to develop policies on conflicts of interest. The American Medical Association (AMA) has been a leader in addressing the problems of conflicts of interest since 1990. As the largest medical association for American physicians, the AMA has published several principles and supporting opinions that establish its code of ethics. Its *Principles of Medical Ethics*, revised in 1980, includes its primary guidelines from which all other codes and recommendations derive. Among the guide's seven basic principles, there is no reference to conflicts of interest. In 1990, the AMA adopted six principles under the heading "Fundamental Elements of the Patient-Physician Relationship." One states: "Patients are also entitled . . . to be advised of potential conflicts of interest that their physicians might have and to secure independent professional opinions" (American Medical Association 2000–01, xiii). The AMA's *Code of Medical Ethics* is a compilation of opinions based on the interpretation of its adopted principles and reports applied to numerous specific cases. In the section devoted to biomedical research, it states: "Avoidance of real or perceived conflicts of interest in clinical research is imperative if the medical community is to ensure objectivity and maintain individual and institutional integrity" (69). It also states that medical researchers receiving funding from a company "cannot ethically buy or sell the company's stock until the involvement ends" and that clinical investigators are obligated to disclose their financial conflicts of interests in all published results including letters (69–70). Because these are solely guidelines, we have no basis for knowing what percentage of the AMA membership complies with its principles.

Other professional societies have issued policy directives on conflicts of interest, particularly those groups that are involved with human-subject research. The American Society of Gene Therapy, which adopted a statement titled *Financial Conflicts of Interest in Clinical Research* in 2000, set its standards higher than the federal guidelines: "all investigators and team members directly responsible for patient selection, the informed consent process and/ or clinical management in a trial must not have equity, stock options or comparable arrangements in companies sponsoring the trial" (American Society of Gene Therapy 2000, 1).

The Association of American Medical Colleges (AAMC) is the professional group representing 125 accredited U.S. medical schools, covering also four hundred teaching hospitals and approximately 90,000 medical school faculties. The AAMC's views on conflicts of interest were issued in its 1990 publication, *Guidelines for Dealing with Faculty Conflicts of Commitment and Conflicts of Interest in Research*. Like many of its sibling university associations, the AAMC supports the basic principles behind the partnership between industry and academia as "essential to preserve medical progress and to continue to improve the health of our citizenry" (Association of American Medical Colleges 2001, 3). But it also asserts that "the mere appearance of a conflict between financial interests and professional responsibilities may weaken public confidence in the researcher's objectivity" (3). How do organizations reconcile the view that some relationships, such as industry-university collaborations, are essential but that they have an *appearance* that weakens the public's trust?

Maintaining that human-subject research requires an especially high standard of moral integrity, the AAMC applies the regulatory concept of "rebuttable presumption" to establish the burden of proof. "Institutional policies should establish the rebuttable presumption that an individual who holds a significant financial interest in research involving human subjects may not conduct such research" (7). Moreover, the AAMC maintains that the principle—namely, "the rebuttable presumption against significant financial interest in human subjects research"—should apply whether the funding is public or private (7).

Under the AAMC's ethical code on conflict of interest, the institution may provide compelling evidence (presumably to itself since the code is voluntary) that, even with significant financial interests, the investigator may be permitted to conduct the research. This hearkens back to the federal ethics guidelines for advisory committees, where the first principle is to prevent scientists with conflicts of interest from participating and the second principle is to permit waivers for the scientists with conflicts of interest when there are "compelling circumstances." The approach taken by the AAMC is to establish a high standard but to leave plenty of latitude for exceptions. Like the federal agencies, the AAMC states: "when the individual holding such interests is uniquely qualified by virtue of expertise and experience and the research could not otherwise be conducted as safely or effectively without that individual, he or she should be permitted the opportunity to rebut the presumption against financial interests by demonstrating these facts to the satisfaction of an institution's conflict of interest committee" (7).

Just how effective will institutional conflict of interest committees be in the face of large grants and contracts and researchers with weighty résumés? Many question the effectiveness of institutional oversight groups against imperial faculty. But there is progress: the AAMC recommends that institutions report conflict of interest information to the university's institutional review board (IRB), a federally mandated body. The IRB is responsible for approving human-subject protocols, and some are already taking on the additional responsibility of making judgments about conflicts of interest.

We continue to hear the argument that the management of conflict of interest and human-subject protection should be kept distinct. But after the death of Jesse Gelsinger in a failed human gene therapy experiment at the University of Pennsylvania, there has been more discussion about folding conflicts of interest into informed consent. Lawsuits filed on behalf of victims who died in clinical trials have argued that failure to disclose a conflict of interest or to prevent a conflict of interest introduce additional risks to the patient, which should be either prevented or disclosed.

The Association of American Universities (AAU) established a special task force on research accountability to produce a report and issue recommendations on individual and institutional financial conflict of interest. The task force was co-chaired by Steven B. Sample and L. Dennis Smith, the presidents of the University of Southern California and the University of Nebraska at Lincoln, respectively. Also included in the task force were the presidents of the University of Iowa, Princeton University, and Columbia University. The association published the task force's findings in October 2001. After reviewing the available information, the task force concluded that, "although the definitive data about the prevalence of conflict of interest is lacking, academic-industry relationships are clearly increasing, and with them, the risk of conflicts of interest compromising the integrity of research conducted in academia continues to rise" (Association of American Universities 2001, 2). While generally favoring an institutional, case-by-case approach to conflicts of interest among university faculty, the task force issued a special warning for situations involving human subjects and presented a zero tolerance recommendation: "Since research involving humans creates risks that non-human research does not, any related financial interest in research involving humans should generally not be allowable" (4).

But like the AAMC, the task force tempered its zero tolerance recommendation by leaving open the opportunity for exceptions: "If compelling circumstances justify an exception to this general rule, the research should be subject to more stringent management measures" (4). Both the AAU and the AAMC positions ask the universities to avoid, whenever possible, financial interests in human trials, to be able to defend trials if necessary, and to apply the ethical rules regardless of the source of funds. In addition, both believe that the IRBs should be involved in reviewing or monitoring conflicts of interests. The

AAU asserts rather confidently that the institutional IRB has jurisdiction over whether a particular financial interest should be managed or disclosed to the human subjects. This jurisdiction is not, however, in the legislation and charter of the IRBs; and many IRBs are not equipped to handle these types of questions. The AAU task force recommends a double layer of protection against financial conflicts in human subject experiments. The first layer of review would be made by the institutional conflict of interest committee. Its recommendation would then be passed on to the IRB, which also makes an independent determination. According to the AAU task force, "in such a system, neither the IRB nor the conflict of interest committee would be able to override the other's management requirements if the result would be to lessen the stringency of the management requirements. Either one could prohibit the research from proceeding, unless the financial conflict was removed or mitigated" (6).

The AAU task force report provides the strongest safeguards to date proposed by any review committee on managing conflicts of interest involving human subjects. The recommendations are designed, however, to keep the government's role to a bare minimum, to avoid further federal regulations, to foster the principle of self-governance, to keep flexibility within the institutions, and to establish ethical principles that extend beyond current federal regulations. For example, the government has not issued any restrictions on institutional financial conflict of interest, while the AAU task force reported that this type of conflict of interest "strikes to the heart of the integrity of the institution and the public's confidence in that integrity" (10). The major categories of institutional financial conflicts of interest include those involving university equity holdings or royalty arrangements and their effect on research programs and those involving university officials with personal financial interests in faculty companies or trustees whose firms could supply the university with goods or services. What is at stake?

In the task force's words, "institutional conflicts can reduce a university's role as an objective arbiter of knowledge on behalf of the public" (12). There are warnings and general guidelines for the institution but no clear prohibitions. For institutional conflicts of interest, the AAU task force cites three principles: always disclose, manage the conflicts in most cases, and prohibit the activity when necessary to protect the public interest or the interest of the university.

But how reasonable is it to expect that universities will choose the higher moral ground of public interest when the institution's bottom line or acquiescence to its big donors is at stake? In the past ten years several of the large professional societies have begun to address the serious erosion of academic integrity for both the individual and institutional conflicts of interest that have become endemic to the university culture. The specialized medical groups have not been as responsive. A 2000 study by the Office of the Inspector General of the Department of Health and Human Services of twenty-one medical associations guidelines found that only two associations (the American College of Emergency Medicine, and the American Psychiatric Association) had codes of ethics with explicit reference to physicians' disclosure of financial conflicts of interest to their patients/subjects (Brown 2000). The federal government's policy actions have been slow and cautious. There have been some incremental changes in response to the demands for more accountability.

Federal Agency Conflict of Interest Policies

Beginning in the late 1990s, in the wake of high-profile scandals and internal investigations, federal agencies began to tighten up their conflict of interest policies. The trend has been toward greater transparency, more comprehensive disclosures of financial relationships to funding and regulatory agencies, and protection of the self-management of conflicts of interest by grantee institutions. The interest of government is twofold. It wants to project an image of fairness and objectivity in policy decisions. And it wants to assure the general public that money going into research, especially clinical research, is not tainted by the real or perceived bias of scientists with a financial interest in the subject matter of their research.

The U.S. General Accounting Office (GAO), an investigative arm of government, reviewed the selection of external advisers on Environmental Protection Agency (EPA) panels in its June 2001 report. The GAO found that conflicts of interest were not identified and mitigated in a timely manner and that the public was not adequately informed about the points of view represented on the EPA's influential panels of experts (General Accounting Office 2001). By June 2002, the EPA drafted new guidelines with changes in how it would deal with conflict of interest.

The EPA's scientific advisory board consists of a staff and about one hundred experts in various fields of science. When advisory panels are chosen to review an area of science that informs a policy, the panel is formed of members of the board with additional experts chosen at large. According to provisions of the Ethics in Government Act of 1978, the board's staff screens panel candidates for conflicts of interest and the appearance of partiality.

The new policy has several changes that will be more attentive to conflicts of interest and afford the public more involvement in the process through which individuals are recommended to serve on expert panels. According to the new policies and procedures, "If a conflict exists between a panel candidate's private financial interests and activities and public responsibilities as a panel member, or even if there is the appearance of partiality, as defined by federal ethics regulations, the [board staff members] will, as a rule, seek to obtain the needed expertise from another individual" (U.S. Environmental Protection Agency 2002, A4). Previously, prospective panel members filled out conflict of interest forms annually. Under the current standards, they file a form each time they are recommended to serve on a scientific advisory board panel. The forms that must be filed by panel members are more detailed. Each prospective panel member is asked to write in narrative form any relationship he or she has that could be perceived as a conflict of interest. If a conflict of interest is identified, staff members must consult with the chair of the board's executive committee. Moreover, the public is given the opportunity to protest against potential panel candidates on grounds of bias. While the EPA has the legal authority to waive the conflict of interest of a potential panel member, by making the process more transparent to the public, the agency will have to think more seriously about exercising its waiver authority because it requires documentation.

The Public Health Service and the National Science Foundation issued conflict of interest regulations in 1995 for all recipients of grants from those agencies. This was a significant step toward establishing a reporting mechanism and a responsible party for managing conflicts of interest within each institution that receives federal grants. The government has not introduced a system for evaluating compliance. Federal guidelines set the standard for disclosure for researchers at equity ownership in companies exceeding 5 percent or aggregate payments received from companies in excess of $10,000 per year. Neither agency's guidelines prohibit any activity or research relationship but let the individual institutions manage what they interpret as a "significant conflict of interest."

As of 1997, under its *Guidelines for the Conduct of Research in the Intramural Research Program*, the National Institutes of Health (NIH) had a full disclosure policy for its scientists. This policy requires NIH employees to file a statement on all of their relevant financial interests (including those of the scientist's immediate family) to any funding agencies to which they submit grant applications, to peer review panels, and to meeting organizers before presentation of results. Finally, they must disclose their financial interests to journal editors when they submit publications and communications, written and oral. The requirement that intramural scientists have to disclose all personal financial interests to journal editors does not translate to extramural research (grants to academic scientists). Government grants do not impose a requirement that academic grantees publish their results in journals that have conflict of interest policies. Such a requirement would undoubtedly create an incentive for more journals to adopt such policies.

Because of the public sensitivity to conflicts of interest in clinical trials and the national priority to protect the integrity of experiments with human subjects, the U.S. Food and Drug Administration (FDA) became a lightning rod for criticism of clinical investigators who had commercial agendas. The FDA published a rule in February 1998, which became effective the following year, requiring disclosure of financial interests of clinical investigators that "could affect the reliability of data submitted to the FDA" by applicants for research support (U.S. Food and Drug Administration 1998, 5233). The FDA rule requires that anyone who submits a marketing application for any drug, biological product, or device must also submit information about the financial interests of any clinical investigator who made a significant contribution to the demonstration of safety. Failure to file the information could result in the FDA's refusal to file the marketing application.

The FDA also requires certification from the applicant that no financial arrangements with a clinical investigator have been made in which the outcome of a study could affect the compensation. In other words, companies should not be giving investigators payments in stock options or special rewards for drugs that "work." Investigators should have no proprietary interest in the tested product and the investigator should not have a significant equity interest in the sponsor of the study. Thus, the FDA has adopted a few prohibitions of the most egregious conflicts of interests. For others, it requires financial disclosure, presumably so the agency can factor in conflict of interest in assessing the reliability of the data.

In May 2000, Department of Health and Human Services secretary Donna E. Shalala outlined her intention to issue additional guidance to clarify its regulations on conflicts of interest. One of her goals was to get the National Institutes of Health and the FDA to work together "to develop new policies for the broader biomedical research community, which will require, for example, that any researchers' financial interest in a clinical trail be disclosed to potential participants" (U.S. Department of Health and Human Services 2000a, n.p.). One of the first initiatives of the secretary was to get IRBs to address conflicts of interests for investigators and institutions. Shalala wrote that the department will "undertake an extensive public consultation to identify new or improved means to manage financial conflicts of interest that could threaten the safety of research subjects or the objectivity of the research itself" (41073).

It was the intention of the secretary to seek new legislation to enable the FDA to issue civil penalties against violations of conflict of interest disclosure.

Shalala hoped to close the loop between conflict of interest, human-subject protection, and IRBs. The failure to disclose a conflict of interest was viewed as either an increased risk or an increased perceived risk to a potential human volunteer. The department issued a draft interim guidance document in January 2001. Strictly speaking, a guidance document is not a regulation, but commentators viewed it as another layer of federal controls on research centers and universities. It said explicitly: "[the department] is offering this guidance to assist Institutions, Clinical Investigators, and IRBs in their deliberations concerning potential and real conflicts of interest, and to facilitate disclosure, where appropriate, in consent forms" (U.S. Department of Health and Human Services 2001, 1). The draft guidance document proposed that the IRBs should be involved in identifying and managing both individual and institutional conflicts of interest and that consent forms for clinical trials should contain the sources of funding of the clinical investigators. A number of commentators were critical of the ill-defined concept of "institutional conflict of interest" and questioned whether IRBs could make decisions based on this concept. Would human volunteers act differently if they learned that clinical researchers or their institution had a financial stake in the outcome of the experiment? Would it be more difficult to recruit volunteers for such studies? Would the IRBs, already overworked in many cases, be able to handle this added responsibility? These were some of the concerns raised by professional societies to the department's draft interim guidance document.

A second draft of the guidance document on financial relationships in research involving human subjects was issued on 31 March 2003. The new draft defines a conflicting financial interest as one that "will or may be reasonably expected to create a bias" (U.S. Department of Health and Human Services 2003, 15457). While an advancement over the purely subjective definition in the prior draft, this definition is limited by linking conflict of interest to the "effect of a relationship" rather than to the "relationship itself." If, during sentencing of a convicted felon, a judge discloses his financial interest in a for-profit prison, we would not need an outcome measure of the effect of such a relationship to declare a conflict of interest. The new draft guidance document stops short of making any clear determinations about what relationships should be prohibited, leaving that decision to individual institutions. The earlier guidance asserts that, in clinical trials, when conflicts of interest cannot be eliminated, they should be disclosed in the consent document. The latest guidance recommends that the investigator *consider* whether to disclose the financial interest to the human subject—a weakening of the transparency concept.

Notwithstanding the initiatives taken by the Public Health Service and the FDA to manage conflicts of interest, according to the Office of Human

Research Protection, "there is currently no uniform comprehensive approach to consideration of potential financial conflicts of interest in human research" (U.S. Department of Health and Human Services 2001, 1). As of 2002, the actions of the federal agencies, by and large, still embrace the belief that data speak for themselves and that good science, not financial interests, determines the reliability of data. The government has taken no formal initiative to address institutional conflicts of interest, notwithstanding the fact that, increasingly, universities are investing in companies funded by faculty members. The responses taken by the FDA and the National Institutes of Health are largely public relations efforts responding to a climate that demands political correctness but does not get to the core of the problem, which is the increasingly commercial face of American universities.

Academic Institutions

American universities are still learning about faculty conflicts of interest. And with respect to institutional conflicts of interest, without a federal mandate or national guidelines, each university is going it alone. The most significant changes have arisen in response to federal mandates that a research university receiving National Science Foundation or National Institutes of Health funding must establish a conflict of interest management plan. Beyond that mandate, some universities are introducing the topic of conflicts of interest in relationship to training programs on scientific integrity designed for doctoral students and clinical investigators.

The research on university conflict of interest policies thus far shows a lack of specificity and wide variation in the content and the management of the policies. For example, a survey examined the conflict of interest policies of one hundred institutions with high levels of National Institutes of Health funding in 1998 and found that 55 percent of the policies required disclosure from all faculty while 45 percent required them only from the principal investigators. A relatively small number (19 percent) of the policies set explicit limits on faculty financial interests in corporate-sponsored research; a mere 12 percent contained language on what type of delay in publication was permissible, while 4 percent had taken the step to prohibit student involvement in work sponsored by a company for which the faculty had a personal financial interest. The study cited the need for uniform guidelines across academia: "Wide variation in management of conflicts of interest among institutions may cause unnecessary confusion among potential industrial partners or competition among universities for corporate sponsorship that could erode academic standards" (Cho et al. 2000, 2208).

In the aftermath of Jesse Gelsinger's death, significant attention at university medical schools has focused on clinical trials and conflicts of interest. The Department of Health and Human Services held hearings on this matter. A study published in 2000 analyzed policies governing conflicts of interest at ten medical schools in the United States that received the largest amount of research funding from the National Institutes of Health. Five of the schools had disclosure policies that exceeded the federal guidelines. Six required disclosure to the IRB as well as to the assigned administrator on conflict of interest policies. Four had stricter requirements for researchers conducting clinical trials than the federal government did (Lo, Wolf, and Berkeley 2000).

Another survey yielding 250 responses from medical schools and research institutions found that 9 percent had policies that exceeded federal guidelines. This indicates that the direction of the moral compass of the universities is favoring more stringent conflict of interest policies to protect the values and integrity of the university than the de minimus standards of the federal government (McCrary et al. 2000). Having learned from the experiences of their peers, university administrators are more cautious with regard to industry contracts containing restrictive covenants giving the sponsor control over data or publication. Two decades ago, Yale University's president Bart Giamatti (1982) wrote, "As an indispensable condition to arrangements for cooperative research with industry . . . the university will not accept restrictions, inhibition, or infringement upon a member of the faculty's free inquiry or capacity orally to communicate the results of his or her research . . . the university will not accept any restriction of written publication, save the most minor delay to enable a sponsor to apply for a patent or a license" (1280). When the faculty member is both the investigator and the corporate head, then the decision to delay publication is not an external control on the university but a part of the academic norm to maximize economic value before communicating the results of science research. The norm of trade secrecy arises as much from within the university as from outside. Delaying publication or denying data to other researchers can have adverse social consequences if they delay potential therapeutic uses or restrict the development of a technique or new product.

Independent Research Institutes

Many leading research institutes receive the majority of their funding from government sources. Typically, they also have ties to universities where researchers have academic appointments. One of these institutions, which has been the target of ongoing investigations by government agencies and investigative journalists, is the Seattle-based Fred Hutchinson Cancer Research Center, a tax-supported nonprofit with ties to the University of Washington. Scientists at "the Hutch," as it is known by locals, were financially involved with companies that financed their research. Since its founding in the 1970s, an estimated twenty scientists working at the Hutch have left to start companies with equity value of more than $18 billion. A series of stories in the *Seattle Times* under the headline "Uninformed Consent" (11 and 15 March 2001) brought these conflicts of interest to the attention of the general public. For many years, physicians at the Hutch were not required to tell patients when they had private financial interests in drugs or medical products. Clinical investigators could supervise clinical trials while they had substantial equity in a company that had a financial interest in the trial's outcome. The *Seattle Times* focused its report on two experiments: one involving a bone marrow transplant protocol, which was carried out between 1981 and 1993; the other a series of experimental treatments for breast cancer, which took place between 1991 and 1998. According to the report, an unusually high number of deaths accompanied these experimental treatments.

A physician at the Hutch, who served on the institution's IRB, contacted federal authorities about what he alleged were egregious conflicts of interest at his institution. The whistleblower was quoted in the *Seattle Times*, 12 March: "In essence, financial conflict of interest led to highly unethical human experimentation, which resulted in at least two dozen patient deaths. Oversight committees were misled, lied to and kept uninformed while in an atmosphere of fear and intimidation." According to records received by the investigative journalists, in addition to the clinical investigators, the Hutch itself had a financial stake in the experiments. Ironically, the board of trustees of the Hutch adopted a conflict of interest policy in 1983 that banned employees from participating in research in which they or their family members had an economic interest of any type. But the policy was not enforced in the cases investigated. Some scientists claimed they did not even know about the policy.

As an outgrowth of the federal investigations and media attention, the Hutch introduced a new conflict of interest policy in May 2002 that markedly restricts a clinical researcher from participating in human-subject research if it is sponsored by or designed to test a product or service of a for-profit entity in which the researcher (or his or her family) has a prohibited financial interest, which includes ownership interest of any amount or any nature in that for-profit entity. This new, rather complex policy signals a move toward the reform of conflict of interest policies among many leading research institutes and medical centers. Nevertheless, the conflict of interest disclosures at these institutes and centers are internal to the institutions and are thus generally shielded from the Freedom of Information Act. Without public disclosure, failure to implement conflict of interest procedures cannot easily be detected unless there is litigation.

Conclusion

The ethics of entrepreneurial research and conflict of interest are still being debated. There are many remaining contested issues:

- Should scientists with a personal financial interest in the subject of federally funded research disclose those interests to the funding agencies or simply to their home institutions? Should clinical scientists who have a commercial interest in drugs, medical procedures, or equipment be required to disclose those interests to human subjects who are invited to participate in a clinical trial? Should the IRBs rule on conflict of interest?
- Should scientists who have equity in a company or who are principals in a company be permitted to accept research grants from the company through their university?
- Should authors with financial interests in the subject matter of their publications be required by journals to disclose those interests? Should they be prohibited from contributing review articles and editorials?
- Should scientific books reviewed in journals be required to disclose the funding sources of the research they discuss?
- Should journals refuse review articles, editorials, and book reviews by authors with a conflict of interest?
- Should government agencies prohibit membership on scientific advisory panels when scientists have a conflict of interest?

Thus far, much of the response to faculty conflict of interest has focused on disclosure. The Department of Health and Human Services has set a priority for addressing conflicts of interest in clinical trials and has issued a draft guidance document that establishes a role for the IRBs in reviewing the competing interests of clinical investigators. The problem of institutional conflicts of interest has not received attention at the federal level and is rarely discussed among other science communities. While journals are beginning to issue policies that require disclosure, compliance by authors may not be high. And university approaches to managing conflicts of interest vary widely.

In the current state of affairs, both institutional and investigator conflicts of interest in basic science and medical research are addressed through a patch-work of voluntary guidelines. An alternative approach would be to apply the concept of *fiduciary responsibility*, a term with strong precedent in the legal com-munity, to academic research and medical sectors. One of the guiding prin-ciples underlying that responsibility is that those who produce knowledge in nonprofit institutions that are largely publicly funded, and those stakeholders who have a financial interest in that knowledge, must be kept separate and distinct. The separation of roles within certain professions that serve a public good such as the judiciary or financial auditors is what prevents even the ap-pearance of conflicts of interest.

References

Parts of this chapter are derived from Krimsky, Sheldon. 2003. *Science in the Private Interest*. Lanham, Md.: Rowman and Littlefield.

American Association of Medical Colleges, Task Force on Financial Conflict of Interest in Clinical Research. 2001. "Protecting Subjects, Promoting Trust, Promoting Progress." Washington, D.C.: American Association of Medical Colleges. December.

American Medical Association, Council on Ethics and Judicial Affairs. 2000–01. *Code of Medical Ethics*. Chicago: American Medical Association.

American Society of Gene Therapy. 2000. "Policy/Position Statement: Financial Con-flict of Interest in Clinical Research." 5 April (*http://www.asgt.org/policy/index.html*).

Association of American Universities, Task Force on Research Accountability. 2001. "Report on Individual and Institutional Conflict of Interest." Washington, D.C.: Association of American Universities. October.

Association of University Technology Managers. "AUTM Licensing Survey: FY 2000" (*http://www.autm.net/survey/2000/summarynoe.pdf*).

Blumenthal, David, Michael Gluck, Karen S. Louis, and David Wise. 1986. "Indus-trial Support of University Research Relationships in Biotechnology: Implications for the University." *Science*, 13 June, pp. 1361–66.

Blumenthal, David, Nancyanne Causine, Eric Campbell, et al. 1996. "Relationships between Academic Institutions and Industry in the Life Sciences: An Industry Sur-vey." *New England Journal of Medicine*, 8 February, pp. 368–73.

Brown, June Gibbs. 2000. "Recruiting Human Subjects." OEI–01–97–00196. Wash-ington, D.C.: U.S. Department of Health and Human Services, Office of the In-spector General. June

Campbell, Eric, G., Brian R. Clarridge, Manjusha Gokhale, et al. "Data Withholding in Academic Genetics." *Journal of the American Medical Association*, 23–30 Janu-ary, pp. 473–80.

Cho, Mildred K., Ryo Shohara, Anna Schissel, and Drummond Rennie. 2000. "Poli-cies on Faculty Conflicts of Interest at U.S. Universities." *Journal of the American Medical Association*, 1 November, pp. 2203–8.

Cole, Jonathan, R. 1994. "Balancing Acts: Dilemmas of Choice Facing Research Uni-versities." In *The Research University in a Time of Discontent*, ed. Jonathan R. Cole, Elinor G. Barber, and Stephen R. Graubard, 1–36. Baltimore: Johns Hopkins Uni-versity Press.

Cole, Jonathan, Elinor Barber, and Stephen Graubard, eds. 1994. *The Research University in a Time of Discontent*. Baltimore: Johns Hopkins University.

Giamatti, A. Bartlett. 1982. "The University, Industry, and Cooperative Research." *Science*. 24 December, p. 1280.

Krimsky, S., L. S. Rothenberg, P. Stott, and G. Kyle. 1996. "Financial Interest of Authors in Scientific Journals: A Pilot Study of 14 Publications." *Science and Engineering Ethics* 2: 395–410.

Krimsky, S., and L. S. Rothenberg. 2001. "Conflict of Interest Policies in Science and Medical Journals: Editorial Practices and Author Disclosure." *Science and Engineering Ethics* 7: 205–18.

Lo, Bernard, Leslie E. Wolf, and Abiona Berkeley. 2000. "Conflicts-of-Interest Policies for Investigators in Clinical Trials." *New England Journal of Medicine*, 30 November, pp. 1616–20.

McCrary, S. Van, Cheryl B. Anderson, Jelena Jakovljevic, et al. 2000. "A National Survey of Policies on Disclosure of Conflicts of Interest in Biomedical Research." *New England Journal of Medicine*, 30 November, pp. 1621–26.

Press, Eval, and Jennifer Washburn. 2000. "The Kept University." *Atlantic Monthly* 285 (March): 54.

Slaughter, Sheila, and Larry Leslie. 1997. *Academic Capitalism: Politics, Policies and the Entrepreneurial University*. Baltimore: Johns Hopkins University.

U.S. Department of Health and Human Services. 2000a. "News Release: Secretary Shalala Bolsters Protection for Human Research Subjects." *HHS News*, 23 May, n.p.

———, Office of the Secretary. 2000b. "Human Subject Protection and Financial Conflict of Interest: Conference." *Federal Register*, 3 July, pp. 41073–76.

———, Office of Human Research Protection. 2001. "Draft Interim Guidance: Financial Relationships in Clinical Research: Issues for Institutions, Clinical Investigators, and IRBs to Consider When Dealing with Issues of Financial Interests and Human Subject Protection." 10 June (*http://ohrp.osophs.dhhs.gov/humansubjects/finreltn/finguid.htm*).

———. 2003. "Draft Guidance Document: Financial Relationships and Interests in Research Involving Human Subjects: Guidance for Human Subject Protection." *Federal Register*, 31 March, pp. 15457–60.

U.S. Environmental Protection Agency, Executive Committee, Science Advisory Board, Policies and Procedures Subcommittee. 2002. "Overview of the Panel Formation Process at the EPA Science Advisory Board." Washington, D.C.: U.S. Environmental Protection Agency. May.

U.S. Food and Drug Administration. 1998. "Financial Disclosure by Clinical Investigators." *Federal Register*, 2 February, p. 5233.

U.S. General Accounting Office. 2001. "EPA's Science Advisory Panels." GAO–01–536. Washington, D.C.: U.S. General Accounting Office. June.

Chapter 12

The Academy and Industry

A View across the Divide

ZACH W. HALL

As EXECUTIVE VICE chancellor at the University of California, San Francisco (UCSF), I oversaw the office of technology transfer and assumed primary responsibility for the development of the university's new Mission Bay campus, a forty-three-acre basic science research campus situated in the center of a three-hundred-acre public-private biomedical research park. In fall 2001, I left UCSF to become president and chief executive officer of EnVivo Pharmaceuticals, a small biotech start-up company. As a result, my experiences on both sides of the academic-industry divide have given me a unique perspective on ties between these diverse institutions.

Close interactions of industry with the academic disciplines of biology, medicine, engineering, chemistry, and agricultural sciences have existed for decades. The close involvement of academic biomedical science with industry, however, is a relatively recent phenomenon. The reasons for this new relationship are complex and interesting, but changes in biomedical science itself constitute part of the driving force. Moreover, although many of the problems arising from this intense interaction are generic and independent of the field, many have specific roots in the intrinsic nature of biomedical research.

The Biomedical Research Revolution

The changes in biomedical research during the past half-century have been extraordinary. The bookends of my own research career perhaps best symbolize the progress and preoccupations of our time. The genetic code was discovered in 1966, when I was in graduate school; and in 2000, shortly before I left my position at UCSF, the human genome sequence was published. The genetic revolution that occurred in the intervening period has transformed every field of biomedical science that it has touched: cell biology, immunology, developmental biology, cancer biology, and, most recently, medical science.

The remaking of the scientific landscape that occurred during the past thirty-four years has had a profound impact on not only the substance of science but also its organization. The way in which science is practiced has changed, with profound consequences for universities and the relationship between academia and industry. In the 1960s, biomedical research was largely a cottage industry, a decentralized enterprise whose fundamental unit was an individual investigator with a research group of three to ten people. With the exception of the National Institutes of Health, laboratories were mostly in universities or nonacademic research institutions, where they were supported by the federal government through grants from the National Institutes of Health and the National Science Foundation, an arrangement resulting from the post–World War II expansion of federal support for science. Each laboratory operated as a largely independent entity, competing, and occasionally cooperating, with laboratories in other universities. With the exception of the National Institutes of Health, whose internal research program also expanded in the postwar era, these laboratories were the source of almost all innovation in biological research as well as advances in technology.

University laboratories were self-contained not only with respect to each other but also with respect to industry, with which, in the biomedical sphere at least, there was little interaction, either individually or institutionally. A researcher who accepted a job in industry was widely regarded as having tacitly admitted failure, either real or anticipated, in the more prestigious and productive world of academic biomedical science. A job in industry was regarded as a one-way ticket to research oblivion, from which friends or colleagues generally never returned. When a prominent biomedical researcher left Washington University to go to Merck in the 1970s, other researchers were genuinely shocked. Why would any successful scientist want to take a position in industry?

The Era of Collaborative Research

The perspective of 2002 is vastly different from that of the late 1960s. First, the modern laboratory is no longer an island unto itself. Any active biomedical laboratory is now engaged in multiple collaborations with a variety of laboratories in other institutions. Because modern research uses multiple and complex technologies and because common biological themes unite research in apparently disparate areas, laboratories must collaborate to be successful. Moreover, the rapid movement of science drives collaborations in different directions at different times. There is thus a premium on the ability of a laboratory to be flexible, to form alliances for specific problems, and then to dissolve and reform them as necessary.

Not only individuals but also institutions have begun to adapt to the same style. For example, three campuses of the University of California (San Francisco, Berkeley, and Santa Cruz) recently established an Institute for Quantitative Biology. Such collaborations among campuses have now become quite common. The Emory University and Georgia Institute of Technology (Georgia Tech) program in bioengineering is one of several joint programs that Emory has with other universities. Individual investigators, institutions, and recently companies create a complex and shifting network of collaborations, alliances, and arrangements that provide access to particular reagents, technologies, and data bases as the occasion demands.

Further, with modern technological advances, large-scale projects can be undertaken in which the resources of many laboratories are coordinated to achieve a specific goal: the Human Genome Project is the preeminent example. Spurred by this success, other ambitious, multi-investigator, multi-institution projects have been created. The Cell Signaling Alliance, organized by Alfred Gilman at the University of Texas, Southwestern, and funded by the National Institute of General Medical Sciences, is one such example. Its purpose is to unite a large number of laboratories into a coordinated and comprehensive effort to understand the signaling pathways in one or two specific cell types.

These projects have several characteristics that are worth noting. The first point is the emphasis on comprehensive rather than clever experiments. The goal is not to determine which gene is likely to be important, for example, but to examine all the genes, all the proteins, all the signaling pathways, all the possible single nucleotide polymorphisms. The result of these large-scale projects is to create data bases of information that are too large for any single laboratory to understand, analyze, or indeed use. Rather, they serve as resources for the whole biomedical community. The second point worth noting is that the size of these projects gives rise to a different kind of science in which the effort of individual investigators is managed and coordinated from above and priorities are set not by the individual lab but by the consortium.

Another notable and important change in modern biomedical research has been the emergence of biotechnology. The original basis for the biotechnology industry was recombinant DNA technology, which arose from research at

UCSF and Stanford University and was based indirectly on work from dozens of other academic laboratories. The biotechnology industry was thus derived directly from university research, with many of its early practitioners recruited from academic laboratories. As biotechnology companies have developed and expanded (there are now approximately four hundred publicly traded companies and more than 1,000 private biotechnology companies), they have become a major source of innovation in biomedical research. Their flexibility and their ability, through the capital markets, to put significant resources into the hands of young investigators have made them an important source of biological and molecular discovery. A look at the contents of current scientific journals or the abstracts of scientific meetings quickly reveals the scope and significance of the contribution of industry to basic and clinical research.

The academic origins of the biotech industry and its research vigor make it possible for researchers to move freely back and forth between industry and academia. UCSF has a number of refugees from industry, perhaps most easily recognized by the size of their houses and the late models of their cars. Further, a number of prominent, high-visibility academic researchers and administrators have recently taken positions in industry. This movement back and forth has increased the rate of cultural exchange across the academic-industry divide and has narrowed the distance separating them. Parenthetically, I note that John Hennessy, the new president of Stanford University, who is an information scientist, interrupted his academic career to start a company before returning to Stanford to become a professor, dean of the School of Engineering, provost, and ultimately president.

Although the movement between academia and industry involves only a small number of researchers, many more have ties to both institutions. Almost every prominent academic scientist these days is a consultant, serves on a scientific advisory board, or is a founder of a company. On an institutional level, universities now actively seek sponsored research agreements with industry. As much as 10 to 15 percent of the research budgets of many major research institutions comes from industry. The early, well-publicized success of several patents held by universities, such as the Boyer-Cohen patent for recombinant DNA, which brought in hundreds of millions of dollars to Stanford and UCSF, spurred universities to expand their offices dealing with intellectual property and technology transfer. Moreover, some universities, often and increasingly encouraged by state legislatures, are actively seeking to expand their contacts and ties with industry. Several are involved, either directly or indirectly, in setting up companies or in constructing research parks (such as Research Triangle Park in North Carolina; Kendall Square in Cambridge, Massachusetts; and Mission Bay in San Francisco), where industry and academia can work side by side in a productive way.

The rapid growth of these various relationships arises in part from economic incentives. Another driving force is the structure of modern science. Academic institutions and private companies have become more collaborative and interdependent for the same reasons that scientific laboratories have: their competitive position depends on it. As one example, one of the most important motivations for plant scientists at the University of California, Berkeley, to enter into the much discussed research agreement with Novartis was the access it gave them to genetic data bases held by the company. The widely publicized competition and cooperation between public and private sectors in the successful execution of the Human Genome Project provides a second example of the scientific benefits of public-private interaction. Its completion four years ahead of the original schedule is a stunning example of the payoff in scientific terms of the partnership between academia, industry, and, in this case, government and philanthropic organizations, such as the Wellcome Trust. Universities and industry have thus both become part of the vast "Internet of biology" that forms the complex working network of modern biomedical research.

Academic-Industry Partnerships

In a larger sense, universities and industries need each other so that each can most successfully fulfill its role of benefiting society. Universities need industry so that discoveries from academic laboratories can be made into useful products; industry needs universities as the continuing source of innovation derived from curiosity-driven research. The key to the successful partnership, however, is the recognition on both sides that universities and industry have distinct missions. The mission of the university is the pursuit of knowledge for its own sake, the best-known strategy for innovation; and the mission of industries is to make money for their stockholders, the best-known strategy for economic progress. In some contexts, these two missions can lead to aims that are antithetical. In other contexts, both aims can be fulfilled in pursuing a common goal, with corresponding benefit to society.

Paradoxically, the partnership between academia and industry is not hampered by the distinctive roles of each but, in fact, is most successful when the distinctions are preserved and recognized. Correspondingly, many of the problems emanating from academic-industry partnerships arise from either a failure of one side to recognize the different values and needs of the other partner or confusion of one partner about the mission of the other.

At the center of any successful academic-industry partnership is recognition of the diverse core values of the two institutions. For academia the pursuit of knowledge wherever it leads, openness of communication, and the protection of students and fellows are paramount. For industry, the core values are a return on investment and protection of proprietary knowledge or technology. Agreements between universities and industry must recognize that university faculty must be free to publish the results of their research and that they must have final control over what they publish, or else they are doomed to failure. UCSF now will not enter into a contract with any company that does not give its investigators the right to publish their data. In spite of protests by industry, UCSF has insisted on this principle; and in every case, the potential corporate partner has agreed. Ironically, during the past three years, UCSF has had two disagreements with the National Institutes of Health in which exactly the same issue was at stake. In one case, the university refused a $1 million contract because the agency would not agree to permit UCSF researchers to maintain the rights to their findings. A year later the agency returned and offered to reword the contract. In the second case, after much discussion, the National Institutes of Health agreed to change a longstanding policy in order to meet the conditions of the university. By the same token, universities need to recognize the proprietary needs of industry, which can sometimes delay publication for several months. The best solution to these problems is for potential partners to start by saying, "Here are our non-negotiable needs. What are yours?" and then to work together to see if a solution can be found that satisfies both.

The Challenge for Universities

The new and close relationships with industry that now pervade the biomedical world pose two types of challenges for universities. First is the threat of corruption of existing structures. Beyond the nuances of structuring specific agreements, universities need to monitor relations with industry to be sure that the schools' core values are preserved. Conflict of interest issues, for both the individual investigator and the institution, must be identified and managed. These are crucial issues both because they are substantively important and because they are crucial to the public perception of universities. If universities are not regarded as a source of objective research that is free of commercial bias, society loses something very precious indeed. The confidence of the public in the integrity and objectivity of university research is most easily achieved by having a common set of standards agreed upon by all major research universities. It is often difficult for individuals to understand why certain behavior is acceptable in one university but is a violation of standards in another.

Most universities now have committees that monitor matters related to individual conflicts of interest. They have spent less time addressing the issue of monitoring institutional conflict of interest. Many universities are actively engaged in generating income from their intellectual property, often by taking equity positions in companies. It is important that universities ensure that the interests of the university not overshadow the faculty member. The money generated by these activities is often directed back to the support of research in the university. Some schools direct the money back to the support of deserving research of all kinds; others direct the money only to research with promising commercial potential. Focusing only on research with commercial potential undermines the values of the university and introduces a commercial bias directly into university policies.

Another issue that often is not addressed is conflict of commitment. In contrast to conflict of interest, to which universal standards should apply, conflict of commitment is an internal matter because it deals with what proportion of a faculty member's time and effort can be spent on non-university matters. In many universities there is no institutional means of monitoring the arrangements that a faculty member may make with an outside company for his or her time, yet these arrangements may be contrary to university policies and may put the university at risk.

Yet another set of challenges arises from university relations with industry. These may be defined as positive challenges in the sense that academic-industry relations offer universities an opportunity to learn from the experience of industry. As universities become increasingly involved in big science, there is more and more call for centralized planning of the sort that is familiar to industry. As science becomes more expensive and more project-oriented, strategic planning by universities becomes a necessity. Decisions must be made centrally about how to deploy scarce resources. The danger, of course, arises when central planning threatens to choke off the vital sources of innovation that arise from creative individuals. How to maintain this balance will be an important challenge. Further, as equipment becomes more expensive, universities are going to have to develop new methods for providing adequate technology for their faculty—not only equipment but also highly skilled people to run it. Many of these people, who hold doctoral degrees, are often not easily accommodated within the tenure system. Finally, it is important for universities to realize that one attraction of industry for many young scientists is the opportunity to work in teams. The team concept often runs counter to the academic ethos, which rewards individual excellence rather than the excellence of the team. Researchers who work on clinical trials are already familiar with the difficulty: how to promote the deserving young assistant professor who does not have a first-authored paper demonstrating his or her individual brilliance and originality but has proven to be an invaluable site leader in a large multicenter clinical trial.

Many of the brightest graduates are attracted to industry because they believe that the technological resources and the team approach offer them the opportunity to do their best work. For similar reasons, several leading scientists in academia are exploring the possibility of setting up research institutes outside the university. These are envisioned as nonprofit institutions that embody some of the advantages of the private-sector approach. The country will soon see a number of efforts to devise new ways of doing modern biomedical research through structures that take into account the changes in the way in which modern biomedical science is now practiced. Many of these efforts will take place outside universities. Universities must understand and respond to the tremendous changes that have taken place in biomedical research over the past half-century in order to continue to attract brilliant researchers. The true challenge facing university administrators is to incorporate new administrative structures that facilitate science in the university without compromising its core values.

Conclusion

Driven by scientific discovery and by changes in how science is done, biomedical research relationships between universities and industry have rapidly grown in extent and complexity. Partnerships between universities and private companies have yielded undoubted benefit to our society, in both scientific and economic terms. The relationship is most successful, however, when the two parties acknowledge and respect their distinct missions. For universities, one challenge of the new relationships will be to protect their core values through clear guidelines for individual and institutional conflict of interest. A second challenge will be to learn from the interaction with industry how universities might change their own research culture in beneficial ways.

Chapter 13

Responsible Innovation in the Commercialized University

DAVID H. GUSTON

In his recent *Science, Truth, and Democracy*, philosopher Philip Kitcher (2001) proposes "well-ordered science" as the ideal to which the organization of the research enterprise should aspire. Distinct from government by "vulgar democracy," in well-ordered science a highly informed public, coupled with a public-spirited research community, sets overall research priorities. As a philosopher, Kitcher avoids a detailed comparison of this ideal to the reality of making science policy in the contemporary United States. But he does imply that the reality falls short of the ideal on the counts of both informed public participation and unselfish scientific service. He therefore recognizes the needs, respectively, for "sociological information required to build realistic models" of the construction of "tutored collective preferences" as well as for "a political theory of science that will consider the various ways in which the interests of actors and social institutions" relate to outcomes in well-ordered science (135, 133 n. 8).

It is true that there are shortcomings in both the public and the scientific community. Yet there is room for optimism about the current state of knowledge on the involvement of the public in making technically complex decisions as well as on the capacity of existing scholarship to guide the connection among researchers, institutions, and outcomes in science policy. What we need to preserve science in the commercialized university are university-based Centers for Responsible Innovation (CRIs) that might contribute a particularly important microcosm of science. This chapter addresses three premises about the commercialized university that form the foundation of my call for CRIs.

It also elaborates the tasks that such centers would perform and grounds their operation in recent scholarship in the social studies of science and technology.

The Challenge of the Commercialized Academy

In December 2000 the vice president for academic affairs at Rutgers University, an economist by training, convened an interdisciplinary group of faculty members in the Scarlet Room, a lush conference room in Rutgers's central administrative building. He questioned why the university, with its two law schools, its recently powerful biomedical sciences, its long tradition in environmental research, its nationally regarded philosophy department, and its up-and-coming planning and policy school, had not yet brought these elements together with law, ethics, and policy. He challenged the faculty in attendance to pursue what he called an initiative in law, ethics, and the sciences. The faculty group met only once more. During the second meeting, the vice president requested that participants circulate among themselves proposals for what such an initiative in law, ethics, and the sciences might accomplish. This chapter is the result of that call.

The concerns that drew the Rutgers group together were only narrowly cast as ethics or law. Something more subtle, perhaps, but more profound than the ad hoc collection of patenting genes, privacy in the Internet era, or ethics training for graduate students suffused the Scarlet Room. Rutgers was acknowledging that the primary task of the university—the creation and dissemination of new knowledge—has normative dimensions that the university was not engaging.

Invigorating the university's primary task with the necessary normative supplements requires accepting three premises. First, large research universities will continue to be in the business of knowledge-based innovation for at least several generations. Even if students turn to distance learning programs on the Internet and pressures on tenure erode the status of faculty, universities and the people affiliated with them will still create new knowledge and seek to express it in scientific, artistic, and professional forms.

Second, universities will continue to market new knowledge. The commercialized academy has, in various ways, been around for a very long time. Brooks and Randazzese (1998) emphasize the role of the land-grant institutions in the nineteenth century and the rise of engineering education in the early twentieth century in creating links between industry and the academy. The Massachusetts Institute of Technology pioneered entrepreneurial relations with industry in the first half of the twentieth century (Etzkowitz 2002); and in the second half of the century, academic capitalism in many nations followed the globalization of research in particular and the economy in general (Slaughter and Leslie 1997). More recently, the Bayh-Dole Act of 1980 has encouraged U.S. universities to become increasingly involved in the commercialization of the new knowledge they produce. In the tenth annual edition of its survey of licensing and other university-based technology transfer practices, the Association of University Technology Managers (2001) provides an overview of the growth of technology transfer activities. Participation in the survey has increased from sixty-six of the top one hundred U.S. research universities to ninety-four, and the total number of respondents increased from 130 to 190 institutions. These respondents report an increase from 6,337 invention disclosures in fiscal year (FY) 1991 to 13,032 disclosures in FY 2000. New U.S. patent applications from these institutions increased from 1,643 to 6,375 over the same period. Licenses and options executed increased from 1,278 to 4,362, and licensing income increased from $186 million to $1.26 billion (in current dollars) from FY 1991 to FY 2000. Respondent universities in the United States received $1.1 billion of the licensing income in FY 2000, a sum equivalent to 50 percent of research expenditures by industry in universities that year and approximately 7 percent of such expenditures by the federal government. As measured by employment and overall economic activity, Bayh-Dole technology transfer is said to have been responsible for approximately 260,000 jobs and $40 billion in economic activity in the United States in 2000.

Although some research (Mowery et al. 2001) has questioned the necessity and uniqueness of Bayh-Dole's contribution to the boom in universities' intellectual property transactions, such activity has created a tightening aggregation of interests around technology transfer. Etzkowitz and Ledesdorff (2000) call this new political economy the triple helix of university-industry-government relations. The new political economy is fueled not just through licenses with royalties but also through licenses with equity. The Association of University Technology Managers, itself an example of the creation of professional and interest groups around the commercialized academy, reports that licenses with equity shares to universities have increased from 142 in FY 1995 to 372 in FY 2000. Of the 454 start-ups formed in FY 2000, 80 percent are located in the same state as the reporting institution, thus contributing to a critical trend in local and regional economic development. The nonprofit State Science and Technology Institute emerged in 1996 to improve collaborative programs in science and technology for regional economic development, connecting with science and technology commissions or offices in dozens of states and with the Science and Technology Council of the States, affiliated with the National Governors Association. At the federal level, even the National

Science Foundation has supported an intersectoral approach to research through its engineering research centers (see Feller, Ailes, and Roessner 2002 for an evaluation) inaugurated in the 1980s, its more recent Partnerships for Innovation program, and other collaborative endeavors.

Even if the new political economy of academic commercialization were not strong enough for observers to presume its durability, one could argue that it demonstrates through the narrow measures of the market that universities are behaving in a responsible way—that is, in accord with the considered values of the wider community. The promise of research to contribute to economic expansion is rooted in the post–World War II social contract for science (Guston 2000), and fulfilling this promise is a critical element of scientific responsibility. But the economic contribution tells only part of the story of responsible innovation.

Third, another premise that dawned on the Rutgers group is that the enterprise of knowledge-based innovation has normative dimensions that science policy confronts only marginally or in ad hoc ways. Such normative consequences begin with the costs, in addition to the benefits, of technology transfer and other university-industry interactions. On campuses, market values intrude on the scholarly enterprise by creating opportunities for conflicts of interest and commitment among faculty and students, changing norms of scholarly communication and materials transfer, turning students into consumers, and potentially devaluing learning for its own sake (Slaughter 2001). In chapter 11, Sheldon Krimsky reminds us that there are both local and broader public consequences to commercialization when universities and their faculties become interested participants in technical decisions and controversies rather than disinterested observers. The ideal of what Joel Primack and Frank Von Hippel (1974) call public science has been almost completely lost: more than two-thirds of national research and development spending in the United States comes from private interests, and a significant fraction of the remaining one-third of public money is potentially compromised by interests in commercialization or by mingling with private funds.

In addition to behaving responsibly with respect to economically relevant research through the creation of offices of technology transfer, universities began a decade earlier to behave responsibly with respect to human and animal research subjects by creating institutional review boards (IRBs). These activities, however, clearly need improvement, as demonstrated by Jesse Gelsinger's tragic death during a genetic therapy trial at the University of Pennsylvania. In this case, the director of the research institute housing the research held financial interests in a firm, founded by one researcher, which helped finance the institute (Sacks 2000).

Technology transfer and IRBs show that universities can adopt a responsible position when the opportunity arrives. Yet the protection of research subjects and the contribution of university-based research to the economy do not exhaust the scope of the ethical, legal, and social implications of innovation. The societal value of knowledge creation cannot be measured merely by licensing income, and the ethical duties of research are not entirely discharged by obtaining informed consent. Derek Bok (1982) realized this two decades ago when he delved into the social responsibilities of the modern university. Bok wondered, in a world remade by knowledge-based innovation, "should academic freedom extend to university laboratories that could produce discoveries of awesome power and destructive force?" There are many grades of distinction between academic freedom and intellectual servitude, just as there are many critical societal effects short of "awesome power and destructive force." The point, familiar to students of science and technology, is simply that knowledge-based innovation helps create many patterns of society to which people must respond, usually without having had any choice in those patterns—whether through design, accident, or neglect (Winner 1977).

Unfortunately, little is known about how these patterns are created. There is a role for knowledge creation and dissemination around the normative dimensions of knowledge creation itself, and universities therefore have a role in this reflexive enterprise. New ways must be found to manage the ethical, legal, and social implications of research that aspires to help people pursue more uplifting lives in more just societies.

Universities' examination of the ethical, legal, and social implications of the knowledge-based innovations they principally pursue is particularly critical given the unbalanced evaluation of costs and benefits to which Bok refers in chapter 3. If it is hard to say no to the incremental commercialization of universities because each new bit is not entirely unprecedented and because the negative consequences of each new increment cannot be as clearly discerned as the positive ones, then at least universities can say yes to the reflexive study of the interaction of innovation and society.

The Roles of the Center for Responsible Innovation

To house the self-scrutiny of the ethical, legal, and social implications of knowledge creation, universities should create centers for responsible innovation (CRIs). CRIs would accomplish this reflexive pursuit in parallel with the universities' traditional missions of teaching, research, and service.

CRIs would function primarily as brokers of interdisciplinary teaching and learning opportunities and educational resources. One obvious area would be supporting departments in their federally mandated and independent efforts to integrate ethics and responsibility issues into their curricula. The National Institutes of Health require that institutions applying for biomedical training grants provide trainees with course work in scientific responsibility. More recently, the Office of Research Integrity (2000) of the U.S. Public Health Service has announced a policy to require similar training in the responsible conduct of research for all grant applicants, although Congress has suspended the policy pending what it considers more appropriate procedures in promulgating it (Brainard 2001). Similarly, the Accrediting Board for Engineering and Technology (2000) requires ethics training in its recent accreditation criteria for undergraduate engineering degrees. CRIs would help such relevant courses find faculty or professional expertise and course material.

CRIs would also propose, plan, promote, or implement novel educational programs. Such programs might include helping to create or support undergraduate course work; minors or majors in science, technology, and society; or graduate programs in science and technology studies. They could also include graduate programs that cross-train, for example, natural scientists and engineers in business, policy, law, and the humanities. At Rutgers, one program combines a master's degree in biomedical sciences with a master's degree in business administration. The Massachusetts Institute of Technology's technology and policy program combines a master's degree in science with course work in public policy and an interdisciplinary thesis.

The primary research contributions of such a center would involve engaging in externally funded cooperative research on the ethical, legal, and social implications of other research on campus. Ethical, legal, and social implications research (known by the acronym ELSI) has expanded over the past decade, funded by 3 to 5 percent set-asides from large federal programs such as human genome, information technology, and nanotechnology initiatives. Although successful in funding a significant amount of research (the human genome ELSI program at the National Institutes of Health and the U.S. Department of Energy has funded more than $150 million of work since FY 1990), ELSI seems to have been more successful in diverting calls for other innovations in ethics and responsible research than in informing the science policy process or encouraging broader and more sophisticated political considerations of issues such as genetic privacy and discrimination (Kitcher 2001). In a detailed study of the human genome ELSI program, Lauren McCain (2002) concludes that "the ELSI experience so far does not support an early contention . . . that public science projects can sufficiently monitor and address their own social impacts. ELSI-type programs are unlikely to help shape public research agendas" (12).

Such expectations for ELSI research, however, may be too high because ELSI work concentrates on innovations after they emerge from the laboratory; it has had few, if any, institutional links back to setting research priorities and other science policy tasks. In contrast, research conducted or encouraged by CRIs could resemble real-time technology assessment, which combines historical research, public opinion and communication, traditional technology assessment, and interactions between the public and active researchers (Guston and Sarewitz 2001). This ensemble of research attempts to encourage responsible knowledge-based innovation by understanding historical precedents for similar innovations; providing links for communication and education among researchers, potential consumers, and the public; and allowing the possibility of public intervention in the innovation process before the innovation is introduced as a market product. Particularly interesting would be interdisciplinary collaborations coordinated by CRIs on knowledge-based innovations with potentially important effects on local communities around universities.

CRIs would also be involved in more traditional scholarly pursuits, such as organizing symposia of university and outside faculty for high-profile intellectual and public events and pursuing an aggressive publishing agenda from them. They would provide advice, assistance, and seed funds for faculty and students commencing externally funded projects that might benefit from ideas in responsible innovation. Specifically, they might assist natural scientists and engineers applying for National Science Foundation grants to articulate responses to the foundation's criterion 2: the broader social merit of the proposed research. Although the foundation does not have a good track record in using criterion 2 to make funding decisions (Mervis 2001), part of the problem may be that applicants do not understand how to frame responses to criterion 2 issues. But political and administrative pressure to use those issues will not subside. CRIs would thus help correct the foundation's mistaken assumption that technically competent researchers also are proficient in discussing the social implications of their work.

In their primary service role, CRIs would reach out beyond the university to local, state, and national decision makers and to the public. This role would, of course, require close collaboration with university communication and government-affairs offices. State legislators and their staff often believe that universities, particularly public ones, should be more helpful to the legislature as informational sources (Jones, Guston, and Branscomb 1996). CRIs would offer informational programs for public officials grounded in research at the university and would collaborate with a university's Washington office on such programs for national decision makers. They would also collaborate with IRBs, offices of technology transfer, and other elements of university administration on local projects of mutual interest. CRIs would pursue a strategy for dissemination that includes nonacademic outlets, such as editorials and cable television, to reach the broadest possible audience.

Interaction with the public mediated by CRIs should not be exclusively one way. CRIs must also be conduits to the university, relaying public concerns and lay perspectives. Not only university officials but also teaching faculty and researchers must hear these voices. There are a variety of models for facilitating such expert-lay interaction, including the consensus conferences pioneered by the Danish Board of Technology and recently imported to the United States and other countries (Joss and Durant 1995, Guston 1999a, Hörnig 1999); scenario development workshops in which experts and lay participants reflect on coherent descriptions of envisioned technological futures (Andersen and Jaeger 1999, Sclove 1999); focus groups (Dürenberger, Kastenholz, and Behringer 1999); and participatory research and design such as that conducted by community-based research centers and "science shops" (Study and Conference on Improving Public Access to Science 2001).

As this list of potential functions suggests, a CRI will not be an organization that does unique things, although some of its tasks will be new in particular institutions. Rather, its novelty will lie in its mission of institutionalizing responsible innovation at research universities and assembling activities in pursuit of this mission. If we remain committed to the idea of the synergy between research and teaching, then this commitment should extend to the university's endeavors to behave responsibly. Failure to institutionalize such an ensemble of activities is not just the failure to pursue responsibility more actively but also the failure to pursue efficiently the mission of the university.

Through CRIs, universities would construct ongoing projects and relationships to help assure members of their own communities, leaders from the public and private sectors, and the public at large that institutions are engaged in responsible innovation, despite continuing commercial ties. CRIs would require some commitment of faculty and staff resources, but they may very well raise a significant share of their own funds from sources such as ELSI programs in the genome, information technology, and nanotechnology initiatives; the Program in Societal Dimensions of Engineering, Science, and Technology at the National Science Foundation; local and regional foundations concerned with the immediate implications of university research; and local corporate givers pursuing an enlightened approach to innovation. The first CRI pioneer would capture headlines and, better, imaginations because such an institution would be novel not just in the United States but perhaps the world. In an increasingly competitive environment, a university with a CRI would be able to position itself at the vanguard of both intellectual creativity and social responsibility.

Will CRIs Succeed?

Having considered the warrant for and functions of CRIs, let us return to Kitcher's concerns about the science policy system more generally. Given that CRIs seek to involve the public in potentially critical roles in knowledge-based innovation, can we have any confidence that they will succeed?

During the past decade, familiarity with and expertise in mechanisms for the participation of the public in various technical decisions has increased tremendously. In science and technology policy circles, perhaps the most notable achievement has been the spread of Danish-style consensus conferences, or citizens' panels, from the smaller nations of northern Europe to larger nations, including the United States and Japan. Governmental bodies, universities, and private groups have implemented such citizens' panels as well as other participatory mechanisms, including scenario workshops, focus groups, and community-based research centers (or "science shops"). With the increase in participatory activities has come increased attention in the science policy literature. Joss (1999) and Chopyak and Levesque (2001), in particular, provide useful summaries of the variety of mechanisms in use, their apparent strengths and weaknesses, and evaluations of their experiences. The literature reveals that such participatory mechanisms have demonstrated, at least under closely supervised and mediated situations, that members of the public can interact helpfully with experts to assess technical controversies and policies, develop plans for technological futures, and design and conduct certain technical inquiries alongside traditional researchers. From these experiences, it is plausible, even likely, that a well-prepared CRI could succeed in engaging the public and communities around universities in substantive activities with university researchers. If created on a number of university campuses, they would thus constitute a distributed capacity for technology assessments, which some observers (such as Sarewitz 1996) have called for.

Since the 1990s, scholars have also made considerable progress in understanding how the institutions of science policy operate between politics and science to produce societal outcomes. Instead of focusing on the "estates" of science, the professions, administration, and politics that have historically characterized the "spectrum from truth to power" (Price 1965, passim), they examine the institutions that manage transactions across these boundaries, which they do not see as static (although Price did). This "important strand of current scholarship about science and society" (Sonnert and Holton 2002,

16) has yielded a description of boundary organizations (Guston 2000, 2001). Examples include offices of technology transfer (Guston 1999b); the Health Effects Institute (Keating 2001); agricultural extension (Cash 2001); the International Research Institute for Climate Prediction (Agrawala, Broad, and Guston 2001); and the Subsidiary Body for Scientific and Technological Advice to the United Nations Framework Convention on Climate Change (Miller 2001). Critical to the success of boundary organizations is their ability to manage the cooperation between scientists and nonscientists in the pursuit of ends of mutual interest—what Guston (2000) calls collaborative assurance. CRIs might engage in collaborative assurance—for example, by providing services to natural science and engineering units (by assisting with ethics curricula, grant applications, and information dissemination to the public and decision makers) while also serving society by helping attune scientists and engineers to societal needs. Although no person may serve two masters, boundary organizations like CRIs can serve both science and society by helping each to achieve the teaching, research, and service goals they want to reach responsibly.

Creating new institutions, even those about which one might have some confidence based in theory and practice, entails some risk. One potential risk of creating CRIs is that they may end up institutionalizing criticism of science. The honest response to such a concern is that CRIs will indeed institutionalize science criticism, but it will be criticism in the sense of constructive engagement with the quality and contribution of the scientific enterprise. Such criticism, which would be along the lines of art or food criticism (Chubin 1994), is exactly what such a center should be after and precisely what the commercialized university needs. The acceptance of ELSI programs within the ranks of scientists suggests that informed criticism can find an institutional home close to the research it engages in. Moreover, there are other, albeit modest, proofs that aspects of this enterprise can succeed. For example, nanotechnology researchers at Arizona State University have collaborated with Columbia University's Center for Science, Policy, and Outcomes to propose a real-time technology assessment agenda and to cross-train Arizona State's graduate students in nanoscience and engineering in science policy under an integrative graduate education and research traineeship grant from the National Science Foundation.

A second possible criticism is that CRIs would contribute to what might be called the "ELSI-fication of the social sciences." That is, the important role of the social sciences in examining the implications of the natural sciences may be taken as the only or the primary role for the social sciences. John Steelman, one of the architects of the modern research establishment in the Truman administration and himself an economist, argued that "competent social scientists should work hand in hand with the natural scientists, so that [societal] problems may be solved as they arise, and so that many of them may not arise in the first instance" (Guston and Sarewitz 2001, 95). More recently, sociologist William Julius Wilson (2002) has argued that the social sciences must respond to the "impetus to address policy-relevant issues . . . that grow out of the struggles of nation states to adapt to the impact of rapid techno-logical and economic changes on individuals, families, communities, institu-tions, and the society at large" (1).

Without predicting the likelihood of demands for greater relevance from social science research, ELSI-like work forms a significant but not overwhelm-ing share of available federal social science research dollars. Since 1991, the National Institutes for Health have spent slightly more than $130 million in ELSI funds, including an estimated $21.5 million for FY 2002. The Depart-ment of Energy has spent nearly $25 million during the same period on genome-related ELSI research, including an estimated $2.8 million in FY 2002.[1] National Science Foundation spending on the social and economic sciences totals more than $70 million per year (American Association for the Advancement of Sci-ence 2002, 144); and of this sum, spending on the Program in Societal Dimen-sions of Engineering, Science, and Technology, the foundation's closest cognate program to ELSI, is close to $2 million per year.

Given that genome-related ELSI funding is nearly an order of magnitude greater than the National Science Foundation's Program in Societal Dimen-sions, a more likely result than the ELSI-fication of the federal social science portfolio is that research on the ethical, legal, and societal aspects of innova-tion will be overwhelmed by particular innovations that the federal govern-ment has already identified and cultivated for support. With significant ELSI-like funds coming only after the federal government has committed to a multiyear, multibillion-dollar investment, the results of such research may be enlightening but have a decreasing chance of influencing the policy environ-ment or the trajectory of the innovation. The risk of ELSI-fication seems less than the risk that only specific technologies will be scrutinized, and then only after they have already been imparted with great momentum. The need for decentralized, university-based CRIs therefore becomes even more apparent.

Conclusion

Universities should make a demonstrated commitment to responsible inno-vation in the face of the challenges wrought by the commercialization of the academy. Such a commitment is warranted because universities will continue to be in the business of knowledge-based innovation for the foreseeable future.

The commercialization of knowledge-based innovations has been, is, and will continue to be integral to some aspects of the university; but "doing no harm" and "contributing to the economy" do not exhaust the normative demands on the research enterprise. University-based CRIs can help satisfy these additional demands, even while helping members of the university community achieve their substantive goals for teaching, research, and service. Grounded in recent scholarship in public participation and the design of science policy boundary organizations, they can draw university research, the values of communities, and the needs of decision makers closer in fruitful ways. CRIs can help create microcosms of well-ordered science, one university at a time.

Note

1. Data were provided by Howard Silver and Angela Sharpe, personal communication (Washington, D.C.: Consortium of Social Science Associations), June 2002.

References

Accreditation Board for Engineering and Technology. 2000. *Criteria for Accrediting Engineering Programs*. Baltimore: Accreditation Board for Engineering and Technology.

Agrawala, Shardul, Kenny Broad, and David H. Guston. 2001. "Integrating Climate Forecasts and Societal Decision Making: Challenges to an Emergent Boundary Organization." *Science, Technology, and Human Values* 26, no. 4: 454–77.

American Association for the Advancement of Science. 2002. *Research and Development, FY 2003*. Washington, D.C.: American Association for the Advancement of Science.

Andersen, Ida E., and B. Jaeger. 1999. "Scenario Workshops and Consensus Conferences: Towards More Democratic Decision-Making." *Science and Public Policy* 26, no. 5: 331–40.

Association of University Technology Managers. 2001. *AUTM Licensing Survey, FY 2000*. Northbrook, Ill.: Association of University Technology Managers.

Bok, Derek. 1982. *Beyond the Ivory Tower: Social Responsibilities of the Modern University*. Cambridge: Harvard University Press.

Brainard, Jeffrey. 2001. "Ethics-Training Rule Is Suspended." *Chronicle of Higher Education*, 2 March, p. A27.

Brooks, Harvey, and Lucian P. Randazzese. 1998. "University-Industry Relations: The Next Four Years and Beyond." In *Investing in Innovation*, ed. Lewis B. Branscomb and James H. Keller, 361–99. Cambridge, Mass.: MIT Press.

Cash, David. 2001. "'In Order to Aid in Diffusing Useful and Practical Information': Agricultural Extension and Boundary Organizations." *Science, Technology, and Human Values* 26, no. 4: 431–53.

Chopyak, Jill, and Peter Levesque. 2002. "Public Participation in Science and Technology Decision Making: Trends for the Future." *Technology in Society* 24, nos. 1–2: 155–66.

Chubin, Daryl. 1994. "How Large an R&D Enterprise?" In *The Fragile Contract: University Science and the Federal Government*, ed. David H. Guston and Kenneth Keniston, 118–44. Cambridge, Mass.: MIT Press.

Dürenberger, G., H. Kastenholz, and J. Behringer. 1999. "Integrated Assessment Focus Groups: Bridging the Gap between Science and Policy." *Science and Public Policy* 26, no. 5: 341–49.

Etzkowitz, Henry. 2002. *MIT and the Rise of Entrepreneurial Science*. New York: Routledge.

Etzkowitz, Henry, and Loet Ledesdorff. 2000. "The Dynamics of Innovation: From National Systems and 'Mode 2' to a Triple Helix of University-Industry-Government Relations." *Research Policy* 29, no. 2: 109–23.

Feller, Irwin, Catherine P. Ailes, and J. David Roessner. 2002. "Impacts of Research Universities on Technological Innovation in Industry: Evidence from Engineering Research Centers." *Research Policy* 31, no. 3: 457–74.

Guston, David H. 1999a. "Evaluating the First U.S. Consensus Conference: The Impact of the Citizens' Panel on Telecommunications and the Future of Democracy." *Science, Technology, and Human Values* 24, no. 4: 451–82.

———. 1999b. "Stabilizing the Boundary between U.S. Politics and Science: The Role of the Office of Technology Transfer As a Boundary Organization." *Social Studies of Science* 29, no. 1: 87–112.

———. 2000. *Between Politics and Science*. New York: Cambridge University Press.

———, ed. 2001. "Special Issue: Boundary Organizations in Environmental Policy and Science." *Science, Technology, and Human Values* 26, no. 4.

Guston, David H., and Daniel Sarewitz. 2001. "Real-Time Technology Assessment." *Technology in Society* 24, nos. 1–2: 93–109.

Hörnig, Susanna. 1999. "Citizens' Panels As a Form of Deliberative Technology Assessment." *Science and Public Policy* 26, no. 5: 351–59.

Jones, Megan, David H. Guston, and Lewis M. Branscomb. 1996. *Informed Legislatures: Coping with Science in a Democracy*. Lanham, Md.: University Press of America.

Joss, Simon, ed. 1999. "Special Issue: Public Participation in Science and Technology." *Science and Public Policy* 26, no. 5.

Joss, Simon, and J. Durant, eds. 1995. *Participation in Science: The Role of Consensus Conferences in Europe*. London: Science Museum.

Keating, Terry. 2001. "Lessons from the Recent History of the Health Effects Institute." *Science, Technology, and Human Values* 26, no. 4: 409–30.

Kitcher, Philip. 2001. *Science, Truth, and Democracy*. New York: Oxford University Press.

McCain, Lauren. 2002. "Informing Technology Policy Decisions: The U.S. Human Genome Project's Ethical, Legal, and Societal Implications Programs As a Critical Case." *Technology in Society* 24, nos. 1–2: 111–32.

Mervis, Jeffrey. 2001. "NSF Scores Low on Using Its Own Criteria." *Science*, 30 March, pp. 2533–35.

Miller, Clark. 2001. "Hybrid Management: Boundary Organizations, Science Policy, and Environmental Governance in the Climate Regime." *Science, Technology, and Human Values* 26, no. 4: 478–500.

Mowery, David C., Richard R. Nelson, Bhaven N. Sampat, and Arvids A. Ziedonis. 2001. "The Growth of Patenting and Licensing by U.S. Universities: An Assessment of the Effects of the Bayh-Dole Act of 1980." *Research Policy* 30, no. 1: 99–119.

Office of Research Integrity. 2000. "PHS Policy on Instruction in the Responsible Conduct of Research." Available at *http://ori.dhhs.gov/html/programs/rcrcontents.asp*.

Price, Don K. 1965. *The Scientific Estate*. Cambridge: Belknap Press of Harvard University.

Primack, Joel, and Frank Von Hippel. 1974. *Advice and Dissent: Scientists in the Political Arena*. New York: New American Library.

Sacks, Stephen Miles. 2000. "The Case of the University of Pennsylvania Health System." *SciPolicy* 1 (fall): 122–53.

Sarewitz, Daniel. 1996. *Frontiers of Illusion: Science, Technology, and the Politics of Progress*. Philadelphia: Temple University Press.

Sclove, Richard E. 1999. "The Democratic Politics of Technology: The Missing Half" (*http://www.loka.org/idt/intro.htm*).

Slaughter, Sheila. 2001. "Professional Values and the Allure of the Market." *Academe* 87 (September/October): 22–26.

Slaughter, Sheila, and Larry L. Leslie. 1997. *Academic Capitalism: Politics, Policies, and the Entrepreneurial University*. Baltimore: Johns Hopkins University Press.

Sonnert, Gerhardt, with Gerald Holton. 2002. *Ivory Bridges: Connecting Science and Society*. Cambridge, Mass.: MIT Press.

Study and Conference on Improving Public Access to Science. 2001. *Living Knowledge: The International Science Shop Network*. Project Technical Reports Compendium, vols. 1A, 1B, and 2. Amherst, Mass: Loka Institute.

Wilson, William Julius. 2002. "Expanding the Domain of Policy-Relevant Scholarship in the Social Sciences." *PS* 35, no. 1: 1–4.

Winner, Langdon. 1977. *Autonomous Technology: Technics-Out-of-Control as a Theme in Political Thought*. Cambridge, Mass.: MIT Press.

Contributors

Marcia Angell, M.D., is senior lecturer in the Department of Social Medicine at Harvard University in Cambridge, Massachusetts, and former editor-in-chief of the *New England Journal of Medicine*. She writes frequently in professional journals on a wide range of topics and is the author of *Science on Trial: The Clash of Medical Evidence and the Law in the Breast Implant Case*.

Ronald A. Bohlander, Ph.D., is the founder and director of the Commercial Realization Office at the Georgia Tech Research Institute in Atlanta.

Derek Bok, Ph.D., is president emeritus and professor of law at Harvard University in Cambridge, Massachusetts. He formerly served as dean of Harvard Law School. Bok has written four books on higher education: *Beyond the Ivory Tower, Higher Learning, Universities and the Future of America*, and *The Future of America*. His latest book is *Universities in the Marketplace*.

Eric C. Dahl, Ph.D., is assistant vice president of research at the University of Georgia in Athens. He formerly served as associate to the provost.

James J. Duderstadt, Ph.D., is president emeritus and university professor of science and engineering at the University of Michigan in Ann Arbor. He formerly served as dean of the College of Engineering, provost, and vice president of academic affairs.

Mary L. Good, Ph.D., is professor and founding dean of the College of Information Science and Systems Engineering at the University of Arkansas in Little Rock.

David H. Guston, Ph.D., is associate professor of public policy and director of the Edward J. Bloustein School of Planning and Public Policy at Rutgers University in New Brunswick, New Jersey. Guston is the author of *Between Politics and Science: Assuring the Integrity and Productivity of Research*. He also is co-author of *Informed Legislatures: Coping with Science in a Democracy*.

ZACH W. HALL, Ph.D., is senior associate dean for research at the Keck School of Medicine of the University of Southern California. Previously he was president and chief executive officer of EnVivo Pharmaceuticals. He formerly served as executive vice chancellor at the University of California, San Francisco, where he oversaw research administration, including the Office of Industry and Research Development.

KAREN A. HOLBROOK, Ph.D., is president of Ohio State University in Columbus. She formerly served as vice president for academic affairs and provost at the University of Georgia in Athens.

SHELDON KRIMSKY, Ph.D., is professor of urban and environmental policy at Tufts University in Medford, Massachusetts. Krimsky writes on scientific ethics and commercialization and their impact on health research and objectivity. His latest book is *Science in the Public Interest: Has the Lure of Profits Corrupted Biomedical Research?*

ARTI K. RAI, J.D., is professor of law at Duke University Law School. She writes extensively on law and biotechnology, patent law, and health care regulation. She is co-author of *Law and the Mental Health System: Civil and Criminal Aspects.*

MURRAY SPERBER, Ph.D., is professor of English and American studies at Indiana University in Bloomington. He is widely recognized as an authority on college sports and their role in American culture. He has written several books, including *Beer and Circus, College Sports, Inc.*, and *Onward to Victory: The Crisis That Shaped College Sports.*

DONALD G. STEIN, Ph.D., is a physiological psychologist and Asa G. Candler professor of neurology and emergency medicine at Emory University in Atlanta, Georgia. Stein formerly served as Emory's vice provost for graduate studies, dean of the Graduate School of Arts and Sciences, and interim vice president for research. He also served as vice provost for research and dean of the Graduate School at Rutgers University in Newark, New Jersey.

JERRY G. THURSBY, Ph.D., is professor and chair of the Department of Economics at Emory University in Atlanta, Georgia. Thursby has published extensively in the areas of econometrics, international trade, and, most recently, the licensing of university technologies. He currently serves on the editorial boards of the *Journal of Technology Transfer and Global Business* and the *Economics Review.*

MARIE THURSBY, Ph.D., is professor of strategic management at the DuPree College of Management of the Georgia Institute of Technology in Atlanta as well as an adjunct professor in economics at Emory University. She is the founding director of a new graduate certificate program at Georgia Tech and Emory University called Technological Innovation: Generating Economic Results (TI:GER^sm). Thursby has been a research associate of the National Bureau of Economic Research for fifteen years and serves on several editorial boards, including *Management Science*, the *Journal of Technology Transfer*, the *Journal of International Economics*, and the *Review of International Economics*.

Index

AAMC. *See* Association of American
  Medical Colleges
AAU. *See* Association of American
  Universities (AAU)
Academe, 2
Academic Capitalism (Slaughter and
  Leslie), 136
Adams, Roger, 49
adjunct faculty, 3
admissions, costs of commercialization,
  37–38, 45
advertising, sports related: beer, 29;
  cigarettes, 18–20; Nike shoes, 23–28
Agrawala, Shardul, 170
agricultural experiment stations, 49
Ailes, Catherine P., 164
Air Force Office of Scientific Research,
  50
Albany Times Union, 25
Alfred University, 136
AMA. *See* American Medical Associa-
  tion
American Medical Association (AMA),
  conflict of interest policy of, 139
American Society of Gene Therapy,
  conflict of interest policy of, 139
American Tobacco Company, 18
Andersen, Ida E., 168
Angell, Marcia, 6, 13, 127–132
Ariad Pharmaceuticals, 119, 120–121
Arizona State University, 170
Association of American Medical
  Colleges (AAMC), conflict of
  interest policy of, 139–140, 141

Association of American Universities
  (AAU), conflict of interest task force
  of, 141–142
Association of University Technology
  Managers, 58, 90–91, 103, 104, 118,
  163
athletics commercialization. *See* sports
  commercialization
Atlantic Monthly, 103
Atomic Energy Commission, 50
Axel, Richard, 120

Bayh Dole Act of 1980: analogy to
  Homestead Act, 68; background and
  context for, 48–51; commercialization goal of, 120; competitiveness
  policy and, 51, 52; exceptional
  circumstance limit on proprietary
  rights, 124; impact of, 52–55, 67, 68–
  69, 90–91, 118, 136–137, 163; library
  model *v*. profit motive, 69–70;
  mandate for university ownership of
  intellectual property, 11–12, 51–52,
  61–62, 66–67, 89–90; medical center
  drug patents under, 130
Becklund, Laurie, 24
Beer companies, sports sponsorships of,
  29
Behringer, J., 168
Berg, Paul, 63
Berkeley, Abiona, 128
Bermuda rules, 123
biomedical research, 117–126; academia
  industry collaboration in, 155–158;

biomedical research (*continued*)
  biotechnology industry ties to, 155–
  156; broad patents in, 118–119;
  institutional review boards (IRBs),
  141–142, 145–146, 164; medical
  center clinical trials, 6, 13, 127–130,
  132; monopoly control of basic
  platforms, 120–121; open exchange
  v. proprietary rights in, 121–125;
  patentable software and data
  structures in, 117–118; pharmaceutical company proprietary rights in, 7,
  117, 121–122; public funding of, 50,
  64, 67, 130, 131; reform of patentability standards, 121; restrictions on
  unpatented research tools, 119, 123,
  124; revolution in, 153–154; trade
  secrets in, 137
biotechnology industry, research
  contribution of, 155–156
Bird, Larry, 23
Blumenstyk, Goldie, 32, 33
Blumenthal, David, 119, 123, 137
Bodenheimer, Thomas, 33, 41, 129
Bohlander, Ronald, 12, 75–88
Bok, Derek, 11, 32–47, 43, 59, 165
boundary organizations, 170
Bowen, William G., 32
Boyer Cohen recombinant DNA patent,
  120, 121, 156
Brainard, Jeffrey, 166
Branscomb, Lewis M., 48, 167
Bristol Myers Squibb, 131
Broad, Kenny, 170
Brooks, Harvey, 162
Brown University, 27
Bryant, Bear, 22
Bryant, Paul, 22
Bush, Vannevar, 66, 67, 68

Cambridge University, 54
Camp, Walter, 18
Campbell, Eric G., 119, 123, 137
Carnegie Foundation report (1929), on
  college sports, 18, 20–21
Carnegie Mellon University, 53, 58
Cash, David, 170

Cell Signaling Alliance, 155
Centers for Responsible Innovation
  (CRIs), proposal for, 161–162, 165–
  171
Center Watch, 127
Chace, William, 10
Cho, Mildred K., 147
Chopyak, Jill, 169
Chronicle of Higher Education, 95
Chubin, Daryl, 170
cigarette advertising, in student
  publications and sports programs, 18–
  20
clinical trials: conflicts of interest in,
  132, 145, 148, 149; FDA approval
  and, 131; human subjects in, 129,
  141; at medical centers, 6, 13, 127–
  130, 132; NIH funding of, 130, 131;
  team concept in, 159–160
coaches, product endorsements by, 21–
  23, 24
Code of Medical Ethics (AMA), 139
Cohen, Wesley, 121
Cole, Jonathan, 137
collaborative assurance, 170
College Sports, Inc., 23
Columbia University, 32, 45, 118, 120,
  170
Columbus Dispatch, 27–28
Colyvas, Jeannette, 120
Commerce Department, U.S., 124
commercialization, academic: Conference on Commercialization of the
  Academy, 9–11; costs of (*See* costs of
  commercialization); economic
  benefits of, 58–59, 75–76, 92–93;
  environmental pressures in, 3–9, 45;
  growth of, 32–33; guidelines for, 14–
  15, 46–47; illusory benefits of, 33–35,
  44; incentives for lesser-known
  institutions, 35–36; indicators of,
  134–138; in postindustrial, knowledge based society, 59–60; responsible
  innovation in, 162–172; in sports
  (*See* sports commercialization); state
  government support for, 58, 91–92;
  See also corporate sponsored research;

government sponsored research; patents and licensing; research and scholarship
community based research centers, 169
Conference on Commercialization of the Academy, 9–11, 47
conflicts of commitment, 5, 159
conflicts of interest, 13, 137–152; contested issues, 150; in corporate sponsored research, 61, 63, 84, 132, 158–159, 164; federal agencies policy on, 143–147; fiduciary responsibility concept in, 151; medical/scientific publications policy on, 138–139; professional societies policy on, 139–143; research institutes policy on, 148–150; universities policy on, 147–148, 159
Constant Gardener, The (Le Carré), 42
continuing education, costs of commercialization, 38, 45
corporate sponsored research: biotechnology industry in, 155–157; collegial relations impacted by, 7, 40, 41; conflicts of interest in, 61, 63, 84, 132, 158–159, 164; debate over improper pressures in, 2, 57; early history of, 49; at Georgia Tech Research Institute, 80–83; growth of, 58–59, 134–136; guidelines for safeguarding integrity of, 129–130; IRS regulations and, 84–85; limits on publication rights in, 13, 148, 158; objectivity and integrity at risk in, 41, 43–44, 129; pharmaceutical company medical center collaboration, 6, 13, 127–130; state government support for, 58; successful partnerships in, 14, 157–158; underwritten by universities and federal government, 62
corporate sponsored sports: by beer companies, 29; coaches' product endorsements and, 21–22; naming rights and, 30; Nike schools, 23–28; revenue offset by public funding loss, 28–29
Corso, Lee, 22

costs of commercialization, 11, 36–45; to admissions standards, 37–38, 45; to curriculum and teaching, 38, 62; ethical, 38–39; government regulation as, 43; to public image, 42–44; to research and scholarship, 39–41, 63; to university community, 41–42
Cox 2 inhibitors, 53
Creamer, Robert W., 21
Creative Sports, Inc., 29
Culbrandsen, C.E., 93
curriculum, costs of commercialization, 38

Dahl, Eric, 12, 89–102
Danish Board of Technology, consensus conferences of, 168, 169
Davidoff, Frank, 128
deadweight loss, 119–120
Dechenaux, Emmanuel, 121
Defense, Department of, 50, 83
defense research, 50
Dillon, Harrison, 113
distance learning, 4, 34, 35; instructional technology development, 95–97
DNA technology, recombinant, 58, 120, 121, 155–156
Drucker, Peter F., 59
drug companies. *See* pharmaceutical companies
Duderstadt, James, 12, 56–74
Duke University, corporate sponsored research at, 134, 135, 136
Dupree, A. Hunter, 55
Durant, J., 168
Dürenberger, G., 168

Eastern Virginia Medical School, 136
economic clusters, 53–54
economic development, university role in, 91–92
Eisenberg, Rebecca S., 123, 124
Elkins, James M., 17
ELSI (ethical, legal, and social implications) research, 166–167
Emory University: in collaborative research programs, 155; Conference

Emory University (*continued*)
on Commercialization of the
Academy at, 9–11, 47
Energy, Department of, 50, 166, 171
Enron Corporation, 30
entrepreneurs, faculty: independent
research by, 60, 63–64; promotion
and tenure of, 12, 94, 95, 98–100,
101; as role models, 100; *See also*
Faculty business enterprises
entrepreneurship, growth of, 133–134
Environmental Protection Agency
(EPA), 50; conflict of interest
guidelines of, 143–144
En Vivo Pharmaceuticals, 153
ethical, legal, and social implications
(ELSI) research, 166–167, 171
ethics: costs of commercialization, 38–
39; training, 166; *See also* conflicts of
interest
Ethics in Government Act of 1978, 143
Etzkowitz, Henry, 162, 163
exclusive licensing, 13, 40, 67–68, 118–
122

faculty: conflicts of commitment, 5, 159;
entrepreneur as role model, 100;
external funding of salaries, 3;
governance, 65; independent
research entrepreneurs, 60, 63–64;
junior, commercial pressures on, 6;
junior, participation in technology
transfer activities, 98; recruitment
and hiring, 4–5, 6, 37; self serving
behavior of, 41–42; teaching "buy
off" by academic stars, 3, 6–7; *See also*
promotion and tenure
faculty business enterprises: at Georgia
Tech Research Institute, 82;
institutional investment in, 5; state
government support for, 58, 91;
wealth from, 56
Feller, Irwin, 164
fiduciary responsibility concept, 151
*Financial Conflicts of Interest in Clinical
Research*, 139
Flexner, Abraham, 32

Florida State University, 53
focus groups, 169
Food and Drug Administration (FDA):
conflict of interest policy of, 145,
147; drug approvals, 127, 130, 131;
patents and licenses, 125
Fred Hutchinson Cancer Center, 129,
149

Gatorade, 27, 53, 58
Gelsinger, Jesse, 129, 141, 148, 164
General Accounting Office (GAO), 143
genome sequencing project, Bermuda
rules in, 123
Georgia Institute of Technology, 10, 12;
in collaborative research program,
155; corporate sponsored research at,
135, 136; *See also* Georgia Tech
Research Institute
Georgia Tech Research Institute
(GTRI), 12, 75–88; analogy to
teaching hospital, 79; client service
in, 78; conflicts of interest and, 84;
cyclical model and, 79–80; faculty
business ventures at, 82; intellectual
property ownership and, 84–87;
management issues in, 82–83;
nonpayment issues in, 87; origins and
early years, 76–77; patents and
licensing at, 81; product developments of, 80–82; research areas of,
77–78; research volume of, 77
Giamatti, Bart, 148
Gilman, Alfred, 155
Glass Bead Game, The (Hesse), 40
Golden, John M., 121
Good, Mary, 11–12, 48–55
governance, shared: faculty, 65, 66;
governing boards, 64–65, 66;
president, 65
governing boards, 64–65, 66
government agencies, conflict of interest
policy of, 143–147
government regulation, as cost of
commercialization, 43
government sponsored research:
biomedical, 50, 64, 67, 130, 131, 154;

conflict of interest regulations in, 143–147; deadweight loss concerns in, 120; decline in, 136; defense, 50; indirect income from, 6; patent rights under Bayh Dole Act, 12, 48, 59, 61–62, 66–67, 89–90; pre 1980 intellectual property policy in, 50–51; *See also* National Institutes of Health

Gray, Denis O., 98, 99

Guidelines for Dealing with Faculty Conflicts of Commitment and Conflicts of Interest in Research (AAMC), 140

Guston, David H., 14, 161–172, 164, 167, 168, 170, 171

Hall, Zach, 14, 153–160

Harvard Clinical Research Institute (HCRI), 130

Harvard University: patents and licensing, 119; sports commercialization at, 17–18

Hatch Act of 1887, 49

Health and Human Services, Department of, conflict of interest policy of, 143, 145–147, 148

Hennessy, John, 156

Hesse, Hermann, 40

Hobey Baker Award, 30

Hofstadter, Richard, 133

Hogan, James, 18

Holbrook, Karen, 12, 15, 89–102, 101

Holton, Gerald, 169–170

Homestead Act of 1882, 68

Hooker, Michael, 26

Hörnig, Susanna, 168

Human Genome Project, 123, 136, 155, 157, 166

human subject research: in clinical trials, 127, 129, 141, 149; conflict of interest policy for, 140, 141–142, 146–147, 149

Hutchinson (Fred) Cancer Center, 129, 149

Illman, D., 93

Indiana University, 22

Indian Institute of Science, 54

industry. *See* corporate sponsored research; corporate sponsored sports; pharmaceutical companies

informed consent, 141, 165

institutional review boards (IRBs), 141–142, 145–146, 164

instructional technology development: peer review for, 96–97; in promotion and tenure decisions, 95–96, 97

intellectual property rights: Bayh Dole Act provisions, 11–12, 51–52, 61–62, 66–67; Georgia Tech policy on, 85–87; IRS regulations and, 84–85; open source movement and, 70–71; pre 1980 government funded research, 50–51; *See also* patents and licensing

Internal Revenue Service (IRS), revenue procedure 97-14, 84–85

International Committee of Medical Journal Editors, 138

Internet: distance learning, 4, 34, 35, 95–97; open courseware project, 70–71

Internet ventures, 33–34

Jaeger, B., 168

Jansen, Christiana, 113

Japanese Technical Literature Act of 1986, 52

Jensen, Richard, 108, 115, 122

Jones, Megan, 167

Joss, Simon, 168, 169

Kansas Institute of Technology, 54

Karel, Frank, 9

Kastenholz, H., 168

Keating, Terry, 170

Kellogg Commission on the Future of the Land Grant University, 71

Kennedy, Donald, 57, 68

Kitcher, Philip, 161, 169

Krimsky, Sheldon, 13, 133–152, 137, 138, 164

Kwiram, A., 93

Land Grant (Morrill) Act of 1862, 48–49

land grant universities, 48–49, 162
Le Carré, John, 42
Ledesdorff, Loet, 163
Lehigh University, 136
Leslie, Larry, 134, 136–137, 163
Levesque, Peter, 169
licensing. *See* patents and licensing
Liebeskind, Julia, 7
Linux operating system, 70
Lipsyte, Robert, 30
Lo, Bernard, 128
Lucas, John A., 17
Lycos Internet technology patent, 53, 58

McCain, Lauren, 166
Malcolm Baldrige National Quality
    Improvement Act of 1987, 52
Malone, Thomas E., 33
Marshall, Eliot, 118
Massachusetts Institute of Technology
    (MIT), 162; corporate sponsored
    research at, 135, 136; in economic
    cluster, 53–54; on intellectual
    property rights, 85; interdisciplinary
    programs of, 166; open courseware
    project of, 70–71; patents and
    licensing at, 119, 121
Max Planck Society, 54
medical centers: conflict of interest
    policy, 139–140, 148; conflicts of
    interest in, 132; faculty stars at, 131–
    132; institutional support for research
    at,15–16; mission and focus of, 131;
    pharmaceutical company collabora-
    tion in clinical trials, 6, 13, 127–130,
    132; pharmaceutical company
    influence in, 45, 130–131
medical journals, conflict of interest
    policies of, 138–139
Merges, Robert P., 120
Mervis, Jeffrey, 167
Michigan State University, 58
Miller, Clark, 170
Minneapolis Tribune, 30
Moe, Michael T., 60
Moos, M., 91
Morrill (Land Grant) Act of 1862, 48–49

Morris, Kit, 24–25
Mowery, David C., 67, 163
Multimedia Educational Resource for
    Learning and Online Teaching
    (MERLOT), 96–97

National Academy Committee on
    Science, Technology, and Economic
    Policy, 103
National Academy of Sciences, 48
National Advisory Committee for
    Aeronautics (NACA), 49
National Aeronautics and Space Agency
    (NASA), 50
National College Athletic Association
    (NCAA) basketball, corporate
    sponsorships in, 24–28, 29
National Competitiveness Technology
    Transfer Act of 1989, 52
National Cooperative Research Act of
    1984, 52
National Institute of General Medical
    Sciences, 155
National Institutes of Health: budget of,
    64; conflict of interest policy of, 144–
    145, 147; drug research funding of,
    130, 131; ELSI funding of, 166, 171;
    ethics training requirement of, 166;
    intellectual property ownership and,
    50–51, 69–70; open exchange
    guidelines of, 123–124; patents and
    licensing of, 125; restrictive contracts
    of, 158
National Institute of Standards and
    Technology Authorization Act of
    1989, 52
National Science Foundation, 50, 83,
    134, 168; budget of, 64; conflict of
    interest policy of, 144, 147;
    intersectoral approach to research,
    163–164; social and economic
    sciences funding by, 171; social merit
    criterion of, 167
Naval Research Laboratory, 50
Nehlen, Don, 22
Nelson, Richard R., 120, 121
New England Journal of Medicine, 132

Newman, John Henry, 58
News and Observer, 25, 26
New York Times, 30
NF-kB cell signaling pathway patent,
    119, 120
Nike: college sports sponsorships of, 23–
    25, 26, 27–28; in labor practices
    controversy, 25, 26–27
nonexclusive licensing policy, 51, 67, 69
nonobviousness standard, 117
North Carolina State University:
    promotion and tenure decision at, 98;
    sports commercialization at, 25
Notre Dame University, sports endorse-
    ments at, 21–22
Nunn, Sam, 10, 100

Ohio State University: corporate
    sponsored research at, 135; promo-
    tion and tenure decisions at, 98–99;
    sports contracts at, 27
Omaha World Herald, 28
Omnibus Trade and Competitive Act of
    1988, 52
open source movement, 70
Oregon State University, 30
Oxford University, 54

patents and licensing: administrative
    costs of, 68; Bayh Dole Act mandate
    for university ownership of intellec-
    tual property, 11–12, 51–52, 61–62,
    66–67, 89–90; benefits of commer-
    cialization, 34, 46; collegial relations
    impacted by, 7–8; court rulings on
    patentable research, 117; deadweight
    loss concerns in, 119–120; entrepre-
    neurial culture promoted by, 5, 63–
    64; exclusive, 13, 40, 67–68, 118–22;
    Georgia Tech Research Institute
    policy on, 81, 85–87; growth of, 103,
    104, 117–118, 136–137, 163; IRS
    regulations and, 84–85; marketing of,
    7, 113–114; nonexclusive, 51, 67, 69;
    v. open source movement model, 70–
    71; reform of patentability standards,
    121; revenue generated from, 7, 12,
    13, 32, 33, 52–54, 58, 90–91, 104–
    105, 118, 156, 163; of Wisconsin
    Alumni Research Foundation
    (WARF), 92–93, 118–119
patents and licensing surveys, 103–116,
    163; on faculty involvement in
    development, 107–108; on failure
    rate, 107, 108; on marketing efforts,
    113–114; on reasons for licensing,
    110–113; on reasons for not licens-
    ing, 108–110; on stage of technology
    development, 106–108; on university
    objectives, 105–106
Pennsylvania State University: corporate
    sponsored research at, 135, 136;
    promotion and tenure at, 99
pharmaceutical companies: clinical trials
    at medical centers, 127–130, 132;
    FDA approval and, 131; influence in
    medical schools, 45, 130–131; in
    patent disputes, 119; proprietary
    rights and, 7, 117, 121–122
Porter, Michael, 48, 53
Porter, Roger T., 33
postindustrial knowledge based society,
    higher education in, 59–60
president, governance by, 65
Press, Eval, 57, 133
Price, Don K., 169
Primack, Joel, 164
Principles of Medical Ethics (AMA), 139
professional societies, conflict of interest
    policies of, 139–143
Program in Societal Dimensions of
    Engineering, Science, and Technol-
    ogy, 171
promotion and tenure: costs of commer-
    cialization, 37; entrepreneurial
    activities as factor in, 12, 94, 95, 98–
    100, 101; grants and contracts as
    factor in, 6; guidelines for commer-
    cialization, 15; instructional technol-
    ogy development as factor in, 95–96,
    97; team concept and, 159–160;
    traditional factors in, 94–95;
    traditional values *v.* commercializa-
    tion goals, 97–98

Public Health Service: conflict of interest policy of, 144; Office of Research Integrity, 166

public image, costs of commercialization, 42–44

public interest, 57–58, 63, 71–73

publicly funded research. *See* government sponsored research

Purdue University, 49

Rader, Benjamin, 18

Rai, Arti K., 13, 117–126, 118, 124

Randazzese, Lucian P., 162

recombinant DNA technology, 58, 120, 121, 155–156

recruitment and hiring: costs of commercialization, 37; funding consideration in, 4–5, 6

research associates, 3

research ethics. *See* conflicts of interest

research institutes: conflicts of interest in, 148–150; private sector approach in, 160

research parks, 156–157

research and scholarship: academia industry partnerships, 155–158; applied *v.* basic, 112; balance of teaching and, 1; biomedical (*See* biomedical research); costs of commercialization, 39–41, 43, 45, 63; decline in recruitment of top students, 9; donor support for, 15; downgrading of esoteric work, 4, 5, 7; ELSI (ethical, legal, and social implications), 166–167, 171; human subject (*See* human subject research); marketing focus of, 1–2; openness and academic freedom, threats to, 56–58, 137; patentable, 7; plagiarized, 4; private sector approach in, 159–160; privatization of, 68–69; *v.* product development, 4; profit motive in, 8–9, 40, 57; royalty research fund grants for, 93; in tenure decision, 94; *See also* corporate sponsored research; government sponsored research; patents and licensing

Research University in a Time of Discontent, The (Cole), 137

revenue, commercial: illusory nature of, 33–34; offset by public funding loss, 28–29, 34; from patents and licensing, 7, 12, 13, 32, 33, 52–54, 58, 90–91, 104–105, 118, 156, 163; *v.* rising costs, 33; royalty research fund grants from, 93

Rhoades, Gary, 4

Robert Wood Johnson Foundation, 9

Rockne, Knute, 20; product endorsements of, 21–22

Roessner, J. David, 164

Rogers, Janice, 77

Rosovsky, Henry, 72

Rothenberg, L.S., 137, 138

royalty research funds, 93

Rutgers University, 162, 166

Ruth, Babe, 21

Sacks, Stephen Miles, 164

St. Pierre, Brian, 37

Sam Nunn/Bank of America Policy Forum, 10, 47

Sample, Steven B., 90, 92, 100, 141

Sarewitz, Daniel, 167, 169, 171

Savage, Howard, 18, 20

scenario workshops, 169

Schmidt, Peter, 58, 91

Science, 68

science policy: Centers for Responsible Innovation proposal, 161, 165–172; competitiveness legislation, 51, 52, 136; defense research and, 50; Hatch Act of 1887, 49; Land Grant Act of 1862, 48–49; linear model in, 67; on patents and licensing, 50–51, 59 (*See also* Bayh Dole Act)

Science and Technology Council of the States, 163

Science—The Endless Frontier (Bush), 66, 67

Science, Truth, and Democracy (Kitcher), 161

scientific publications, conflict of interest policies of, 138–139

Seattle Times, 149

Shalala, Donna, 145–146

Shulman, James L., 32

Slaughter, Sheila, 134, 136–137, 163, 164

Small Business Innovation Development Act of 1982, 52

Smith, L. Dennis, 141

Smith, Ronald A., 17, 18

Sonnert, Gerhardt, 169–170

Sperber, Murray, 11, 17–31, 19, 22, 27

sports commercialization, 11, 17–31; admission standards and, 37–38, 45; Carnegie Foundation report (1929), 18, 20–21; cigarette advertising and, 18–20; coaches' product endorsements, 21–23, 24; consultants and agencies in, 29; corporate sponsorship by beer companies, 29; corporate sponsorship by Nike, 23–28; early history of, 17–18; facilities construction, 25, 29–30; illusory benefits of, 34, 35; immunity from budget cuts and, 25–26; naming rights, 30; revenue offset by public funding oss, 28–29, 34; revenue *v.* rising costs, 33; tramp athletes, 18

Sports Illustrated, 23

Stanford University, 120, 156

state governments, support for academic commercialization, 58, 91–92

State Science and Technology Institute, 163

Steelman, John, 170–171

Stein, Donald G., 1–16

stem cell research, 118–119, 121–122, 125n.3

Stevenson Wydler Technology Innovation Act of 1980, 52

Stokstad, Erik, 57

Stone, John, 9

Strasser, J.B., 24

Studebaker, Rockne's endorsement of, 21–22

Syracuse University, 25

Tampa Tribune, 29

Taxol patent, 53

teaching: by adjunct faculty, 3; balance of research and, 1; costs of commercialization, 38, 62; by graduate students, 6–7; in promotion and tenure decision, 94

technology transfer: open source movement model for, 70–71; pre 1980, 50, 66; professional level of participants, 98; in promotion and tenure decisions, 97–100; public interest and, 57–58, 63, 71–73; *See also* commercialization, academic; Georgia Tech Research Institute; patents and licensing

tenure. *See* promotion and tenure

Terrazas, 100

Texas A&M University, 135

Thursby, Jerry, 13, 103–116, 122

Thursby, Marie, 13, 103–116, 108, 115, 122

tobacco companies, college sports and student publications supported by, 18–20

Tornatzky, Louis G., 91, 92, 98, 99

Trademark Clarification Act of 1984, 52

trade secrets, 137, 148

tramp athletes, 18

Underwood, John, 22

Uniform Biological Material Transfer Act of 1995, 123

universities: conflict of interest policies of, 147–148, 159; economic development role of, 91; land grant, 48–49, 162; market driven restructuring of, 60–61; in postindustrial knowledge based society, 59–60; shared governance in, 64–66; social responsibility of, 161–172; *See also* commercialization, academic; *specific names*

University of Alabama, 22

University of California at Berkeley, 157

University of California at San Francisco: biomedical research at, 58, 153, 156; corporate sponsored research at, 135, 158

University of California System:
  collaborative biomedical research in,
  155; patents and licenses of, 118
University of Chicago, 32
University of Connecticut at Storrs,
  28
University of Florida: faculty participa-
  tion in technology transfer, 98;
  patents and licensing at, 53, 58
University of Georgia, 10, 91, 98
University of Illinois, 49
University of Maryland, 30
University of Michigan: corporate
  sponsored research at, 135; Nike
  sports sponsorship at, 24, 26;
  technology transfer policy at, 71–72
University of Nebraska at Lincoln, 28
University of North Carolina at Chapel
  Hill, Nike sports sponsorship at, 24,
  25, 26
University of Oklahoma, 30
University of Oregon, 30
University of Pennsylvania, 141, 164
University of Rochester, 53
University of South Florida, 29
University of Texas at Austin: corporate
  sponsored research at, 134, 135, 136;
  naming rights at, 30
University of Tulsa, 136
University of Washington: corporate
  sponsored research at, 135; Royalty
  Research Fund, 93
University of Wisconsin: patents and
  licensing at, 53, 118–119, 125n.3;
  promotion and tenure decisions at,

99; royalty research fund grants at,
  92–93
utility standard, 117

Vaccaro, Sonny, 23
van Opstal, Debra, 48, 53
Venter, Craig, 123
Vest, Charles, 70–71
Virginia Polytechnic Institute, 99
Von Hippel, Frank, 164

Walsh, Christy, 21
Walsh, John P., 121
Warfarin patent, 53
Washburn, Jennifer, 57, 133
Waugaman, Paul G., 91, 92, 98, 99
Wellcome Institute, 123, 157
West Virginia University, 22
Whitehead Institute for Biomedical
  Research, 119
White, John, Jr., 79
Wilson, William Julius, 171
Winner, Langdon, 165
Wisconsin Alumni Research Foundation
  (WARF), 92–93, 118
Wolf, Leslie E., 128
Woody, Todd, 45
work-for-hire mode, 85

Yale University, 17–18, 32
Young, J.R., 95, 96

Zacks, Rebecca, 52–53
Zemsky, Robert, 73
Zimbalist, Andrew, 29